T0212958

Lecture Notes in Computer Science 9959

Commenced Publication in 1973
Founding and Former Series Editors:
Gerhard Goos, Juris Hartmanis, and Jan van Leeuwen

More information about this series at http://www.springer.com/series/7408

Jens Grabowski · Steffen Herbold (Eds.)

System Analysis and Modeling

Technology-Specific Aspects of Models

9th International Conference, SAM 2016
Saint-Melo, France, October 3–4, 2016
Proceedings

 Springer

Editors
Jens Grabowski
Georg-August-Universität Göttingen
Göttingen
Germany

Steffen Herbold
Georg-August-Universität Göttingen
Göttingen
Germany

ISSN 0302-9743   ISSN 1611-3349   (electronic)
Lecture Notes in Computer Science
ISBN 978-3-319-46612-5   ISBN 978-3-319-46613-2   (eBook)
DOI 10.1007/978-3-319-46613-2

Library of Congress Control Number: 2016951709

LNCS Sublibrary: SL2 – Programming and Software Engineering

Printed on acid-free paper

This Springer imprint is published by Springer Nature
The registered company is Springer International Publishing AG
The registered company address is: Gewerbestrasse 11, 6330 Cham, Switzerland

Preface

The System Analysis and Modeling (SAM) conference provides an open arena for participants from academia and industry to present and discuss the most recent innovations, trends, experiences, and concerns in modeling, specification, and analysis of distributed, communication, and real-time systems using the Specification and Description Language (SDL-2010) and Message Sequence Charts (MSC) notations from the International Telecommunication Union (ITU-T), as well as related system design languages such as UML, ASN.1, TTCN-3, SysML, and the User Requirements Notation (URN).

The first seven editions of SAM (Berlin 1998, Grenoble 2000, Aberystwyth 2002, Ottawa 2004, Kaiserslautern 2006, Oslo 2010, and Innsbruck 2012) were workshops. Since the 2014 edition of SAM in Valencia, SAM has become a conference to better reflect its structure, audience, and overall quality.

This 9th SAM conference (http://sdl-forum.org/Events/SAM2016/) was co-located with the ACM/IEEE 19th International Conference on Model-Driven Engineering Languages and Systems (MODELS 2016) in Saint-Malo, France, during October 3–4, 2016.

Theme for 2016: Technology-Specific Aspects of Models

Modern modeling languages are used in many different domains and for many different applications. Technology-specific aspects of models include domain-specific aspects of models and peculiarities of using models for different technologies, including, but not limited to the Internet of Things (IoT), automotive software, cloud applications, and embedded software. Moreover, the usage of models for different purposes and the combination with different software engineering technologies, including but not limited to software testing, requirements engineering, and automated code generation are also of interest within this theme.

SAM 2016 especially invited contributions that cover such domain and application-specific aspects. Additionally, academics and industry representatives were invited to provide contributions regarding models and quality, language development, model-driven development, and applications.

Review Process

SAM 2016 used a multi-tier review process. First, all papers were reviewed by at least three Program Committee members. The papers and reviews were then made available to Program Committee members who did not have a conflict of interest with the authors. The papers were discussed online during a one-week online meeting before final decisions were made. Out of 31 full papers, 15 papers were selected (48% acceptance rate).

Proceedings Overview

This volume contains 15 papers selected for presentation at SAM 2016. The volume reflects the five sessions of the conference. The first two sessions are closely aligned with the conference theme with a session on the "Internet of Things" and a session on "Technology-Specific Aspects." The other three sessions cover aspects regarding modeling languages and model-driven development in general and were organized in the sessions "Languages, Configurations and Features" and "Patterns and Compilation."

Acknowledgement

The ninth edition of SAM was made possible by the dedicated work and contributions of many people and organizations. We thank the authors of submitted papers, the 41 members of the Program Committee, the three additional reviewers, and the board members of the SDL Forum Society. We thank the MODELS 2016 local Organizing Committee for their logistic support. The submission and review process was run with the EasyChair conference system (http://www.easychair.org/) and we thank the people behind this great tool.

October 2016

Jens Grabowski
Steffen Herbold

Organization

Organizing Committee

Chairs

Jens Grabowski	Georg-August-Universität Göttingen, Germany
Steffen Herbold	Georg-August-Universität Göttingen, Germany

SDL Forum Society

Reinhard Gotzhein (Chairman)	University of Kaiserslautern, Germany
Joachim Thees (Treasurer)	University of Kaiserslautern, Germany
Ferhat Khendek (Secretary)	Concordia University, Canada
Rick Reed (Non-voting board member)	TSE, UK

Program Committee

Program Chairs

Jens Grabowski	Georg-August-Universität Göttingen, Germany
Steffen Herbold	Georg-August-Universität Göttingen, Germany

Program Committee

Shaukat Ali	Simula Research Laboratory, Norway
Daniel Amyot	University of Ottawa, Canada
Rolv Bræk	Norwegian University of Science and Technology, Norway
Reinhard Brocks	HTW des Saarlandes, Germany
Tibor Csöndes	Ericsson, Hungary
Dennis Christmann	University of Kaiserslautern, Germany
Pau Fonseca I Casas	Universitat Politècnica de Catalunya, Spain
Janusz Dobrowolski	StateSoft, USA
Stein Erik Ellevseth	ABB Corporate Research, Norway
Joachim Fischer	Humboldt University of Berlin, Germany
Emmanuel Gaudin	PragmaDev, France
Abdelouahed Gherbi	Ecole de Technology Supérieure, Université du Quebec, Canada

Reinhard Gotzhein	University of Kaiserslautern, Germany
Jameleddine Hassine	KFUPM, Saudi Arabia
Øystein Haugen	SINTEF, Norway
Loïc Hélouët	Inria, France
Peter Herrmann	NTNU Trondheim, Norway
Ferhat Khendek	Concordia University, Canada
Gábor Kovács	Budapest University of Technology and Economics, Hungary
Alexander Kraas	T-Systems, Germany
Finn Kristoffersen	Cinderella ApS, Denmark
Anna Medve	University of Pannonia, Hungary
Birger Møller-Pedersen	University of Oslo, Norway
Gunter Mussbacher	McGill University, Canada
Helmut Neukirchen	University of Iceland, Iceland
Ileana Ober	University of Toulouse, IRIT, France
Iulian Ober	University of Toulouse, IRIT, France
Dorina Petriu	Carleton University, Canada
Andrej Pietschker	Giesecke & Devrient, Germany
Andreas Prinz	University of Agder, Norway
Rick Reed	TSE, UK
György Rethy	Ericsson, Hungary
Axel Rennoch	Fraunhofer FOKUS Berlin, Germany
Manuel Rodríguez Cayetano	University of Valladolid, Spain
Ina Schieferdecker	Freie Universität Berlin, Germany
Edel Sherratt	University of Wales Aberystwyth, UK
Maria Toeroe	Ericsson, Canada
Andreas Ulrich	Siemens AG, Germany
Hans Vangheluwe	University of Antwerp, Belgium and McGill University, Canada
Thomas Weigert	Uniquesoft LLC, USA
Marc-Florian Wendland	Fraunhofer FOKUS Berlin, Germany

Reviewers

Bart Meyers	McGill University, Canada
Martin Schneider	Fraunhofer FOKUS Berlin, Germany
Bruno Barroca	McGill University, Canada

Contents

Evaluating Variability Modeling Techniques for Supporting Cyber-Physical System Product Line Engineering

Safdar Aqeel Safdar[1(✉)], Tao Yue[1,2], Shaukat Ali[1], and Hong Lu[1]

[1] Simula Research Laboratory, Oslo, Norway
{safdar, tao, shaukat, honglu}@simula.no
[2] University of Oslo, Oslo, Norway

Abstract. Modern society is increasingly dependent on Cyber-Physical Systems (CPSs) in diverse domains such as aerospace, energy and healthcare. Employing Product Line Engineering (PLE) in CPSs is cost-effective in terms of reducing production cost, and achieving high productivity of a CPS development process as well as higher quality of produced CPSs. To apply CPS PLE in practice, one needs to first select an appropriate variability modeling technique (VMT), with which variabilities of a CPS Product Line (PL) can be specified. In this paper, we proposed a set of basic and CPS-specific variation point (VP) types and modeling requirements for proposing CPS-specific VMTs. Based on the proposed set of VP types (basic and CPS-specific) and modeling requirements, we evaluated four VMTs: Feature Modeling, Cardinality Based Feature Modeling, Common Variability Language, and SimPL (a variability modeling technique dedicated to CPS PLE), with a real-world case study. Evaluation results show that none of the selected VMTs can capture all the basic and CPS-specific VP and meet all the modeling requirements. Therefore, there is a need to extend existing techniques or propose new ones to satisfy all the requirements.

Keywords: Product Line Engineering · Variability modeling · Cyber-Physical Systems

1 Introduction

Cyber-Physical Systems (CPSs) integrate computation and physical processes and their embedded computers and networks monitor and control physical processes by often relying on closed feedback loops [1, 2]. Nowadays, CPSs can be found in many different domains such as energy, maritime and healthcare. Many CPS producers employ the Product Line Engineering (PLE) practice, aiming to improve the overall quality of produced CPSs and the productivity of their CPS development processes [3].

In [4], a systematic domain analysis of the CPS PLE industrial practice is presented, which focuses on capturing static variabilities and facilitating product configuration at the pre-deployment phase. The systematic domain analysis identifies the following key characteristics of CPS PLE: (1) CPSs are heterogeneous and hierarchical systems; (2) the hardware topology can vary from one product to another; (3) the generic

© Springer International Publishing AG 2016
J. Grabowski and S. Herbold (Eds.): SAM 2016, LNCS 9959, pp. 1–19, 2016.
DOI: 10.1007/978-3-319-46613-2_1

software code base might be instantiated differently for each product, mainly based on the hardware topology configuration; and (4) there are many dependencies among configurable parameters, especially across the software code base and the hardware topology. Various challenges in CPS PLE were also reported in [4] such as lacking of automation and guidance and expensive debugging of configuration data. In general, cost-effectively supporting CPS PLE, especially enabling automation of product configuration, is an industrial challenge.

Cost-effectiveness of PLE is characterized by its support for abstraction and automation. Generally speaking, abstraction is a key mean that enables reuse. Concise and expressive abstractions for CPS PLE are required to specify reusable artifacts at a suitable level of abstraction as commonalities and variabilities. Such abstractions are quite critical and provide the foundation for automation. To capture variabilities at a high level of abstraction, a number of variability modeling techniques (VMTs) are available in the literature, including Feature Modeling (FM) [5], Cardinality Based Feature Modeling (CBFM) [6], a UML-based variability modeling methodology named SimPL [7], and Common Variability Language (CVL) [8]. These VMTs were proposed for a particular context/domain/purpose. For example, SimPL was designed for the architecture level variability modeling. It is however no evidence showing which VMT suits CPS PLE the best.

In this paper, we propose a set of basic variation point (VP) types, CPS-specific VP types, and modeling requirements of CPS PLE. To define basic VP types, we constructed a conceptual model for basic data types in mathematics. Corresponding to each basic data type, we defined one basic VP type (Sect. 4.1). We also constructed a conceptual model for CPS based on the knowledge gathered from literature about CPSs and our experience of working with industry [4]. The second and third authors of the paper have experience of working with industrial CPS case studies and have derived the conceptual model. From the CPS conceptual model, we systematically derived a set of CPS-specific VP types (Sect. 4.2). We also derived a set of modeling requirements based on the literature and our experience in working with industry [4] (Sect. 5). Based on the proposed basic and CPS-specific VP types and the modeling requirements, we evaluated FM [5], CBFM [6], CVL [8], and SimPL [7]. FM was selected as it is the most widely used VMT in industry [9] and CBFM is an extension of FM. CVL is a language for modeling variability using any domain specific language based on Meta Object Facility (MOF), which was submitted to Object Management Group for standardization but did not go through due to Intellectual Property Rights issues. SimPL is a specific VMT dedicated for CPS PLE and has been applied to address industrial challenges. To evaluate the VMTs, we modeled a case study (Material Handling System-MHS) with all the VMTs and evaluated them using the proposed eight basic and 16 CPS-specific VP types, and nine modeling requirements.

Results of the evaluation show that (1) only SimPL and CVL can capture all the basic VP types, whereas FM and CBFM provide partial support. None of the four VMTs can capture all the CPS-specific VP types; (2) SimPL and CVL provide support for 81% and 75% of the total CPS-specific VP types respectively, whereas CBFM supports 50% and FM supports only 15% of the total CPS-specific VP types; (3) SimPL satisfies all but one of the modeling requirements, FM and CBFM only covers one modeling requirement, and CVL fully or partially fulfills four requirements out of nine requirements. Based on above results, we can conclude that it is required to either extend an existing technique or propose a new one to facilitate the variability modeling in the context of CPS PLE. The proposed VP types and modeling requirements can be also used as evaluation criteria for selecting existing VMTs or defining new ones for a particular application when necessary.

The rest of the paper is organized as follows: Sect. 2 presents the related work. Section 3 presents the context of the work. Section 4 presents the proposed VP types. Section 5 presents the modeling requirements. In Sect. 6, we report evaluation results. Threats to validity are given in Sect. 7. Section 8 concludes the paper.

2 Related Work

This section discusses the existing literature that compares or classifies VMTs, systematic literature reviews (SLRs) and surveys of VMTs.

Galster et al. [10] conducted a SLR of 196 papers published during 2000–2011, on variability management in different phases of software systems. Results show that most of the papers focus on design time variabilities and a small portion of the papers focus on runtime variabilities. In [11], Chen et al. conducted a SLR of 33 VMTs in software product lines and highlighted the challenges involved in variability modeling such as evolution of variability, and configuration. Arrieta et al. [12] conducted a SLR of variability management techniques, but limited their scope to techniques for Simulink published after 2008. Berger et al. [9] conducted a survey on industry practices of variability modeling using a questionnaire, aiming to discover characteristics of industrial variability models, VMTs, tools and processes. Another industrial survey of feature-based requirement VMTs was conducted to find out the most appropriate technique for a company [13]. They evaluated existing techniques based on requirements collected from the company's engineers, including readability, simplicity and expressive, types of variability and standardization.

Eichelberger and Schmid [14] classified and compared 10 textual VMTs in terms of scalability. They compared the selected techniques in five different aspects: configurable elements, constraints support, configuration support, scalability, and additional language characteristics. Similarly, Sinnema and Deelstra [15] classified six VMTs and compared them based on key characteristics of VMTs such as constraints, tool support, and configuration guidance. Czarnecki et al. [16] reported an experience report, in which they compared two types of VMTs: decision modeling and feature modeling. They compared them in 10 aspects: application, hierarchy, unit of variability, data types, constraints, modularity, orthogonality, mapping to artifacts, tool support, and binding time and mode. A comparative study [17] was reported to compare two VMTs, i.e., Kconfig and CDL, in the context of operating systems, in terms of constructs, semantics, and tool support.

All the above studies classify and evaluate various types of VMTs either in general or for a particular domain other than CPSs. We however, in this paper, propose a set of basic and CPS-specific VP types as well as a list of modeling requirements for evaluating VMTs in the context of CPS PLE, based on which we evaluated four representative VMTs with a non-trivial case study.

3 Context

Sections 3.1 and 3.2 introduce the case study and the four VMTs. In Sect. 3.3, we present the study procedure.

3.1 Case Study

The case study is a product line of Handling Systems, which consist of various types of sub-systems such as Automatic Storage Retrieval System (ASRS), Automatic Guided Vehicle (AGV), Automatic Identification and Data Collection (AIDC) and Warehouse Management System. We selected three of these systems: AGV, AIDC, and ASRS for the evaluation of the selected VMTs. AGV is a fully automatic transport system that uses unmanned vehicles to transport all types of loads without human intervention. It is typically used within warehouse, production and logistics for safe movement of goods. AIDC is used to identify, verify, record, and track the products. Typically, these systems are used in supply chain, order picking, order fulfillment, and determination of weight, volume, and storage. ASRS is an automated system for inventory management, which is used to place and retrieve the loads from pre-defined locations in the warehouse. The descriptive statistics of the MHS case study's class diagram are given in Table 1. We modeled the case study (MHS) using the four selected VMTs (i.e., FM, CBFM, SimPL, and CVL). The case study models corresponding to selected VMTs are available at [18].

Table 1. Descriptive statistics of the MHS

Element	Count
Class	132
Generalization	56
Composition	62
Association	69
Simple attribute	113
Enumerated attribute	82
Enumeration	23
Enumeration Literal	73

3.2 Variability Modeling Techniques

Feature Modeling (FM) is widely applied in practice [9]. A feature model is organized hierarchically as a tree. The root node of the tree represents the system, whereas the descendent nodes are functionalities of the system (features). A feature can be mandatory, optional or alternative. A feature can either be a compound feature that has one or more descendent features or a leaf feature with no descendent features. Figure 1 shows an excerpt of the FM model for AGV modeled using Pure::Variants [19]. As shown in Fig. 1, *AGVHardware, Sensor,* and *Connectivity*

Fig. 1. An excerpt of FM for AGV

are mandatory features. The *Connectivity* feature has three alternative features, i.e., *Bluetooth, Wifi,* and *NFC*. The *Sensor* feature has two optional features: *MultiRay-LEDScanner and LaserScanner.*

Cardinality Based Feature Modeling (CBFM) is an extension to FM, which introduces new concepts such as Feature Cardinalities, Groups and Groups Cardinalities, Attributes, and References. For Feature Cardinalities, features can be annotated with cardinalities such as <1..*> whereas alternative features and optional features are special cases with cardinality <1..1> and <0..1> respectively. A feature group can be or-group with cardinality <1..k> or

Fig. 2. An excerpt of CBFM for AGV

alternative-group with cardinality <1..1>. For an alternative-group, one can select only one feature, whereas for or-group, one can select 1 to *k* number of features where *k* is the maximum number of features in the group. A feature can have one attribute of either String or Integer type. To achieve better modularization, a special leaf node (i.e., Reference) was introduced to refer to another feature model. This can be used to divide a large feature model into smaller ones to support modularization. As shown in Fig. 1 *AGVHardware, Sensor*, and *Connectivity* are mandatory features. *AGVHardware* and *Sensor* have feature cardinality <1..10>. *Connectivity* has an alternative-group that consists of three features: *Bluetooth, Wifi*, and *NFC*. The *Sensor* feature has an or-group consisting of two features with group cardinality <0..2> (Fig. 2).

Common Variability Modeling (CVL) is a generic variability modeling language and is composed of three interrelated models: base model, variability model, and resolution model. The base model can be defined in UML or any MOF based Domain Specific Language (DSL). Corresponding to the base model a variability model is defined. The variability model has a tree structure to specify variabilities. The resolution model specifies configurations of variabilities corresponding to a particular product. To support CVL, an Eclipse-based

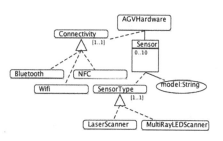

Fig. 3. An excerpt of CVL for AGV

plugin CT-CVL is available [20]. In Fig. 3, rounded rectangles (e.g., *AGVHardware, SensorType, Connectivity*) represent *Choice* elements and a rectangle (e.g., *Sensor*) represents a *VClassifier* element whereas an ellipse represents a variable. Multiplicity inside the *VClassifier Sensor* (0..10) indicates that the number of instances of sensors can be between zero to 10 where for each instance one needs to configure sensor type and model. *Connectivity* and *SensorType* are *ChoiceVP* with group cardinality (1..1), which means only one option can be selected from given alternative options.

SimPL is a UML based VMT, which provides notations and guidelines for modeling variabilities and commonalities of CPS product lines at the architecture and design level. To support SimPL, several modeling tools [21] (RSA, MagicDraw, and Papyrus) are available. It captures four types of VPs: Attribute-VP, Type-VP, Topology-VP, and Cardinality-VP. A SimPL product line model can be specified with a subset of UML structural elements and stereotypes defined in the SimPL profile. Constraints are specified in the Object Constraint Language (OCL). SimPL has two major views: SystemDesignView and VariabilityView. SystemDesignView is composed of HardwareView, SoftwareView, and AllocationView to represent hardware components, software components and their relationship. VariabilityView is for capturing and structuring variabilities using UML packages and template parameters. Stereotype « ConfigurationUnit » is applied on UML packages to group relevant variabilities. Variabilities are defined as template parameters of a package template and can trace back to hardware or software elements in the SystemDesignView. Figure 4 presents an excerpt of the *HardwareView* of MHS, in which *AGV* is a hardware component composed of zero to many *Sensors*. *Sensor* can be of two types: *LaserScanner* and *MultiRayLEDScanner*. *AGV* has one Attribute-VP (*connectivity*) and one Cardinality-VP (*sensors*) denoting the number of instances of *Sensor*. For *Sensor*, two variabilities are specified: model (Attribute-VP) and type of sensor (Type-VP). *AGVConfigurationUnit* and *SensorsConfigurationUnit* are the template packages that are used to organize the variabilities corresponding to hardware component *AGV* and hardware *Sensor* respectively.

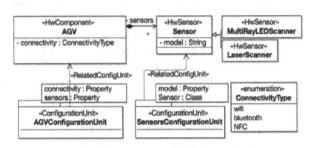

Fig. 4. An excerpt of SimPL for AGV

3.3   Procedure of the Study

Figure 5 describes the procedure that we followed to conduct the study. First, we constructed a conceptual model for defining data types in mathematics and then we validated the data types with MARTE [22] and SysML [23], as these two standards are often used for modeling embedded systems and therefore can be used for modeling CPSs. In the third step, we defined a set of basic VP types (Sect. 4.1), based on the mathematical basic data types. We used basic data types for defining the basic VP types, as configuring a VP always requires assigning/selecting a value to/for a basic type variable. In the fourth step, we derived a set of modeling requirements (Sect. 5) based on knowledge collected from the literature and our experience of conducting industry-oriented research in the field of CPS PLE [4]. In the fifth step, we constructed a conceptual model for CPS, which is used to systematically derive the CPS-specific VP types (Step 6, more details in Sect. 4.2). In Step 7, we modeled the MHS case study with the selected VMTs, followed by the evaluation of the selected VMTs (Step 8, details in Sect. 6), based on the basic VP types, CPS-specific VP types, and the set of modeling requirements.

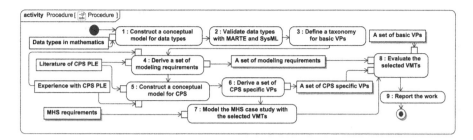

Fig. 5. Procedure of the study

4 Basic and CPS-Specific Variation Point Types

4.1 Basic Variation Point Types

Based on the basic data types in mathematics, we constructed a conceptual model to classify them, as shown in Fig. 6. A *Variable* can be a *VariationPoint* or a *Non-configurableVariable*, which represents the configurable and non-configurable variable in CPS PLE. Each *Variable* has a *Type*, which is classified into two categories: *Atomic* (taking a single value at a given point of time) and *Composite* (composed of more than one atomic type, where each

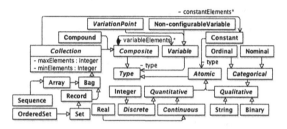

Fig. 6. Basic data types

atomic type variable takes exactly one value at a given point in time). Atomic types are further classified into *Quantitative* types (taking numeric values) and *Qualitative* types (taking non-numeric values). *Quantitative* types can be *Discrete* (taking countable values) or *Continuous* (taking uncountable values). *Integer* is the concrete *Discrete* type, whereas *Real* is the concrete *Continuous* type. *Qualitative* types are categorized into *String*, *Binary* and *Categorical* that is further classified into *Ordinal* and *Nominal*.

A *Composite* data type combines several variables and/or constants, which is classified as: *Compound* and *Collection*. *Compound* takes only variables (e.g., complex numbers in SysML containing two variables realPart and imaginaryPart [23]) whereas *Collection* takes *Variables* and/or *Constants* (e.g., collection of colors). Attributes *minElements* and *maxElements* of *Collection* specify the minimum and maximum numbers of elements in a

Table 2. Collection types

Collection	Hom.	Uni.	Ord.
Bag	No	No	No
Record	No	Yes	No
Set	Yes	Yes	No
OrderedSet	Yes	Yes	Yes
Array	Yes	No	No
Sequence	Yes	No	Yes

collection. As shown in Fig. 6, we have classified *Collection* into six types (i.e., *Bag*, *Array*, *Record*, *Set*, *OrderedSet* and *Sequence*) based on three properties: homogeneity, uniqueness and order. The homogeneity, uniqueness, and order properties of each collection type are specified as OCL constraints (Appendix A). Table 2 summarizes the six types of *Collection* along with their properties.

To validate the conceptual model of the basic data types, we mapped the data types defined in the MARTE Value Specification Language-VSL [22] and SysML [23] to the basic data types presented in Fig. 6. We used MARTE and SysML for validation because these two modeling languages can be used for modeling CPSs [24, 25]. During the validation, we do not include the extended data types provided in MARTE, as they are defined by extending the data types used in our

Table 3. Mapping MARTE and SysML data types to the basic data types

MARTE	SysML	Basic data types
Integer	Integer	Integer
UnlimitedNatural	UnlimitedNatural	Integer
Boolean	Boolean	Binary
String	String	String
Real	Real	Real
DateTime	Complex	Compound
EnumerationType	Enumeration	Ordinal/Nominal
	ControlValue	Nominal/Ordinal
IntervalType	UnitAndQuantityKind	Compound
TupleType		Compound
ChoiceType		Compound
CollectionType		Collection

mapping. In case of SysML we include all the data types. Results of the mapping are presented in Table 3, from which one can see that each data type in MARTE and SysML has a correspondence in our basic data type classification, which suggests that our classification of the basic data types is complete.

In Fig. 7, we present a classification of basic VP types where one basic VP type is defined corresponding to each basic data type presented in Fig. 6. A *VariationPoint* can be a *CompositeVP* or an *AtomicVP*. An *AtomicVP* can come with any of the six concrete types: *StringVP, BinaryVP, NominalVP, OrdinalVP, IntegerVP, and RealVP* corresponding to *String, Binary, Nominal, Ordinal, Integer,* and *Real* respectively. A *CompositeVP* can be *CompoundVP* or *CollectionVP*, which are defined corresponding to *Compound* and *Collection* data types respectively. As shown in Fig. 7, a *CompositeVP* may have several *AtomicVPs* and/or *CompositeVPs* depending on the number of *variableElements* (Fig. 6) involved in the *Composite* data type. *CollectionVP* may have two additional *IntegerVP*(s), i.e., *lowerLimitVP* and *upperLimitVP* corresponding to the minimum and maximum numbers of the elements in the collection.

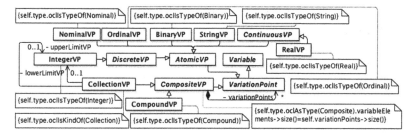

Fig. 7. Classification of the basic VP types

4.2 CPS-Specific Variation Point Types

In this section, first we present a conceptual model for CPS (Fig. 8), based on which we then derive a set of CPS-specific VP types (Table 4). As shown in Fig. 8, a CPS can be defined as a set of physical components (e.g., human heart, engine), interfacing components (e.g., sensor, actuator, network), and cyber components (with deployed software), which are integrated together to accomplish a common goal.

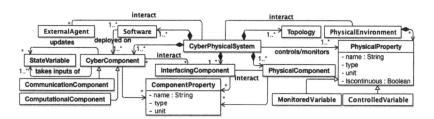

Fig. 8. A CPS conceptual model

A CPS can have one or more topologies, which define how various components are integrated. A CPS controls and monitors a set of physical properties. A *CyberComponent* can either be a *CommunicationComponent* or *ComputationalComponent*, which takes values of *StateVariables* as input and updates their values when needed. Each component in CPS has several component properties. CPS may interact with *PhysicalEnvironment* and *ExternalAgent*s (e.g., external systems). Both *PhysicalProperty* and *ComponentProperty* have attributes *name*, *type*, and *unit* to specify the name, type (e.g., descriptive, numeric, Boolean), and unit of a specific property. *PhysicalProperty* has an extra Boolean attribute *isContinuous* to specify either it is a continuous or a discrete type of property.

In Table 4, the first column represents the CPS concepts used to derive CPS-specific VP types and the second column shows the derived CPS-specific VP types. The last column presents the basic VP type corresponding to a particular CPS-specific VP type.

Table 4. CPS-specific VP types

CPS concept	CPS-specific VP type	Basic VP type
CP	Descriptive-VP	StringVP
CP, PP	DiscreteMeasurement-VP	IntegerVP
CP, PP	ContinuousMeasurement-VP	RealVP
CP, PP	BinaryChoice-VP	BinaryVP
CP, PP	PropertyChoice-VP	NominalVP/OrdinalVP
CP, PP	MeasurementUnitChoice-VP	OrdinalVP
CP, PP	MeasurementPrecision-VP	RealVP
CP, PP, COM	Multipart/Compound-VP	CompoundVP
COM	ComponentCardinality-VP	IntegerVP
COM	ComponentCollectionBoundary-VP	IntegerVP
COM	ComponentChoice-VP	NominalVP/OrdinalVP
COM	ComponentSelection-VP	CollectionVP
Topology	TopologyChoice-VP	NominalVP
Deployment	AllocationChoice-VP	NominalVP
Interact	InteractionChoice-VP	NominalVP
Constraint	ConstraintSelection-VP	CollectionVP

*CP = ComponentProperty, PP = PhysicalProperty, COM = Physical,
Interfacing, or Physical Component

PhysicalProperty and **ComponentProperty:** Descriptive-VP, DiscreteMeasurement-VP, ContinuousMeasurement-VP, BinaryChoice-VP, PropertyChoice-VP, MeasurementUnitChoice-VP, and MeasurementPrecision-VP are defined for physical properties and/or component properties of CPS. Descriptive-VP is a *StringVP*, which requires setting a value in order to configure it. It can be defined for a textual *ComponentProperty* such as ID of a sensor. DiscreteMeasurement-VP and ContinuousMeasurement-VP are *IntegerVP* and *RealVP* respectively. Both these two types of VPs can be defined for numeric component properties (e.g., data transmission interval of a sensor) or physical properties (e.g., length and weight of a physical component) of CPS. BinaryChoice-VP is a *BinaryVP*, which can be defined for Boolean physical properties (e.g., the presence of a magnetic field) and component properties (e.g., whether a sensor keeps the events' log). PropertyChoice-VP is a *NominalVP* or an *OrdinalVP*, which requires selecting one value from a list of pre-defined values. For example, a *ComponentProperty* can be connectionType, which can be configured as wired, 3G, or Wi-Fi, which can be captured as a PropertyChoice-VP. MeasurementUnitChoice-VP is an *OrdinalVP*, which is derived from the *unit* of *PhysicalProperty* and *ComponentProperty*. For example, one can select meter, centimeter or millimeter as a unit for length (a *PhysicalProperty*). MeasurementPrecision-VP is a *RealVP*, which is related to the degree of measurement precision for a *PhysicalProperty* or *ComponentProperty*.

Component: ComponentCardinality-VP, ComponentCollectionBoundary-VP, ComponentChoice-VP, and ComponentSelection-VP are derived from the different types of CPS components: *CyberComponent*, *InterfacingComponent*, *PhysicalComponent*.

ComponentCardinality-VP is an *IntegerVP*, which is related to varying number of instances of a CPS component (e.g., number of temperature sensors). Component-CollectionBoundary-VP is an *IntegerVP*, which is related to the upper limit and/or the lower limit of a collection of CPS components. For example, the maximum and minimum numbers of sensors supported by a controller. ComponentChoice-VP is a *NominalVP/OrdinalVP*, which is about selecting a particular type of CPS component such as selecting a speedometer sensor from several speedometers with various specifications. ComponentSelection-VP is a *CollectionVP*, which is about selecting a subset of CPS components from a collection of CPS components such as selecting sensors for a product from available sensors.

Multipart/Compound-VP is a *CompoundVP*, which can be specified for a *PhysicalProperty*, *ComponentProperty*, or a component (Physical, Cyber, or Interfacing) that requires configuring several constituent VPs involved in it. As in the domain of CPS, it is common that different properties do not give complete meaning unless they are combined together. For example, length is a *PhysicalProperty*, which is meaningless without a unit. Hence, we need a Compound-VP type, which involves two VPs including length and its unit. A Compound-VP can also be defined for a component (e.g., sensor), which contains several other VPs defined for its properties.

Topology: TopologyChoice-VP is a *NominalVP*, which is related to selecting a topology from several alternatives. For example, how *CyberComponent* (e.g., controller) is connected with *InterfacingComponent*s (e.g., sensors and actuators).

Deployment: AllocationChoice-VP is a *NominalVP*, which is about the deployment of software on a *CyberComponent* (e.g., controller). For example, the same version of software can be deployed on different controllers or different versions of software can be deployed on the same controller.

Interaction: InteractionChoice-VP is a *NominalVP*, which is about the interaction (presented as association named interact in Fig. 8), of two CPS components (e.g., *CyberComponent* and *InterfacingComponent*) or interaction of CPS with an external agent, which can be for example an external system.

Constraint: ConstraintSelection-VP is a *CollectionVP*, which is about selecting a subset of constraints in order to support the configuration of a specific product, from a set of constraints defined for the corresponding CPS product line.

5 Modeling Requirements

In addition to capturing different types of VPs, a VMT should also accommodate some modeling requirements to enable automation of configuring CPS products. These requirements (Table 5) are derived from the literature and our experience of working with industry [4].

In Table 5, R_1 is related to support different binding times of a VP, as a VP can be configured at three different phases [26]: the pre-deployment phase, the deployment phase and the post-deployment phase. Requirements R_2 focuses on a traceability mechanism to link the variability model and its base whereas R_3 is related to realizing the separation of concerns principle in the product line model. R_4–R_8 are relevant to different types constraints that a VMT should be able to capture for enabling automation of the configuration process in CPS PLE [3]. In [3], a constraint classification was presented and we extended it by adding two more categories: inference and conformance. These constraints are needed to facilitate different functionalities of an interactive, multi-step and multi-staged configuration solution, such as consistency checking, decision inferences. R_9 is related to modeling different types of configurable elements of CPSs.

Table 5. Modeling requirements

ID	Name	Description
R_1	VP binding time	Support different binding times for a VP (e.g., pre-deployment, deployment, and post-deployment phases).
R_2	Linkage between VP and the base	Provide a mechanism to relate a VP to the corresponding base model element.
R_3	Separation of Concerns	Provide a mechanism to realize the principle of separation of concerns to enable multi-staged and cross-disciplinary configuration of CPS.
R_4	Variability dependency	Capture dependencies between a VP and a variant, two VPs, and two variants.
R_5	Ordering	Specify constraints on the order of configuration steps.
R_6	Inference	Specify constraints that can be used to configure VPs automatically.
R_7	Conformance	Specify conformance rules for ensuring the correctness of configuration data.
R_8	Consistency	Specify consistency rules for checking the consistency of the configuration data and variability models.
R_9	Multidisciplinary	Model *Software*, *PhysicalComponent*, *InterfacingComponent*, *CyberComponent*, and *PhysicalEnvironment* elements of CPS.

6   Evaluation

The purpose of the evaluation is to compare the selected four VMTs with the aim to help modelers to select an appropriate VMT or propose a new one if necessary for CPS PLE, which can capture different types of VPs (Sect. 4) and meet the modeling requirements (Sect. 5). Corresponding to this goal, we pose the following research questions: **RQ1**: To what extent can each selected VMT capture the basic VPs? **RQ2**: To what extent can each selected VMT capture the CPS-specific VPs? **RQ3**: To what extent does a selected VMT comply with the modeling requirements? We answer RQ1, RQ2 and RQ3 in Sects. 6.1, 6.2, and 6.3, respectively.

6.1   Evaluation Based on Basic VP Types (RQ1)

To answer RQ1, we evaluate the selected VMTs based on the basic VP types. In Table 6, the first column represents the basic VP type and the second column indicates if a basic VP type is required by the MHS case study, whereas columns 3–6 show how each selected VMT supports each basic VP type.

As one can see from Table 6, modeling the MHS case study requires all the basic VP types. However, FM supports only three out of eight basic VP types: *BinaryVP*, *NominalVP* and *OrdinalVP*. Optional feature and alternative-group with two features of FM map to *BinaryVPs*. In FM, alternative-group corresponds to *NominalVPs* and *OrdinalVPs*, but FM does not differentiate *NominalVP* from *OrdinalVP*. CBFM provides support for all the basic VP types except for *CompoundVP*. Corresponding to *RealVPs* and *StringVPs*, CBFM provides attributes (one attribute per feature) of Real and String respectively. However, for *IntegerVPs*, it offers feature and group cardinalities together with Integer attributes. For *BinaryVP*, CBFM has optional features, alternative-groups, feature cardinalities (0..1), and Boolean attributes. Similar to FM, CBFM also provides alternative-groups, which map to *NominalVPs* and *OrdinalVPs* and CBFM does not differentiate these two types. For *CollectionVP*, CBFM provides alternative-groups and or-groups.

Both SimPL and CVL support all the basic VP types. In SimPL, Attribute-VP defined with Real and String attributes map to *RealVPs* and *StringVPs*. *IntegerVPs* can map to Attribute-VPs defined on Integer attributes or Cardinality-VP. To support *BinaryVP*, SimPL provides Attribute-VP defined on attributes of the binary type, Cardinality-VP with two options, Type-VP with two types, and Topology-VP with two topologies. Cardinality-VP, Type-VP, and Topology-VP offered by SimPL can be mapped to *NominalVPs* and *OrdinalVPs*. SimPL does not differentiate *NominalVP* and *OrdinalVP*. To support *CompoundVP*, SimPL defines «ConfigurationUnit», which can be applied on packages, to organize a set of relevant VPs. In SimPL, *CollectionVP* corresponds to Cardinality-VP.

To support *RealVP* and *StringVP*, CVL provides ParametricVP. For *IntegerVP* it provides ParametricVP and cardinalities. For *BinaryVP*, CVL has different types of ChoiceVPs (i.e., ObjectSubstitution, SlotAssignment, ObjectExistence, SlotValue-Existence, and LinkExistence) along with multiplicity and ParametricSlotAssignment (i.e., ParametricVP). In CVL, both *NominalVPs* and *OrdinalVPs* can be mapped to SlotAssignments (i.e., ChoiceVP) with group multiplicity (1..1) or ParametricObjectSubstitution (i.e., ParametricVP). Similar to all the other VMTs, CVL does not differentiate *NominalVP* and *OrdinalVP*. In CVL, *CompoundVP* maps to CompositeVP and a VClassifier with several RepeatableVP(s) can also be used to model *CompoundVPs*. For *CollectionVP*, CVL has VClassifier with the multiplicity other than (1..1) and a group of SlotAssignment (i.e., ChoiceVP).

To summarize, both SimPL and CVL support all the basic VP types whereas FM and CBFM provide partial support. None of the selected four VMTs differentiate NominalVP and OrdinalVP.

Table 6. Evaluation based on the basic VP types (RQ1)

Basic VP Type	MHS	VMT			
		FM	CBFM	SimPL	CVL
IntegerVP	Yes	No	One At/F, G & F Cardinality	Attribute-VP, Cardinality-VP	Multiplicity, ParametricVP
RealVP	Yes	No	One At/F	Attribute-VP	ParametricVP
StringVP	Yes	No	One At/F	Attribute-VP	ParametricVP
BinaryVP	Yes	OF, Alt. F	One At/F, OF, Alt. G, F-Cardinality	Attribute-VP, Cardinality-VP, Type-VP, Topology-VP	ChoiceVP (ObjectSubstitution, SlotAssignment, ObjectExistence, SlotValueExistence, LinkExistence), Multiplicity, ParametricSlotAssignment
NominalVP	Yes	Alt. G	Alt. G	Attribute-VP, Type-VP, Topology-VP	Group of SlotAssignment (i.e., ChoiceVP) with group Multiplicity (1,1), ParametricObjectSubstitution (i.e., ParametricVP).
OrdinalVP	Yes	Alt. G	Alt. G		
CompoundVP	Yes	No	No	Configuration Unit	CompositeVP, VClassifier with several Repeatable-VP(s).
CollectionVP	Yes	No	Alt. G, OR G	Cardinality-VP	VClassifier with configurable Multiplicity, group of SlotAssignment (i.e., ChoiceVP).

*F = feature, OF = optional feature, G = group, At = attribute, Alt = Alternative, / = per, & = and

6.2 Evaluation Based on the CPS-Specific VP Types (RQ2)

To answer RQ2, we evaluate the selected four VMTs based on the CPS-specific VP types (Sect. 4.2) and VPs modeled for the MHS case study. In Table 7, the first column represents the CPS-specific VP types and the second column indicates if a particular CPS-specific VP type is required by the MHS case study. Columns 3–6 are related to the four VMTs to signify if they support a particular CPS-specific basic VP type. The seventh column shows the number of VPs in the MHS case study corresponding to a particular CPS-specific VP type, whereas columns 8–11 show the number of VPs modeled using the four VMTs.

As one can see from Table 7, our case study (MHS) contains VPs corresponding to all the CPS-specific VP types. FM does not cater majority of the CPS-specific VP types and only supports fully or partially three out of 16 CPS-specific VP types: BinaryChoice-VP, PropertyChooice-VP, and ComponentChoice-VP.

CBFM supports six of 16 CPS-specific VP types: ComponentCardinality-VP, ComponentCollectionBoundary-VP, MeasurementPrecision-VP, PropertyChoice-VP, ComponentChoice-VP, and ComponentSelection-VP. It provides partial support for three CPS-specific VP types (i.e., Descriptive-VP, DiscreteMeasurement-VP, and ContinuousMeasurement-VP) because CBFM allows adding only one attribute for each feature. BinaryChoice-VP is also partially supported, as it can be captured using optional feature or cardinality but CBFM does not allow adding Boolean attribute. The remaining six CPS-specific VP types are not supported by CBFM.

Both SimPL and CVL support Descriptive-VP, DiscreteMeasurement-VP, ContinuousMeasurement-VP, ComponentSelection-VP, ComponentCardinality-VP, ComponentCollectionBoundary-VP, BinaryChoice-VP, MeasurementPrecision-VP, MeasurementUnitChoice-VP, PropertyChoice-VP, ComponentChoice-VP, and Compound-VP. SimPL also supports TopologyChoice-VPs, which cannot be captured using CVL. The remaining three CPS-specific VP types (i.e., AllocationChoice-VP, InteractionChoice-VP, and ConstraintSelection-VP) are not catered by either SimPL or CVL.

Table 7. Evaluation of VMTs based on the CPS-specific VP types and VPs (RQ2)

CPS-specific VP type	VP types coverage					VP coverage				
	MHS	FM	CBFM	SimPL	CVL	MHS	FM	CBFM	SimPL	CVL
Descriptive-VP	Yes	No	Partial	Yes	Yes	34	0	4	34	34
Discrete Measurement-VP	Yes	No	Partial	Yes	Yes	23	0	5	23	23
Continuous Measurement-VP	Yes	No	Partial	Yes	Yes	51	0	18	51	51
ComponentCardinality-VP	Yes	No	Yes	Yes	Yes	42	0	42	42	42
ComponentCollectionBoundary-VP	Yes	No	Yes	Yes	Yes	42	0	42	42	42
MeasurementPrecision-VP	Yes	No	Yes	Yes	Yes	2	0	2	2	2
BinaryChoice-VP	Yes	Partial	Partial	Yes	Yes	3	0	0	3	3
PropertyChoice-VP	Yes	Yes	Yes	Yes	Yes	82	82	82	82	82
ComponentChoice-VP	Yes	Yes	Yes	Yes	Yes	12	12	12	12	12
TopologyChoice-VP	Yes	No	No	Yes	No	9	0	0	9	0
AllocationChoice-VP	Yes	No	No	No	No	3	0	0	0	0
InteractionChoice-VP	Yes	No	No	No	No	15	0	0	0	0
MeasurementUnitChoice-VP	Yes	No	No	Yes	Yes	59	0	18	59	59
ConstraintSelection-VP	Yes	No	No	No	No	1	0	0	0	0
ComponentSelection-VP	Yes	No	Yes	Yes	Yes	42	0	42	42	42
Multipart/Compound-VP	Yes	No	No	Yes	Yes	64	0	0	64	26
Total (count)	**16**	**2.5**	**8**	**13**	**12**	**484**	**94**	**267**	**465**	**418**
Coverage (%)	**100 %**	**15 %**	**50 %**	**81 %**	**75 %**	**–**	**19 %**	**55 %**	**96 %**	**86 %**

As shown in Table 7, none of the selected VMTs supports all the CPS-specific VP types. SimPL supports 81 %, FM supports only 15 %, CVL caters 75 %, and CBFM covers 50 % of the total CPS-specific VP types. Using SimPL and CVL we were able to model 96 % and 86 %, whereas with FM and CBFM, we could model only 19 % and 55 % of total VPs in our case study.

6.3   Evaluation Based on the Modeling Requirements (RQ3)

Table 8 summarizes the results of our evaluation of the four VMTs in terms of modeling requirements (Sect. 5) with MHS. In Table 8, the first two columns are used to identify the requirements and the third column indicates if a requirement is required by MHS. Columns 4–7 signify if the VMTs support a particular requirement.

None of the selected VMTs except for CVL allows specifying the binding time (R_1) of a VP to enable its configuration in different phases. CVL and SimPL support linking a VP to the corresponding base model element explicitly (R_2), which is however not supported by FM and CBFM, as they do not have separate base models. FM and CBFM

Table 8. Results for the evaluation of the VMTs based on the modeling requirements (RQ3)

ID	Name	MHS	FM	CBFM	CVL	SimPL
R_1	VP binding times	Yes	No	No	Yes	No
R_2	Linkage between VP and the base	Yes	No	No	Yes	Yes
R_3	Separation of Concerns	Yes	No	No	Partial	Yes
R_4	Variability dependencies	Yes	Partial	Partial	Partial	Yes
R_5	Ordering	Yes	No	No	Depends on base modeling language	Yes
R_6	Inference	Yes	No	No		Yes
R_7	Conformance	Yes	No	No		Yes
R_8	Consistency	Yes	No	No		Yes
R_9	Multidisciplinary	Yes	No	No		Partial

do not support the separation of concerns (R_3) and CVL supports partially as it models variabilities separately from the base model. SimPL supports R_3 as it provides hardware, software and allocation views in addition to the variability view. For MHS, we captured all the four views defined in SimPL. But, it still requires a view for specifying environment elements and corresponding VPs.

R_4–R_8 are related to capturing different types of constraints to enable automation in CPS PLE. FM and CBFM provide partial support for capturing variability dependencies such as requires and excludes, but they are unable to capture other complex constraints such as consistency rules. In the case of CVL, it uses the Basic Constraint Language [8] for capturing simple propositional and arithmetic constraints but it is unable to capture all the types of constraints discussed in Sect. 5. If the base model is modeled in UML, then OCL can be integrated with CVL, thereby allowing the specification of all the types of constraints. SimPL is based on UML and OCL, which makes it possible to capture all the types of constraints.

MHS is a multidisciplinary system, which contains *Software*, *CyberComponent*, and different types of *PhysicalComponent* and *InterfacingComponent* interacting with *PhysicalEnvironment* but none of the selected VMTs explicitly model these multidisciplinary elements of CPS (R_9). SimPL supports all, except for *PhysicalEnvironment* elements. In case of CVL, it depends on the DSL used for modeling the base model, which may or may not have the capability of modeling different elements of CPS.

7   Threats to Validity

One threat to validity of our study is the selection of the VMTs. Since it is not practically feasible to evaluate all existing VMTs, we therefore selected four representative VMTs. Another threat to validity is the completeness of the basic and CPS-specific VP types and modeling requirements. Note that our approach for deriving the basic VP types is systematic, which to certain extent ensures their completeness. In addition, we validated them using SysML and MARTE, which are two existing standards often used for embedded system modeling. We derived CPS-specific VP types based on thorough domain analyses and our experience in working with industry. We also verified that the MHS case study covers all the CPS-specific VP types.

8 Conclusion

In this paper, we present a set of basic and CPS-specific VP types that need to be supported by a VMT in the context of CPS PLE. Moreover, we present a set of modeling requirements, which need to be catered to enable the automation of configuration in CPS PLE. Based on the proposed basic and CPS-specific VP types and modeling requirements, we evaluated four VMTs: feature model, cardinality based feature model, CVL, and SimPL, with a real-world case study. Results of our evaluation show that the selected four VMTs cannot capture all the VP types and none of the four VMTs meets all the requirements. This necessitates the extension of an existing technique or proposal of a new one to facilitate CPS PLE. The proposed VP types and modeling requirements can be used as evaluation criteria to select a suitable VMT or develop a new one if necessary.

Acknowledgement. This work was supported by the Zen-Configurator project funded by the Research Council of Norway (grant no. 240024/F20) under the category of Young Research Talents of the FRIPO funding scheme. Tao Yue and Shaukat Ali are also supported by the EU Horizon 2020 project U-Test (http://www.u-test.eu/) (grant no. 645463), the RFF Hovedstaden funded MBE-CR (grant no. 239063) project, the Research Council of Norway funded MBT4CPS (grant no. 240013/O70) project, and the Research Council of Norway funded Certus SFI (grant no. 203461/O30).

Appendix A: OCL Constraints

Homogeneity: context Array, Set (Sequence, OrderedSet)(**self**.constantElements->size()=0 **and self**.variableElements->select(a|a.**oclIsKindOf**(Collection))->size()=0 **and self**.variableElements->forAll(a,b| a.type=b.type))**or** (**self**.variableElements->size()=0 **and self**.constantElements->forAll(a,b| a.type=b.type)) **or** (**self**.constantElements->size()=0 **and self**.variableElements->size()=**self**.variableElements->select(a:Variable|a.type.**oclIs KindOf**(Collection))->size() **and self**.variableElements->forAll(v1, v2|(v1.type.**oclAsType**(Collection).constant Elements->size()=0 **and** v1.type.**oclAsType**(Collection).variableElements->forAll(v3:Variable | v3.type = v2.type.**oclAsType**(Collection).variableElements->asSequence()->first().type)) **or** (v1.type.**oclAsType**(Collection).variableElements->size()=0 **and** v1.type.**oclAs Type**(Collection).constantElements->forAll(v3:Constant| v3.type=v2.type.**oclAsType** (Collection).constantElements->asSequence()->first().type))))

Uniqueness: context Record (Set, OrderedSet) **self**.variableElements->select (**self**.variableElements ->forAll(a,b| a=b))->isEmpty() **and self**.constant Elements->select (**self**.constantElements->forAll(a,b| a=b))->isEmpty()

Order: context Sequence **self**.variableElements->asSet()->size() >1 **implies self**.variableElements->asSequence()->reverse() <> **self**.variableElements->asSequence() **and self**.constantElements->asSet()->size() >1 **implies self**.constantElements->asSequence()->reverse() <> **self**.constantElements->asSequence()

context OrderedSet **self**.variableElements->asOrderedSet()->reverse() <> **self**.variableElements->asOrderedSet() **and self**.constantElements->asOrderedSet()->reverse() <> **self**.constantElements->asOrderedSet()

References

1. http://cyberphysicalsystems.org/
2. Rawat, D.B., Rodrigues, J.J., Stojmenovic, I.: Cyber-Physical Systems: From Theory to Practice. CRC Press, Boca Raton (2015)
3. Nie, K., Yue, T., Ali, S., Zhang, L., Fan, Z.: Constraints: the core of supporting automated product configuration of cyber-physical systems. In: Moreira, A., Schätz, B., Gray, J., Vallecillo, A., Clarke, P. (eds.) MODELS 2013. LNCS, vol. 8107, pp. 370–387. Springer, Heidelberg (2013)
4. Yue, T., Ali, S., Selic, B.: Cyber-physical system product line engineering: comprehensive domain analysis and experience report. In: Proceedings of the 19th International Conference on Software Product Line, pp. 338–347. ACM (2015)
5. Kang, K., Cohen, S., Hess, J., Novak, W., Peterson, A.: Feature-Oriented Domain Analysis (FODA) Feasibility Study (CMU/SEI-90-TR-021). Carnegie Mellon University (1990)
6. Czarnecki, K., Helsen, S.: Staged configuration using feature models. In: Nord, R.L. (ed.) SPLC 2004. LNCS, vol. 3154, pp. 266–283. Springer, Heidelberg (2004)
7. Behjati, R., Yue, T., Briand, L., Selic, B.: SimPL: a product-line modeling methodology for families of integrated control systems. Inf. Softw. Technol. **55**, 607–629 (2013)
8. Haugen, O.: Common Variability Language (CVL). OMG Revised Submission (2012)
9. Berger, T., Rublack, R., Nair, D., Atlee, J.M., Becker, M., Czarnecki, K., Wąsowski, A.: A survey of variability modeling in industrial practice. In: Proceedings of 7th International Workshop on Variability Modelling of Software Intensive Systems, pp. 7. ACM (2013)
10. Galster, M., Weyns, D., Tofan, D., Michalik, B., Avgeriou, P.: Variability in software systems-A systematic literature review. IEEE Trans. Softw. Eng. **40**, 282–306 (2014)
11. Chen, L., Ali Babar, M., Ali, N.: Variability management in software product lines: a systematic review. In: 13th International Software Product Line Conference, pp. 81–90 (2009)
12. Arrieta, A., Sagardui, G., Etxeberria, L.: A comparative on variability modelling and management approach in simulink for embedded systems. V Jornadas de Computación Empotrada, ser. JCE (2014)
13. Djebbi, O., Salinesi, C.: Criteria for comparing requirements variability modeling notations for product lines. In: 4th International Workshop on Comparative Evaluation in Requirements Engineering, pp. 20–35. IEEE (2006)
14. Eichelberger, H., Schmid, K.: A systematic analysis of textual variability modeling languages. In: Software Product Line Conference, pp. 12–21. ACM (2013)
15. Sinnema, M., Deelstra, S.: Classifying variability modeling techniques. Inf. Softw. Technol. **49**, 717–739 (2007)
16. Czarnecki, K., Grünbacher, P., Rabiser, R., Schmid, K., Wąsowski, A.: Cool features and tough decisions: a comparison of variability modeling approaches. In: Proceedings of 6th International Workshop on Variability Modeling of Software Intensive Systems, pp. 173–182. ACM (2012)
17. Berger, T., She, S., Lotufo, R., Wąsowski, A., Czarnecki, K.: Variability modeling in the real: a perspective from the operating systems domain. In: International conference on Automated software engineering, pp. 73–82. ACM (2010)
18. http://www.zen-tools.com/SAM2016.html
19. http://www.pure-systems.com
20. http://modelbased.net/tools/ct-cvl/

21. Safdar, S.A., Iqbal, M.Z., Khan, M.U.: Empirical evaluation of UML modeling tools–a controlled experiment. In: Taentzer, G., Bordeleau, F. (eds.) ECMFA 2015. LNCS, vol. 9153, pp. 33–44. Springer, Heidelberg (2015)
22. The UML MARTE profile. http://www.omgmarte.org/
23. OMG: Systems Modeling Language (SysML) v1.4 (2015). http://sysml.org/
24. Selic, B., Gérard, S.: Modeling and Analysis of Real-Time and Embedded Systems with UML and MARTE: Developing Cyber-Physical Systems. Elsevier, Amsterdam (2013)
25. Derler, P., Lee, E.A., Vincentelli, A.S.: Modeling cyber–physical systems. Proc. IEEE **100**, 13–28 (2012)
26. Murguzur, A., Capilla, R., Trujillo, S., Ortiz, Ó., Lopez-Herrejon, R.E.: Context variability modeling for runtime configuration of service-based dynamic software product lines. In: Proceedings of the 18th International Software Product Line Conference: Companion Volume for Workshops, Demonstrations and Tools, pp. 2–9. ACM (2014)

Complex Event Processing in ThingML

An Ngoc Lam[(✉)] and Øystein Haugen

Østfold University College, Halden, Norway
{anl,oystein.haugen}@hiof.no
http://www.hiof.no

Abstract. Complex Event Processing (CEP) is concerned with real-time detection of complex events within multiple streams of atomic occurrences. Numerous approaches in CEP have been already proposed in the literature. In this paper, we examine the CEP Extension of ThingML which is a cross-platform modeling language for deploying Cyber Physical System (CPS). In particular, we focus on both language characteristic and performance of the ThingML Extension while processing CEP queries. Experiments show that although ThingML does not outperform other well-known CEP engines, it is still a potential CEP solution for CPS which has limited physical resources. In addition, ThingML also shows its efficiency in term of language expressiveness in comparison with State Machine based CEP queries.

Keywords: ThingML Modeling Language · Complex Event Processing · Language expressiveness · Processing performance · Cyber Physical System

1 Introduction

Complex Event Processing (CEP) is a set of methods and techniques for tracking and analyzing real-time streams of information and detecting patterns or correlations of unrelated data (complex events) that are of interest to a particular business [21]. Besides being an attractive research topic, CEP concept is already applied in many areas such as finance, manufacturing processes, energy management, etc. [6]. It also has a strong impact on information systems design especially with the pervasive evolution of decentralized data nowadays [6]. Today, with the convergence of *Internet of Thing* (IoT) and *Big Data*, the ability to large-scale real-time stream processing and analysis become more and more demanding; especially in *Cyber Physical Systems* (CPS) where fast response is sometimes crucial (e.g., traffic management systems). Therefore, CEP has evolved to cope with these situations in order to build highly scalable and dynamic systems.

Although CEP systems have been designed to accomplish the same goal, they present different solutions regarding data model, processing algorithm and system architecture [8]. *Event Pattern Language* (EPL) which is the language to define atomic or complex event and specify the process of filtering (determine

© Springer International Publishing AG 2016
J. Grabowski and S. Herbold (Eds.): SAM 2016, LNCS 9959, pp. 20–35, 2016.
DOI: 10.1007/978-3-319-46613-2_2

event of interest) and extracting events properties for constructing high-level events [19] is one of the key elements of the CEP solution. *RAPIDE-EPL* is an example of EPL with the ability to declare event types (integer, string, boolean, array, record) and attributes as well as matching rule [19]. *SASE* is a CEP system with a SQL-similar language that combines filtering, correlation, and transformation of RFID data for delivery of relevant, timely information as well as storing necessary data for future querying [25]. *The Cayuga System* is a high-performance system for complex event processing which has a well-defined query language for event pattern detection [9].

In recent years, *HEADS* project [1] has presented *ThingML* [2], a domain-specific language and compiler for the IoT, which includes concepts to describe both software components and communication protocols. ThingML provides developers the abilities to deploy the same implementation onto various platforms (Java, Javascript C/C++ and Arduino) as well as extend to new platforms. The formalism used is a combination of architecture models, state machines and an imperative action language. Recently, ThingML has been extended to include CEP capabilities supplementing the state machines. ThingML provides mechanisms to declare events, extracting attributes and some basic event operations such as: join, merge, filtering, etc.

This paper investigates CEP capabilities of ThingML. In particular, we aim to evaluate whether ThingML with CEP Extension could be sufficient for deploying CEP applications for CPS systems. Our approach is conducting a detailed study of both language characteristics and processing performance of this extension in order to answer following two research questions:

- **RQ$_1$.** Is ThingML CEP Extension an efficient language for developing CEP applications?
- **RQ$_2$.** Is ThingML CEP Extension powerful enough for CPS systems?

To answer RQ$_1$, we conduct a study analyzing how CEP operators would be described in ThingML using the CEP extension and comparing them with descriptions using only pure ThingML. Regarding RQ$_2$, a benchmark including data rate (events per second), latency (response time) and resource consumption is running for each CEP operator in order to evaluate the ability to execute complex event queries over real-time streams of sensing data.

2   Related Work

In the context of event processing systems, there are some frequently applied benchmarks that are relevant to CEP: the Linear Road benchmark for Stream Data Management Systems [4], the BEAST benchmark for Object-Oriented Active Database Systems [12,13], the SPECjms2007 benchmark for Message-Oriented Middleware [20], the NEXMark benchmark for Queries over Data Streams [23] and BiCEP - a CEP system benchmark [5]. However, currently there is no standardized benchmark that allows an objective comparison of different CEP systems.

In 2006, Wu et al. [25] presented SASE - a CEP system that executes monitoring queries over streams of RFID reading and provided a comparison between SASE and a relational stream processor TelegraphCQ [7] developed at the University of California, Berkeley. In this study, solely latency test was conducted to compare the performance of the two systems. The experiments showed that SASE performed much better than TelegraphCQ, eventually achieved much better scalability [25]. Later, Suhothayan et al. [22] when presenting Siddhi - a CEP Engine that incorporated several improvements including the use of pipeline architecture - also provided a comparison with Esper - the most widely used open source CEP Engine. Similar to previous work, the experiments conducted in this work only focused on latency metric as a criterion to evaluate the effectiveness of their proposed approach.

In 2007, Bizarro introduced BiCEP [5], a project to benchmark CEP systems. His main goal was to identify the core CEP requirements and to develop a set of synthetic benchmarks that allowed a comparison of CEP products and algorithms in spite of their architectural and semantic differences. In his paper, he described the design and the benchmark metrics such as: sustainable throughput, response time, scalability, adaptivity, computation sharing, etc. In the following years, Mendes et al. built FINCoS, a framework that provides a flexible and neutral approach for testing CEP systems [16]. FINCoS introduces particular adapters to achieve a neutral event representation for various CEP systems. In a further publication, Mendes et al. [18] used their framework to conduct different performance tests on three CEP engines - Esper and two developer versions of not further specified commercial products. In this work, they focused on the impact of variations of CEP rules by varying query parameters such as window size, windows expiration type, predicate selectivity, and data values. In a further work, Mendes et al. [17] introduced Pairs benchmark aiming at assessing the ability of CEP engines in processing progressively larger volumes of events and simultaneous queries while providing quick answers.

In the following years, there were also some works introducing benchmarks for CEP systems. However, similar to aforementioned works, they only concentrated on performance metrics as the criteria for evaluation. In 2011, Grabs et al. [14] proposed using metrics: data rate, latency and resource consumption to measure performance of CEP systems. In 2012, Wahl et al. [24] described their concept to measure the performance of different CEP systems in an automated manner by introducing a testing environment that included an event emitting component with stable interface, an interchangeable CEP component based on this interface and a measurement and evaluation component. Recently, in 2013, Mathew also conducted several experiments to evaluate the open source CEP system Esper based on four metrics: CPU utilization, Memory Utilization, Selectivity and Number of Classes [15].

In our work, we also perform experiments to evaluate the performance of ThingML on CEP capabilities. Although we measure metrics that aforementioned benchmarks also used [15,18], our work achieve a step further by more comprehensively focusing on language characteristic and application of

ThingML. In particular, we introduce several metrics to assess the expressiveness of the language and compare with ThingML without CEP features.

3   Background

3.1   CEP Operators

Complex Event Processing is one of the most rapidly emerging fields in data processing, and it is a principal technology solution for processing real time data streams [22]. A Complex Event Processor could be able to identify meaningful patterns, relationships and data abstractions from various streams of unrelated events. Once such information is extracted, the CEP engine would encapsulate it into a *composite event* and send to the interested components. To describe those behaviors, CEP uses a number of primitive operators as envisaged in [8]:

- *Selection* filters relevant events based on the values of their attributes. As an example, consider the following pseudocode pattern which selects `Thermometer` events that carry the temperature reading between 50 and 100.
  Pattern 1:
  ```
  Select Thermometer(temp >= 50 and temp <=100)
  From DataSource
  ```
- *Projection* extracts or transforms a subset of attributes of the events. For example, Pattern 2 selects only the humidity attributes of `Thermometer` events.
  Pattern 2:
  ```
  Select Thermometer(humid)
  From DataSource
  ```
- *Window* defines which portions of the input events to be considered for detecting a pattern.
- *Conjunction* considers the occurrences of two or more events. As an example, Pattern 3 can be used to capture a hypothetical event of `Fire` where both `Smoke` and high `temp` events are notified within the window frame of 5 min.
  Pattern 3:
  ```
  Within 5m. Smoke() and Thermometer(temp > 50)
  From DataSource
  ```
- *Disjunction* considers the occurrences of either one or more events in a predefined set.
- *Sequence* introduces ordering relations among events of a pattern which is satisfied when all the events have been detected in the specified order.
- *Repetition* considers a number of occurrences of a particular event. Pattern 4 illustrates an usage example of Repetition which detects a number of occurrences of high temperature.
  Pattern 4:
  ```
  Select Thermometer(temp > 60) as Temp
  From DataSource
  Where count(Temp) > 5
  ```

– *Aggregation* introduces constraints involving some aggregated attribute values. As an example, Pattern 5 computes the average value of humidity from `Thermometer` events.

  Pattern 5:

```
Select avg(Thermometer.humid)
From DataSource
```

– *Negation* prescribes the absence of certain events. Pattern 6 enhances the detection of `Fire` events by introducing the absence of `Rain` events.

  Pattern 6:

```
Within 5m. Smoke() and Thermometer(temp > 50) and not Rain()
From DataSource
```

A CEP query may contain several of these primitive operators in order to describe more complex patterns or behaviors. CEP engines provide the runtime to perform complex event processing where they accept these queries and match them against the event streams and trigger an event or execution whenever the conditions specified by the queries have been satisfied [22].

3.2   ThingML

ThingML is a domain-specific modeling language which provides a practical model-driven software engineering toolchain targeting resource constrained embedded systems such as low-power sensors, microcontroller based devices, gateways, etc. and facilitates their integration with more powerful resources (e.g. servers, cloud) [1,2]. ThingML provides mechanisms to describe both software components and communication protocols. The language also provides a template mechanism to integrate with third-party API, rather than re-developing them from scratch [1,2]. Currently, it supports transformation from ThingML model to targeting platforms such as C (Linux and Arduino) and Java.

ThingML language provides mechanism to describe the software components as state machine based models whose internal states and communication protocols are based on event triggers. Please refer to [2] for a full explanation of the language syntax and semantics, and [11] for the example of an adaptive temperature sensor network running on a microcontroller platform. Recently, in order to enhance the capability of event processing, ThingML has been extended with CEP logic. Currently, ThingML supports following operators:

– *Selection*: filters events according to their parameters, discarding elements that do not satisfy a given constraint. The following example presents a ThingML selection query which processes the stream of event `E1` from the event port `eventPort`, keeps only the events which have attributes values from 10 to 80, and forwards these events to `cep` port:

```
stream SelectionStream
from m : eventPort?E1::keep if (m.att1 > 10 and m.att5 < 80)
produce cep!cepEvt(m.att1, m.att2, m.att3, m.att4, m.att5)
```

- *Projection*: extracts only part of the information contained in the event. As an example, it is used to extract and transform only attributes of interest:

```
stream ProjectionStream
from m : eventPort?E1
select var att1: Integer = m.att1 + 2
       var att2: Integer = m.att2 * m.att2
produce cep!cepEvt(att1, att2)
```

- *Conjunction*: A conjunction of events $E_1, E_2, ...E_n$ is satisfied when all the events $E_1, E_2, ...E_n$ have been detected (in any order). For example, the following code snippet illustrates the usage of conjunction to detect the occurrences of both events E_1 and E_2:

```
stream ConjunctionStream
from m : [e1 : eventPort?E1 & e2 : eventPort?E2
          -> cepEvt(e1.att1, e2.att1)]
produce cep!cepEvt(m.att1, m.att2)
```

- *Disjunction*: A disjunction of events $E_1, E_2, ...E_n$ is satisfied when at least one of the events $E_1, E_2, ...E_n$ has been detected. The following example illustrates the disjunction of E_1 and E_2:

```
stream DisjunctionStream
from m : [e1 : eventPort?E1 | e2 : eventPort?E2 -> cepEvt]
produce cep!cepEvt(m.att1, m.att2, m.att3, m.att4, m.att5)
```

- *Window*: defines which portions of the input flows have to be considered during the execution of operators. There are two types of windows supported by ThingML: time and length windows. The window attribute is defined by two values: size (time span) and step (time shift). As an example, the following code snippet illustrates the usage of window to compute the average, minimum and maximum values of the attribute att1 of event E_1 within the window:

```
stream LengthWindowStream
from m : eventPort?E1 :: buffer 5 by 5
select var avg : Double  = average(m.att1[])
       var min : Integer = min(m.att1[])
       var max : Integer = max(m.att1[])
produce cep!cepEvt(avg, min, max)

stream TimeWindowStream
from m : eventPort?E1 :: during 5000 by 5000
select var avg : Double  = average(m.att1[])
       var min : Integer =   min(m.att1[])
       var max : Integer = max(m.att1[])
produce cep!cepEvt(avg, min, max)
```

4   A Study on CEP Functional Capacities of ThingML

This study aims to evaluate how CEP applications could be deployed with ThingML. Particularly, the study examines CEP capabilities of ThingML language by analyzing the capacities and performance of the ThingML CEP Extension. Detailed experiments are also conducted in order to compare ThingML CEP Engine with other existing CEP engines in term of language characteristic and processing performance.

In this study, we assess the CEP capability of ThingML based on the CEP operators that the language supports. In particular, we evaluate the using efficiency and processing performance of six CEP operators (as envisaged in [15]) which are currently supported by ThingML. The queries of all operators that are used throughout the experiments of this study are the ones presented in Sect. 3.2.

The following sections discuss the evaluation of language expressiveness and performance of ThingML CEP capacity in order to answer the two aforementioned research questions:

4.1 RQ_1: Is ThingML CEP Extension an efficient language for developing CEP applications?

By "efficient language", we mean an Event Pattern Language which provides concise and meaningful definitions of atomic and complex events. To answer this question, we present a language characteristic analysis of the CEP extension of ThingML. We demonstrate the language expressiveness of ThingML by comparing the CEP operators of ThingML with our implementation of the operators without using CEP extension in order to provide insights into the strength and limitations of the two implementation strategies. For evaluation, we use the following metrics for each of the specified queries:

- *Lines of Codes (LoC)*: number of lines of code written in both implementations (with and without using CEP extension).
- *Number of Keywords (NoK)*: number of keywords used in each implementation.

Table 1 shows the comparison of LoC and NoK between the two CEP queries implementations in ThingML. As can be seen from this table, the implementation of CEP queries with CEP extension always uses smaller number of code and keywords. The smallest and largest differences in LoC are 3 (Selection query) and 14 (Time Window query), the respective numbers in NoK are 6 (Selection query) and 45 (Conjunction query). Although these differences are not substantial, they do state the efficiency of using CEP capacity of ThingML in term of language expressiveness. In particular, by using CEP extension of ThingML to deploy CEP application, we could improve the conciseness of the source code, which could improve the understandability of the source code, produce less error or even save time for development.

Table 1. Language expressiveness measurement of ThingML with/without CEP.

Operator	LoC		NoK	
	With CEP	Without CEP	With CEP	Without CEP
Selection	55	58	54	60
Projection	61	64	50	58
Conjunction	62	98	50	95
Disjunction	60	64	58	70
Length window	104	126	110	135
Time window	105	119	115	136

```
internal event m:eventPort?E1 action do
   if(m.att1 > 10 and m.att5 < 80) do
      cep!cepEvt(m.att1, m.att2, m.att3, m.att4, m.att5)
   end
end
```

Fig. 1. Implementation of selection query without using CEP extension.

Table 1 only shows the differences of both implements of every single query, which leads to the small differences between the two columns. However, in practice, an application would contain more than one query or the expressions and computations of the queries could be much more complicated. Therefore, without CEP extension, these numbers could become considerably large.

Figure 1 shows the partial implementation of the selection query presented in Sect. 3.2 without using CEP extension. As can be seen, for this type of operator, there is not much difference between the two implementations even if the Boolean expression becomes more complex, resulting in the small difference between LoC and NoK.

However, for disjunction operator which is a similar type of occurrence detection, using CEP extension could be much more efficient. As can be seen from Fig. 2 which shows the partial implementation of disjunction query without using CEP extension, the occurrences of each event should be checked individually, which leads to code duplication and errors if the number of events in the disjunction query increases.

```
internal event m:eventPort?E1 action do
   cep!cepEvt(m.att1, m.att2, m.att3, m.att4, m.att5)
end
internal event m:eventPort?E2 action do
   cep!cepEvt(m.att1, m.att2, m.att3, m.att4, m.att5)
end
```

Fig. 2. Implementation of disjunction query without using CEP extension.

```
property att1 : Integer[1000]
property att2 : Integer[1000]
property i : Integer = 0
...
internal event e:eventPort?E1 action do
    att1[i] = e.att1
    att2[i] = e.att2
    i = i + 1
end
internal event timer?timer_timeout action do
    i = 0
    var avg : Double = average(att1)
    var min : Integer =  min(att1)
    var max : Integer = max(att1)
    cep!cepEvt(avg, min, max)
    timer!timer_start(1000)
end
```

Fig. 3. Implementation of time window query without using CEP extension.

The same problem of code duplication also occurs for time window and conjunction (Figs. 3 and 4). Especially for conjunction query which involves only two events, the implementation is relatively large. Thus, with the increase of the number of events, without using CEP Extension, the implementation of this operator would be much more cumbersome and difficult to manage. Moreover, for these types of operations, we should also use global variables for storing intermediate attributes. Thus, causing more memory consumption increasing with the number of involving events or the number of attributes of the events. Especially for time windows and length windows where the number of events in each window is undetermined, memory reservation for storing these events could be problematic as ThingML does not support dynamic allocation.

Currently, in the implementations of time window (see Fig. 3) and length window, we assume that the size and step of the windows are equal, thus, the windows do not overlap each other. For simplicity, we have not analyzed the other case as the algorithm could require more than two timers or become much more complicated. However, as presented above, this would be easily resolved by using CEP extension.

4.2   *RQ$_2$*: Is ThingML CEP Extension powerful enough for CPS systems?

To answer this question, we present a detailed performance analysis of ThingML. We also compare ThingML CEP extension with our implementation without CEP extension and Esper [10] which is an open source CEP Engine. We choose to compare to Esper because it is an open-source full-fledged stream processor. In addition, Esper is a Java-based software that has a well-supported user community, well-documented manuals, which facilitated this comparative study.

```
property isEvent1 : Boolean = false
property isEvent2 : Boolean = false
property event1Att : Integer
property event2Att : Integer
...
internal event e1 : eventPort?E1 action do
   isEvent1 = true
   event1Att = e1.att1

   if(isEvent2) do
      timer!timer_cancel()
      isEvent1 = false
      isEvent2 = false
      cep!cepEvt(event1Att, event2Att)
   end

   if(not isEvent2) do
      timer!timer_start(1000)
   end
end

internal event e2 : eventPort?E2 action do
   //analogous to waitE1 State
end

internal event timer?timer_timeout action do
   isEvent1 = false
   isEvent2 = false
end
```

Fig. 4. Implementation of conjunction query without using CEP extension.

Experiment Settings. All the experiments were performed on a workstation with a CPU Intel Core I5 2.60 GHz processor and 8 GB memory running Sun J2RE 1.8 on Window 10. We set the JVM maximum allocation pool to 1 GB, so that virtual memory activity has no influence on the results.

In order to test the system, we implemented an event generator that creates a stream of events with different throughputs from 1 to 1000 events per second. In our experiments, we considered 5 events types each of which has 5 attributes excluding the timestamps. For each attribute, the number of possible values (the domain size) was chosen from the range [1, 100]. We did not consider events with more attributes because the additional attributes were not used in our queries and can be projected out.

We measured the following metrics for each of the specified queries under different throughputs:

- *Latency* is the time taken to detect a complex event since the last event in the set of triggering events are sent to the CEP engine.

- *CPU Utilization* is the CPU Utilization for different kinds of CEP query over different event rates for a given pattern. It is measured by using a profiler called YourKit [3].
- *Memory Utilization* is the memory profile for different kinds of CEP query over different event rates for a given pattern; which is also measured with YourKit.

The criterion for stopping each experiment was such that the system has detected 1000 instances of the complex event specified in each query. The latency was obtained by averaging the latency values of 1000 runs. For memory utilization we captured the maximum heap memory allocated during the runs.

Result. Figure 5 presents the performance analysis of ThingML CEP Extension of the specified queries. As can be seen, the CPU utilization is around 50–60% which is medium CPU requirement. The CPU performance increases very slightly as the throughput changes from 1 to 1000, which shows that CPU requirement is not substantially affected by the occurrences of the events. For all types of queries, the CPU utilization is always at highest performance when the throughput is at highest rate (1000 events/s). This could be easily explained as the more processing performance is required when the events occur more frequently.

Similarly, the memory requirement for CEP Extension is also relatively low (around 35–90 MB). Memory usage is also increasing as the throughput rate raises. Length window and time window queries always amount to the largest memory because these queries need to store information of the events occur within the windows. In contrast, as the throughput increases, the latency is found to decrease. Which means as the events occur more frequently, the event processing time becomes shorter. This shows the effectiveness of the CEP engines which try not to lose too much meaningful information as the events come out so close to each other.

For the implementation without CEP Extension and Esper, the same pattern also happens. Therefore, for saving space, we do not include all the bar charts into this paper. Instead, we only show the comparison of the three implementations under the highest throughput (see Fig. 6). However, from the ThingML implementation without CEP Extension, we observe that there are remarkable differences in the three metrics. In particular, this implementation always requires slightly more physical resources (CPU, Memory) while the latency is slower. The differences could be clearly observed in conjunction, time window and length window queries which require more processing performance. This finding is also consistent with our discussion from the language characteristic analysis that our own implementation without using CEP extension may not be effectively optimized for CEP operations.

Compared with the other two implementations, Esper engine requires much more physical resources: CPU utilization is ranging from 75–90 % and memory usage is around 50–120 MB. However, the latency is much better (approximately

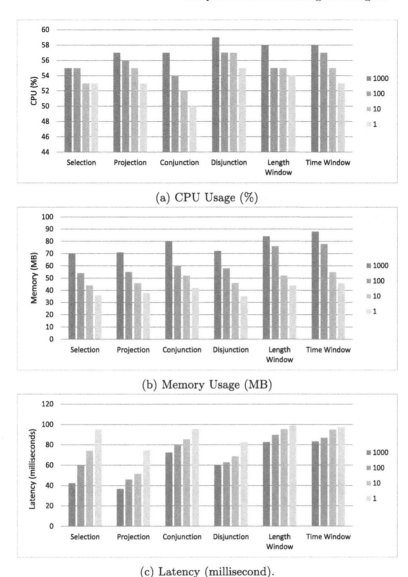

(a) CPU Usage (%)

(b) Memory Usage (MB)

(c) Latency (millisecond).

Fig. 5. Performance analysis of ThingML with CEP Extension.

two times faster than CEP extension), which shows the effectiveness of the architecture (event processing algorithm, data structure, etc.) of this CEP engine.

4.3   Discussion

In this study, we perform the analysis of language characteristic and processing performance of ThingML CEP extension. Finding from the first analysis reveals

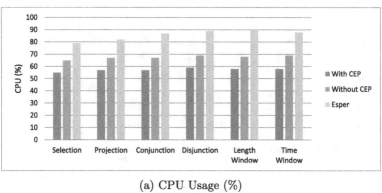

(a) CPU Usage (%)

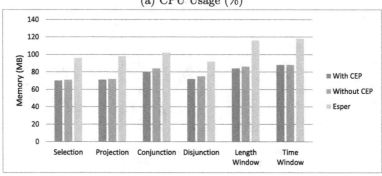

(b) Memory Usage (MB)

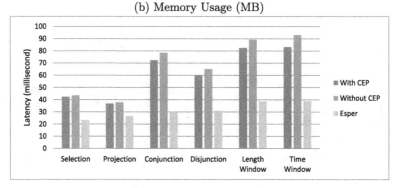

(c) Latency (millisecond).

Fig. 6. Performance analysis of different implementations (1000 events/sec).

that the source code written by using CEP extension is much shorter and more concise than the implementation without using the extension, hence improving the understandability, saving development time, removing code duplication and less error prone. In this study, we only evaluate every single query separately and the queries are also simple, thus the differences between the two implementations may not be substantial. However, a real CEP application could involve tens of queries. Therefore, in these practical situations, using CEP extension would improve the efficiency of the development process. Moreover, CEP applications could also involve hundreds of event types with really complicated patterns for complex events (complex boolean expressions, nested operations, etc.) which may not be implemented without using CEP extension. Therefore, this CEP extension not only helps to save much more effort but also enables the implementation of CEP applications.

As can be seen from the second experiment, CEP extension of ThingML is not the most effective CEP Engine. However, this implementation requires relatively low physical resources which are extremely limited for CPS devices. In addition, although the latency of ThingML CEP is larger than that of Esper, it is still within the range required for CPS applications, which need responses within milliseconds. Also, because the event generator and CEP processor were implemented in the same application, the measured performance and physical consumption for CEP Engine also contained those of the event generator. Thus, the actual numbers for the CEP engine could be even smaller than those presented, which could be a threat to validity. However, because all tested CEP applications contain the same implementation of the event generator, the existence of the event generator does not influence the value of this comparative study, but rather emphasizes the power of the extension to perform CEP tasks.

5   Conclusion

In this paper, we presented the analysis of ThingML CEP extension, a complex event processing capacity of the modeling language for embedded and distributed systems. We first assessed the language expressiveness of this CEP extension by considering the two quantitative attributes of the source code written with and without the CEP extension. The assessment revealed that by using CEP extension, CEP application written in ThingML could be much more concise. In addition, this capacity could enable the implementation of some complex event patterns which require complicated algorithm or even could not be implemented without using CEP extension. We also performed the analysis of physical resource consumption and processing performance of ThingML in comparison with usual implementation (without using CEP extension) and Esper. Findings from this experiment also showed that ThingML required much smaller physical resources and reasonable latency values, which makes it a potential language for deploying CEP applications for CPS systems.

For future study, we should also need to evaluate the performance of a real ThingML CEP application which involves a variety of complex events because currently our experiments were tested on only single and simple queries. In addition, as presented above, ThingML is a modeling language which could be deployed on different physical platforms. However, in this paper, we only tested the performance experiments on computer workstation which has generous physical resources. Therefore, it is also necessary to consider the performance of this language on different CPS platforms (e.g., Arduino, Raspberry Pi).

References

1. Head project. http://heads-project.eu/
2. ThingML. http://thingml.org/pmwiki.php
3. Yourkit profiler. https://www.yourkit.com/
4. Arasu, A., Cherniack, M., Galvez, E., Maier, D., Maskey, A.S., Ryvkina, E., Stonebraker, M., Tibbetts, R.: Linear road: a stream data management benchmark. In: Proceedings of the Thirtieth International Conference on Very Large Data Bases, Vol. 30, pp. 480–491. VLDB Endowment (2004)
5. Bizarro, P.: BiCEP-benchmarking complex event processing systems. In: Dagstuhl Seminar Proceedings. Schloss Dagstuhl-Leibniz-Zentrum für Informatik (2007)
6. Buchmann, A., Koldehofe, B.: Complex event processing. IT-Information Technology Methoden und innovative Anwendungen der Informatik und Informationstechnik **51**(5), 241–242 (2009)
7. Chandrasekaran, S., Cooper, O., Deshpande, A., Franklin, M.J., Hellerstein, J.M., Hong, W., Krishnamurthy, S., Madden, S.R., Reiss, F., Shah, M.A.: TelegraphCQ: continuous dataflow processing. In: Proceedings of the 2003 ACM SIGMOD International Conference on Management of Data, p. 668. ACM (2003)
8. Cugola, G., Margara, A.: Processing flows of information: from data stream to complex event processing. ACM Comput. Surv. (CSUR) **44**(3), 15 (2012)
9. Demers, A.J., Gehrke, J., Panda, B., Riedewald, M., Sharma, V., et al.: Cayuga: a general purpose event monitoring system
10. EsperTech: Esper (2016). http://www.espertech.com/esper/. Accessed 3 Feb 2016
11. Fleurey, F., Morin, B., Solberg, A.: A model-driven approach to develop adaptive firmwares. In: Proceedings of the 6th International Symposium on Software Engineering for Adaptive and Self-Managing Systems, SEAMS 2011, pp. 168–177. ACM, New York (2011). http://doi.acm.org/10.1145/1988008.1988031
12. Geppert, A., Berndtsson, M., Lieuwen, D., Zimmermann, J.: Performance evaluation of active database management systems using the beast benchmark. Technical report. Citeseer (1996)
13. Geppert, A., Berndtsson, M., Lieuwen, D.F., Roncancio, C.: Performance evaluation of object-oriented active database systems using the beast benchmark. TAPOS **4**(3), 135–149 (1998)
14. Grabs, T., Lu, M.: Measuring performance of complex event processing systems. In: Nambiar, R., Poess, M. (eds.) TPCTC 2011. LNCS, vol. 7144, pp. 83–96. Springer, Heidelberg (2012). doi:10.1007/978-3-642-32627-1_6
15. Mathew, A.: Benchmarking of complex event processing engine-esper. Technical report, Technical Report IITB/CSE/2014/April/61, Department of Computer Science and Engineering, Indian Institute of Technology Bombay, Maharashtra, India (2014)
16. Mendes, M., Bizarro, P., Marques, P.: A framework for performance evaluation of complex event processing systems. In: Proceedings of the Second International Conference on Distributed Event-Based Systems, pp. 313–316. ACM (2008)
17. Mendes, M., Bizarro, P., Marques, P.: Towards a standard event processing benchmark. In: Proceedings of the 4th ACM/SPEC International Conference on Performance Engineering, pp. 307–310. ACM (2013)
18. Mendes, M.R.N., Bizarro, P., Marques, P.: A performance study of event processing systems. In: Nambiar, R., Poess, M. (eds.) TPCTC 2009. LNCS, vol. 5895, pp. 221–236. Springer, Heidelberg (2009). doi:10.1007/978-3-642-10424-4_16

19. Robins, D.: Complex event processing. In: Second International Workshop on Education Technology and Computer Science. Wuhan (2010)
20. Sachs, K., Kounev, S., Bacon, J., Buchmann, A.: Performance evaluation of message-oriented middleware using the SPECjms2007 benchmark. Perform. Eval. **66**(8), 410–434 (2009)
21. Schmerken, I.: Deciphering the myths around complex event processing. Wall Street & Technology, May 2008. http://www.wallstreetandtech.com/latency/deciphering-the-myths-around-complex-event-processing/d/d-id/1259489?
22. Suhothayan, S., Gajasinghe, K., Loku Narangoda, I., Chaturanga, S., Perera, S., Nanayakkara, V.: Siddhi: a second look at complex event processing architectures. In: Proceedings of the 2011 ACM Workshop on Gateway Computing Environments, GCE 2011, pp. 43–50. ACM, New York (2011). http://doi.acm.org/10.1145/2110486.2110493
23. Tucker, P., Tufte, K., Papadimos, V., Maier, D.: Nexmark-a benchmark for queries over data streams (draft). Technical report, OGI School of Science & Engineering at OHSU, September 2008
24. Wahl, A., Hollunder, B.: Performance measurement for cep systems. In: Proceedings of the 4th International Conferences on Advanced Service Computing, pp. 116–121 (2012)
25. Wu, E., Diao, Y., Rizvi, S.: High-performance complex event processing over streams. In: Proceedings of the 2006 ACM SIGMOD International Conference on Management of Data, pp. 407–418. ACM (2006)

SDL: Meeting the IoT Challenge

Edel Sherratt$^{(\boxtimes)}$

Department of Computer Science, Aberystwyth University, Aberystwyth, UK
eds@aber.ac.uk
http://users.aber.ac.uk/eds

Abstract. SDL 2010 offers excellent support for modelling, simulating
and testing systems of communicating agents. However, it is not perfectly
adapted to meeting the specific challenges presented by the Internet of
Things (IoT). Three areas that pose a challenge are considered, and language adaptations that aim to address the specific needs of IoT systems
developers are explored.

The first challenge concerns signal delay or signal loss on crowded networks. Signals in SDL 2010 are by default delayed by an indeterminate
duration, but a facility to model delays that depend on network traffic
would be desirable. A modification is proposed to enable this.

The second concerns undesirable interactions with external IoT systems. SDL 2010 supports modelling of a system within an environment
populated by multiple agents. It also allows modelling of multiple interacting subsystems. However, it would be useful to be able to model interactions with external agents in a way that supported identification of
threats to reliability, privacy and security of an IoT system. An adaptation of channel substructures, a construct that was dropped from SDL
96, is proposed to facilitate this.

The third and final challenge concerns the signal handling by multiple
recipients. Different approaches to supporting this are considered with a
view to further investigation to determine their desirability.

Keywords: SDL (Z.100) · Internet of Things (IoT) · Modelling ·
Simulation

1 Introduction

The Internet of Things (IoT) is made up of systems that affect many different
aspects of life. IoT systems include smart homes and cities, domestic appliances,
children's toys, field robotics and more [1]. All these systems collect sensor data.
Some transmit the data to repositories for offline processing to support activities
such as decision making or scientific investigation. Others react to the data
they receive by generating signals that control physical systems such as lighting
or heating in buildings, road traffic signals or physical locks or barriers. All
have requirements for safety, security and reliability, and appropriate engineering
processes should be followed when they are developed and deployed.

© Springer International Publishing AG 2016
J. Grabowski and S. Herbold (Eds.): SAM 2016, LNCS 9959, pp. 36–50, 2016.
DOI: 10.1007/978-3-319-46613-2_3

SDL 2010, a member of the ITU Z.100 family of standards [2], is a non-proprietary formalism for modelling, simulating, implementing and deploying systems that involve parallel activities and communication. With its strong theoretical basis, its excellent tool support and its established track record in distributed systems development, SDL 2010 is ideally placed to provide support for creating critical elements of the Internet of Things (IoT). SDL's capacity for modelling and simulating communicating systems that interact with the physical world has been demonstrated by numerous examples, including a railway crossing [3], a toffee vending machine [4], and automotive and building control systems [5].

More recent work [1] explored the many benefits of SDL for developing and deploying IoT systems, but also identified specific technical areas where SDL could be more closely aligned with the needs of IoT developers. Challenges include

- loss or delay of signals depending on load on a communication channel;
- unwanted interaction between a new IoT system and environmental agents.

These both stem from the fact that IoT systems depend on a shared, publicly accessible communications infrastructure.

A related concern is that signals in an SDL model are consumed by a single recipient, but addressing requirements for reliability and for privacy in an IoT system entails taking account of the fact that signals might be consumed by multiple environmental agents as well as by their intended recipient.

It should be emphasised that all these situations can already be modelled using SDL 2010, but that modelling and simulation could be made more direct and intuitive for the IoT developer by introducing the changes discussed below.

Each of the following sections addresses one of these challenges. Section 2 addresses signal delay in a busy network. It outlines a smart city scenario, identifies support provided by SDL 2010, and proposes a modification to the SDL delaying channel. Section 3 explores the problem of unwanted interactions with external systems. It introduces a simple situation involving two scientific investigations in a remote location, explores the differences between classical telecommunications feature interaction and the kinds of unwanted interaction likely to occur in the IoT, and proposes a language extension based on the channel substructure of SDL 96. Section 4 considers situations where multiple recipients respond to an event. For each of these challenges, the aim is to provide language facilites to support the work of the IoT developer while retaining the benefits of SDL. Other important IoT challenges that were also identified in [1], such as power management, co-design of hardware and software, and targeting of new IoT platforms, that relate to use of SDL and to tool support for SDL rather than to the language itself, are not addressed here but will be the subject of future work.

2   Signals in a Busy Network

"The impact of deployment of an IoT system in contexts with numerous of other systems making use of the same communication resources causing potential delays and loss of messages is supported in SDL only to a limited degree. SDL may be extended with features to specify possible loss and delay of signals based on the load on a communication path." [1].

In a busy network, delay or even loss of signals is likely. An engineer uses modelling and simulation to predict the behaviour of an IoT system in a network whose communications resources are shared with many other systems.

2.1   Scenario: Bristol Is Open

Bristol Is Open, a joint venture between the University of Bristol and Bristol City Council[1], collects sensor data from waste bins, street lights, volunteers' smart phones and GPS devices, and from many other sources. This data can be used for research or for creative activity, but a key intention is to create an *open programmable city*. Ideas include automatic diversion of traffic in response to road congestion, or text messages to notify people of problems with air quality in particular areas.

With so much data being collected from so many sources, and so many actuating signals being sent in response to that data, delay or loss of signals is highly likely. This is a real-time problem. Significant delays in notifying citizens about problems with air quality, or in establishing road traffic diversions are not acceptable, and a good model allows such delays to be predicted.

Real-time behaviour is modelled in SDL in terms of a global time that increases as a simulation proceeds. The current value of global time is accessed by means of the SDL **now** expression, and is used in conjunction with SDL timers. This model of time is not expressive enough to meet all the needs of real-time systems developers [6], and over the years modelling and simulation of real-time activities in SDL have attracted considerable attention. An intermediate representation for SDL enabled investigation of alternative meanings of time in SDL [7] as well as facilitating different kinds of model analysis by supporting tool-set integration. Real-time extensions to SDL introduced in [6] were further developed in [8]. Such approaches provide powerful mechanisms for modelling and simulating passage of time. However, providing controllable time would require a significant change to the SDL semantics [9].

2.2   Modelling Delay with Delaying Channels in SDL 2010

Using SDL 2010 without modification or extension, the kind of delay that might be expected in a busy network can be modelled using a delaying channel, as

---

[1] http://www.bristolisopen.com/.

illustrated in Fig. 1a. A signal placed on a delaying channel is delayed for an indeterminate period of time, and delaying channels are used to simulate the behaviour of IoT systems communicating over a busy, shared network.

However, in order to model the behaviour of systems that are deployed in a network that also supports large and varying populations of external agents, it would be useful to be able to model delays whose variability was conditioned by network traffic density. That is, engineers need to be able to design and run simulation experiments that reveal the behaviour of a system under different network traffic conditions. In other words, they need to run experiments in which network traffic acts as the independent variable controlled by the engineer, and signal loss or delay depends on network traffic.

2.3   Proposed Modification

A modification to SDL delaying channels is proposed that allows the engineer to specify a delay function that takes account of traffic on the channel. This modification provides some control over how the passage of time is modelled but does not change the underlying SDL time semantics. Figure 1(b) illustrates a proposed modification to SDL2010 that provides a reference to a named delaying function.

(a) Signals placed on a delaying channel are delayed for an indeterminate duration

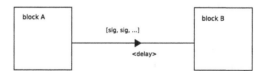

(b) Signals are delayed by a duration that depends on channel traffic

Fig. 1. Simulating a busy network with a delaying channel

2.4   Implementing the Proposed Change

The textual representation (SDL-PR) for a channel is defined in Z.106 [2] using the following grammar rule

```
<channel definition> ::=
    channel [<channel name> [<encoding rules>]]
```

```
[nodelay]
    <channel path> [<channel path>]
endchannel [<channel name>] <end>
```

In the following version of the rule, an optional <specified delay> has been added as an alternative to **nodelay** in the rule specifying a channel definition. The nonterminal <specified delay> names a predefined function that takes an integer as input and returns a value of type duration. The function is evaluated at run time, delaying each signal by a duration that depends on the rest of the traffic on the channel.

```
<channel definition> ::=
    channel [<channel name> [<encoding rules>]]
        [nodelay|<specified delay>]
        <channel path> [<channel path>]
    endchannel [<channel name>] <end>
```

The specified delay could be implemented as a predefined runtime library from which the engineer could name the required delay. A collection of named probability distribution functions, or cumulative distribution functions would be useful for this purpose. Each distribution function could take as input the length of the delaying queue, or some combination of the delays already applying to signals in the queue, and delay the next signal accordingly.

An alternative approach, that would have allowed the developer to specify the delay was considered and rejected. The alternative approach was to define <specified delay> as a reference to an SDL procedure that could be defined by the developer, rather than as a reference to a predefined function. Although this approach would have provided more expressive power to the IoT developer, it was rejected because it would have demanded a fundamental change to SDL. A procedure has to be evaluated in the context of an SDL agent, that is, a block or process, and not a channel. Introducing a channel agent, analogous to block or process agents, would be a significant change to the current SDL semantics. For this reason, the previous suggestion – a predefined set of delay functions – is preferred.

3   Unwanted Interaction with External Agents

IoT systems are deployed in an environment that exposes them to external agents at every system level. SDL 2010 supports modelling of a system in an environment populated by multiple agents. It also allows modelling of multiple interacting subsystems. This section explores the extent to which SDL enables the engineer to model interactions with external agents in a way that supports identification of threats to reliability, privacy and security of an IoT system.

3.1   Scenario: Scientific Investigation in a Remote Location

Two different investigations were conducted in a remote location[2]. Each involves data collection using a wireless sensor network.

Browsing Patterns of Sheep. The purpose of the first investigation was to discover the browsing patterns of sheep. Each sheep was provided with an ear tag that broadcast a signal at regular 15 min intervals. The broadcast signals were picked up by devices mounted on poles, and the position of each sheep was calculated by triangulation. The positions were then forwarded to outlying stations where data was collected for further processing.

For 100 sheep, collisions were infrequent, which meant that power usage was acceptable and useful data was collected. But once the number of sheep or the reporting frequency was increased, collisions were frequent, demands on batteries became unacceptably high and data was less useful.

Environmental Monitoring. A number of sensors were placed in a remote location to collect data about temperature, humidity, wind speed and other environmental factors [10]. The data collected by the sensors was forwarded for central processing.

This second investigation had the potential to interfere with the first, leading to frequent collisions, re-sends, excessive power consumption and possibly unusable data.

As it happens, although the two investigations were carried out on behalf of two different organizations, they were in fact conducted by the same investigators, who ensured that the signals broadcast by the two experiments did not interfere with each other. But if the contracts had been awarded to different investigators, contention would have been likely.

3.2   Interaction in the IoT

The scenario described above is a simple one, but despite its simplicity, it provides scope for unwanted interaction between different communicating systems. The previous scenario, Bristol is Open, is complex, and provides even more opportunity for interference between different systems. The current IoT is populated by all manner of systems built using low-cost micro-controllers, single board computers and other components. Many of these devices and systems are created as a learning exercise, or as a proof of concept. Some are likely to be poorly designed, and some may even be malicious [1]. An engineer designing a system with a view to deployment in the Internet of Things must take account of such external systems, and of their implications for reliability and security of the new system. This means taking account not only of requirements for interaction within the new system, but also addressing the problem of unwanted interactions with other devices and systems in the IoT

---

[2] This scenario is based on recent, as yet unpublished, work.

Unwanted interaction between a new IoT system and other systems deployed on the same communications infrastructure is closely related to the well-researched problem known as *feature interaction* in the world of telecommunications services. Feature interaction occurs when new software added to an existing telecommunication system interacts in an undesirable way with the existing software. That is, new features interact with existing features, and the outcome is not what the developers intended.

3.3 Modelling and Simulating Feature Interaction with SDL

SDL has an established record in feature interaction detection [11,12]. When the CRESS notation was developed to communicate feature interaction problems with non-specialists, translation to SDL enabled practical simulation and exploration of those problems [12]. As Internet telephony became more prominent, SIP (Session Initiation Protocol) services and their feature interactions were modelled using SDL with the aim of detecting and prevent unwanted interactions [13].

In these examples, SDL provides a way to model an existing system and a new feature, and, with the help of tools, to simulate the behaviour of the whole system, with its old and new elements, and to discover problems such as livelock, deadlock, and interactions that reflect conflicts between the underlying requirements or assumptions for the new feature and the rest of the system.

3.4 Differences and Challenges

However, there are important differences between the conventional feature interaction problems in telecommunications and the interaction problems faced by a system deployed in the IoT, and these differences present challenges to the engineer who uses SDL to detect and prevent interaction problems.

The first concerns the resolution of unwanted interactions. In a typical feature interaction investigation, the engineer aims to detect and prevent undesirable interactions involving new and existing features, but includes both sets of features in the final system. An engineer concerned with unwanted interactions between a new IoT system and the external systems with which it will share a communications infrastructure wants to predict and prevent those interactions, but in a way that as far as possible makes the external systems invisible to a user of the new system. Ideally, the new IoT system would not have to share infrastructure; in practice, the new system must share, but should be insulated against interference.

The second difference concerns access to the communications infrastructure. In a telecommunications system, certain communications cannot be intercepted without physical intervention. In SDL terms, internal channels cannot be accessed by environmental agents. In the IoT, communications are by way of the public Internet, and can be intercepted by systems other than the one to which they belong. Moreover, the source of an externally generated signal may appear to be other than it actually is.

SDL presents a problem to the engineer who needs to explore potentially threatening interactions between a new IoT system and other systems that share the same communications infrastructure. SDL guides development towards systems that to minimize the likelihood of unwanted interactions. Channels can only transfer named signals. Internal channels are not accessible to the wider environment. Communication between a system and its environment is by way of a well defined interface across the system boundary. Interactions with the system environment are modelled as signals that are passed across the system boundary via a well defined interfacece, and environmental agents are typically only of interest insofar as different system features may demand conflicting responses to environmental stimuli. But once the new system is deployed on the public Internet, its internal communications become vulnerable to interference that was not possible in the original SDL model.

A further difference between conventional feature interaction and unwanted interaction between a new system and other, external IoT systems is that features are not created specifically to damage other features, whereas malicious systems are likely to be found in the IoT. Such systems specifically aim to intercept signals, or to create false signals, or to impersonate agents of the system under development, and modelling such systems with a view to preventing their success poses an additional challenge to the developer of new IoT systems.

A fourth and final difference between conventional feature interaction problems and unwanted interaction between a new system and its environment concerns visibility of the internal behaviour of interacting sub-systems. When interactions between features of a telecommunications system are investigated, the engineer (investigator) has access to the internal behaviour of both the existing system and the new features, and can used that access to detect and prevent unwanted interactions between new and previously existing features. When investigating differences between a new IoT system and its environment, the engineer does not have access to the internal structure of environmental agents, and must instead consider the kind of interface a potentially interfering agent might have.

3.5   Using SDL 2010 to Model Unwanted Interaction

From the previous discussion, the following requirements can be identified:

- an ability to detect and resolve interactions in which signals from the environment affect the behaviour of new IoT system;
- an ability to model environmental interference that affects internal channels within a new IoT system, and, having ensured that the new system is resilient in the face of such interference, to remove models of external systems before implementing and deploying the new system;
- an ability to model malicious agents that deliberately subvert the proposed new IoT system, possibly impersonating parts of the new IoT system, or parts of its intended environment;
- an ability to detect of undesirable interactions without knowledge of the internal structure of environmental agents.

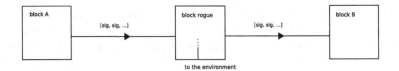

Fig. 2. A rogue block interferes with a channel in SDL 2010

Key to meeting these needs is an ability to model interception of signals on internal channels by environmental agents.

With SDL 2010, undesirable transmission of signals between the environment and the system can be modelled by directly adding such unwanted transmission to the model of a system that is being developed. However, this entails modifying internal system agents and adding channel definitions to signals that represent the unwanted transmission. Even though use of signal lists makes this a reasonably clean procedure, creating the modification in order to investigate unwanted interaction, and later reversing the modification in order to generate the required system, is a source of error and vulnerability.

Similarly, it is possible to model signal interception, or injection of unwanted signals into a channel by adding a rogue block to an SDL model of new IoT system, as illustrated in Fig. 2. Again, this intervention clutters the model and its later removal is another likely source of error.

3.6   Proposed Solution

A better solution is to reinstate something very like the channel substructure of SDL 96 [4]. Channel substructures enabled the user of SDL to specify the behaviour of a channel explicitly. A channel substructure specification was like a block specfication except that it connected to external blocks, or the environment, rather than to channels. Channel substructures were dropped from SDL 2000 [14] because they were never used in practical models.

The difference between what is proposed here and the SDL 96 channel substructure is that, instead of aiming to specify the behaviour of a channel, the intention is to provide a clearly identifiable model of environmental interference with the channel.

Figure 3(a) shows an SDL 96 diagram illustrating channel substructure. Figure 3(b) uses a similar diagram to illustrate interference with the channel by an external source. The only difference between the rogue and the SDL 96 channel substructure is that the rogue has an external connection that ultimately leads to the system environment, whereas a channel substructure connected only to the two blocks connected to the channel. The rogue is transformed in the same way as a channel substructure was transformed in SDL 96, leading to the structure shown in Fig. 2.

The benefit of this is that the rogue is clearly identifiable, and its removal is likely to be less error-prone than removal of the rogue block in Fig. 2.

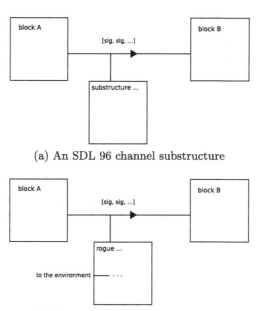

(a) An SDL 96 channel substructure

(b) A rogue interferes with a channel

Fig. 3. A rogue block can be represented like an old SDL 96 channel substructure

To complete a model of rogue behaviour, a way for the rogue to 'spoof' the value of sender would also be needed. That is, a signal sent by the rogue would differ from the old channel substructure in that it would masquerade as the block from which signals were placed on the original channel. This represents a significant departure from normal SDL behaviour, and would require allowing the anonymous variable whose value is accessed by **self** to be updated by processes in a rogue block. However, the benefits of being able to model unwanted behaviour in this way, and then to remove the unwanted behaviour safely before deploying the new system indicate that this change is worth further consideration.

4 Multiple Recipients

Different modelling formalisms have different approaches to handling events. In SDL 2010, an event, modelled as a signal, is handled by a single agent selected from a set of potential recipients [2]. This contrasts with Harel state machines in which a signal is handled by every agent that is capable of receiving it [15].

Ambient and broadcast communications characterise the Internet of Things. For example, the smart city broadcasts information about atmospheric conditions to all users who wish to receive that information in order to avoid areas with high levels of allergens. Also, some activities require different agents to coordinate their response to signals. For example, in the sheep monitoring investigation, the position of each sheep was determined by triangulation, so more than one recipient had to react to the sheep's beacon.

However, event sharing also leads to potential conflict between the different agents that could potentially react to an event [16]. For example, when sensors in the programmable city detect road traffic congestion, a coordinated response is needed to create appropriate diversions, and road safety will dictate that response should be controlled by a single agent[3].

4.1 Using SDL 2010 to Model Multiple Recipients

Sending Signals to Multiple Known Recipients. Figure 4 illustrates a block that sends the same signals to three other blocks. The model illustrated in Fig. 5 uses an intermediate block to achieve the same communication between block A and blocks B, C and D. The second approach has the advantage that all the logic relating to copying and forwarding signals is contained in the intermediate block.

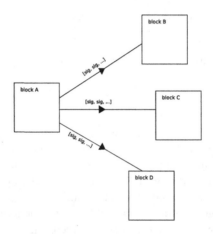

Fig. 4. Signals are sent directly to known recipients

Represent a Broadcasting Channel as a Signal Repository. A variation on the approach illustrated in Fig. 5 can be used to model broadcast wireless communications. Signals on a broadcast wireless channel can be accessed by any device that is tuned to that channel. This can be modelled in SDL by defining a block to represent the wireless channel. The broadcasting agent sends signals to that block via a non-delaying channel, and the block stores those signals, each with a time-stamp indicating when the signal arrived. Other agents send requests to the block which retrieves and delivers the stored signals. Constraints governing the usability of signals apply and old signals are eventually discarded as they expire.

---

[3] It is conceivable that roads and junctions, or vehicles, could negotiate diversions, but establishing that this was safe and effective would require further research.

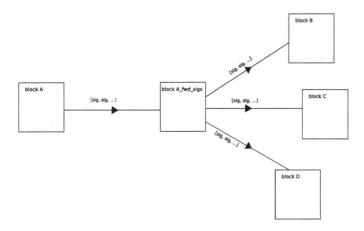

Fig. 5. Signals are sent to an intermediate block, which copies the signals to their recipients

4.2   Possible Extensions to SDL

The approaches outlined above all conform to the SDL principle that each signal is consumed by a single agent. Reaction by a single agent leads to robust systems in which a single recipient modelled as a state aggregation coordinates the actions of all the agents, modelled as state partitions, that should respond to an event. However, it also leads to rather rigid systems, in which formation and dissolution of ad-hoc collections of cooperating or competing agents cannot be modelled directly.

Some approaches to providing flexible, controllable signal handling in SDL are discussed below.

Allow the Sender to Specify Multiple Recipients. In SDL 2010, the sender of a signal can specify a recipient. This could be extended to allow the sender to specify that more than one recipient should respond to the signal. This would allow an IoT developer to specify the relationship between the sender and recipients directly, without the need to also specify a separate agent to replicate signals for each recipient.

This could be implemented in SDL 2010 by introducing transformations that inserted a new block between the sender of the signal and its intended recipients. Adding new channels from the new block to the recipients, and re-naming the signals would complete the transformation.

This change does not require any change to basic SDL, but could be implemented as a syntactic extension.

Allow Agents to Indicate that they will Always Respond to a Signal. A signal recipient could specify that it always responds to a signal. This could be implemented in a similar way to the previous suggestion, with each recipient receiving its own version of the signal. This approach also has the advantage that it facilitates model re-use, as it allows an existing model to be encapsulated and extended by the addition of new signal recipients.

The Intermediate Block. Both these approaches make use of an intermediate block, as in Fig. 6, that duplicates signals sent by an originator to multiple intended recipients. This block either acts as a server, accepting requests from those recipients and treating stored signals as data to be forwarded to recipients on demand, or as a router, that forwards copies of the original signal to individual recipients.

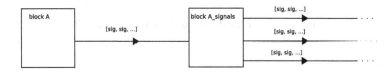

Fig. 6. An intermediate block makes signals available to different recipients

As illustrated in Fig. 5, an intermediate block can be modelled directly using SDL 2010 without modification. However, it would be useful to introduce some convenient syntax with appropriate transformations to define the corresponding semantics in terms of an intermediate block[4]. Further consideration is need to decide which, if any, syntactic modifications of SDL are desirable.

5   Next Steps

The engineer who wishes to model and simulate new systems for deployment in the IoT faces some specific communications challenges. Some of these were explored in the previous sections, and adaptations of SDL 2010 with a view to making it easier to meet those challenges were discussed.

The challenges, originally identified in [1], represented areas where SDL appeared to be less than ideally suited to modelling situations that are likely to occur in the IoT. However, for the most part, these can be addressed with fairly minor changes to SDL 2010.

Simulating system behaviour on a busy communications network can be modelled by providing a runtime library of delay functions that delay signals on a channel by a duration that depends on the signals already in the channel's delay queue. A minor change to SDL 2010 would make these available to the engineer using SDL. Further consideration needs to be given to the functions to

---

[4] Additional syntax that makes basic SDL more usable is formally defined by means of transformations to the core language.

be provided, but probability distributions, or cumulative distributions are likely candidates.

Undesirable interactions with external agents can already be modelled by representing those agents as part of a new IoT system. Re-instatement of a construct similar to the SDL 96 channel substructure, would make it possible to do this in a way that clearly indicates the external agent and that facilitates its removal prior to deployment.

Allowing signals to be handled by multiple recipients can also be achieved by adding an intermediate block between the sender and the recipients. Syntactic constructs to be transformed so as to introduce such a block could be defined, but further discussion and exploration is needed to identify which constructs are likely to be of interest.

As a final word of caution, past experience indicates that added constructs do not always live up to their original promise. For example, the original channel substructure construct was never used. This may have been because detailed control of channel behaviour was not actually needed, or because tool support was never provided for the construct. Before introducing changes to SDL 2010, careful evaluation of potential tool support and of demand for the proposed modifications is needed.

References

1. Sherratt, E., Ober, I., Gaudin, E., Fonseca i Casas, P., Kristoffersen, F.: SDL-the IoT language. In: Fischer, J., Scheidgen, M., Schieferdecker, I., Reed, R. (eds.) SDL 2015. LNCS, vol. 9369, pp. 27–41. Springer, Heidelberg (2015). doi:10.1007/978-3-319-24912-4_3

2. ITU-T: Z.100 series for SDL 2010, International Telecommunications Union 2011–2015

3. Williams, A.W., Probert, R.L., Li, Q., Kim, T.-H.: The winning entry of the SAM 2002 design contest. In: Reed, R., Reed, J. (eds.) SDL 2003. LNCS, vol. 2708, pp. 387–403. Springer, Heidelberg (2003). doi:10.1007/3-540-45075-0_23

4. Ellsberger, J., Hogrefe, D., Sarma, A.: SDL: Formal Object-oriented Language for Communicating Systems. Prentice Hall, Upper Saddle River (1997)

5. Metzger, A.: Feature interactions in embedded control systems. Comput. Netw. **45**, 625–664 (2004). Elsevier

6. Bozga, M., Graf, S., Mounier, L., Ober, I., Roux, J.-L., Vincent, D.: Timed extensions for SDL. In: Reed, R., Reed, J. (eds.) SDL 2001. LNCS, vol. 2078, pp. 223–240. Springer, Heidelberg (2001). doi:10.1007/3-540-48213-X_14

7. Bozga, M., Fernandez, J.-C., Ghirvu, L., Graf, S., Krimm, J.-P., Mounier, L., Sifakis, J.: IF: an intermediate representation for SDL and its applications. In: Dssouli, R., Bochmann, G., Lahav, Y. (eds.) SDL 1999 - The Next Millennium, Proceedings of the Ninth SDL Forum, Montreal. Elsevier (1999)

8. Graf, S.: Expression of time and duration constraints in SDL. In: Sherratt, E. (ed.) SAM 2002. LNCS, vol. 2599, pp. 38–52. Springer, Heidelberg (2003). doi:10.1007/3-540-36573-7_3

9. Prinz, A.: SDL time extensions from a semantic point of view. In: Sherratt, E. (ed.) SAM 2002. LNCS, vol. 2599, pp. 53–60. Springer, Heidelberg (2003). doi:10.1007/3-540-36573-7_4

10. Blanchard, T.: Endocrine Inspired Control of Wireless Sensor Networks: Deployment and Analysis Aberystwyth University, Ph.D. thesis (2016)
11. Kelly, B., Crowther, M., King, J.: Feature interaction detection using SDL models. In: Proceedings of IEEE GLOBECOM, vol. 3, pp. 1857–1861 (1994)
12. Turner, K.J.: Formalizing graphical service descriptions using SDL. In: Reed, R., Reed, J. (eds.) SDL 2003. LNCS, vol. 2708, pp. 183–202. Springer, Heidelberg (2003). doi:10.1007/3-540-45075-0_11
13. Chan, K.Y., Bochmann, G.V.: Methods for designing SIP services in SDL with fewer feature interactions. In: Proceedings of the 7th Feature Interactions in Telecommunications and Software Systems, pp. 59–76. IOS Press (2003)
14. Doldi, L.: SDL Illustrated: Laurent Doldi (2001)
15. Harel, D., Feldman, Y.: Algorithmics: The Spirit of Computing. Pearson Education Ltd., Essex (2004)
16. Sherratt, E.: SDL in a changing world. In: Amyot, D., Williams, A.W. (eds.) SAM 2004. LNCS, vol. 3319, pp. 96–105. Springer, Heidelberg (2005). doi:10.1007/978-3-540-31810-1_7

Applying MDA and OMG Robotic Specification for Developing Robotic Systems

Claudia Pons[1,2,3(✉)], Gabriela Pérez[1], Roxana Giandini[1], and Gabriel Baum[1]

[1] LIFIA, Facultad de Informática, Universidad Nacional de La Plata, La Plata, Argentina
{cpons,gperez,giandini,gbaum}@info.unlp.edu.ar
[2] CIC, Comisión de Investigaciones Científicas PBA, La Plata, Argentina
[3] UAI, Universidad Abierta Interamericana, Buenos Aires, Argentina

Abstract. Robotics systems have special needs often related with their real-time nature and environmental properties. Often, control and communication paths within the system are tightly coupled to the actual physical configuration of the robot. As a consequence, these robots can only be assembled, configured, and programmed by robot experts. Traditional approaches, based on mainly writing the code without using software engineering techniques, are still used in the development process of these systems. Even when these robotic systems are successfully used, several problems can be identified and it is widely accepted that new approaches should be explored. The contribution of this research consists in delineating guidelines for the construction of robotic software systems, taking advantage of the application of the OMG standard robotic specifications which adhere to the model-driven approach MDA. Thereby the expert knowledge is captured in standard abstract models that can then be reused by other less experienced developers. In addition part of the code is automatically generated, reducing costs and improving quality.

Keywords: Robotic software system · Model driven software development · OMG standard

1 Introduction

Robotics systems are essentially real-time, distributed embedded systems. They have special needs often related with their real-time nature and environmental properties; they have to be able to cope with the uncertain and dynamic physical environment where they are immersed. Furthermore, robotic systems consist of different hardware components. There are a wide variety of controllers, sensors and actuators which results in very complex and highly variable architectures. Often, control and communication paths within the system are tightly coupled to the actual physical configuration of the robot. As a consequence, these robots can only be assembled, configured, and programmed by experts.

Traditional approaches, based on mainly coding the applications without using modeling techniques, are still used in the development process of these software systems. Even when the applications are running and being used in the different robotic systems,

J. Grabowski and S. Herbold (Eds.): SAM 2016, LNCS 9959, pp. 51–67, 2016.
DOI: 10.1007/978-3-319-46613-2_4

several problems can be identified. On the one hand, there is no clear documentation of design decisions taken during the coding phase, making the evolution and the mainte-nance of the systems difficult. On the other hand, when using specific programming languages, such as C in Microsoft RDS [27], the possibility of generalizing concepts - that could be extracted, reused and applied in different systems - is wasted and the code is written from scratch over and over again.

Thus, currently used methodologies and toolsets are not enough, and it is widely accepted that new approaches should be explored. The goal of our work is to investigate on the current use of modern software engineering techniques for developing robotic systems and their actual automation level. Especially, we have explored the OMG standards in this domain [32] and as a consequence we have delineated a methodology for the construction of robotic software systems, taking advantage of the application of the model-driven approach MDA and the OMG robotic specifications, in particular the RTC proposal.

The rest of the paper is organized as follows. Section 2 summarizes the most relevant software engineering techniques for developing robots. Section 3 presents our guidelines for the construction of robotic systems, applying the MDA approach together with the OMG robotic specifications, through a simple case study. Section 4 discusses a set of related works. Finally, conclusions are presented in Sect. 5.

2   Software Engineering Techniques for Developing Robots

Although the complexity of robotic software is high, in most cases reuse is still restricted to the level of libraries. At the lowest level, a multitude of libraries have been created for robot systems to perform tasks like mathematical computations for kinematics, dynamics and machine vision [14]. Instead of composing systems out of building blocks with assured services, the overall software integration process for another robotic system often is still re-implementation of the glue logic to bring together the various libraries. Often, the kind of overall integration is completely driven by a certain middleware system and its capabilities. This is not only expensive and wastes tremendous resources of highly skilled roboticists, but this also does not take advantage from a maturing process to enhance overall robustness.

From this perspective, it is widely accepted that new approaches should be estab-lished to meet the needs of the development process of today's complex robotic systems. Component-based development (CBD) [45], Service Oriented Architecture (SOA) [10], as well as Model Driven Architecture (MDA) [31] are among the key promising tech-nologies in the robotic systems domain. These technologies have been adopted by the Robotics Domain Task Force (RTF) [32], which promotes the integration of modular robotic systems components through the use of OMG standards.

In first place, the CBD paradigm states that application development should be achieved by linking independent parts, the components. Strict component interfaces based on predefined interaction patterns decouple the sphere of influence and thus diminishing the overall complexity. This results in loosely coupled components that interact via services with contracts. Components such as architectural units allow specifying very precisely, using the concept of port, both the services provided and the services required by a given component and defining a composition theory based on the notion of connector. Component technology offer high rates of reusability, but little flexibility with regard to the implementation platform: most existing components are linked to C/C++ and Linux, e.g. Microsoft robotics developer studio [27], EasyLab [7], Player/Stage project [20]. On the other hand, some proposals achieve more independence, thanks to the use of some middleware, e.g. Smart Software Component model [43], Orocos [14], Orca [12] and CLARAty [29].

In second place, SOA is a flexible set of design principles used during the phases of systems development and integration. SOA separates functions into distinct units, or services which developers make accessible over a network in order to allow designers to combine and reuse them in the production of applications. These services and their corresponding consumers communicate with each other by passing data in a well-defined, shared format.

Finally, the MDE [44] approach has emerged as a paradigm shift from code-centric software development to model-based development. Such approach promotes the systematization and automation of the construction of software artifacts. Models are considered as first-class constructs in software development, and developers' knowledge is encapsulated by means of model transformations. Models are implementation-independent and they are automatically transformed to executable code. The MDA is the OMG realization of the MDE. The MDA process can be divided into three phases: the first phase builds a PIM, which is a high-level technology-independent model; then, the previous model is transformed into one or more PSMs; these models are lower level and describe the system in accordance with a given deployment technology; finally, the source code is generated from each PSM.

3   OMG Standards for Robotic Components

The Object Management Group (OMG) is an international, open membership, not-for-profit technology standards consortium. OMG Task Forces develop enterprise integration standards for a wide range of technologies and industries. OMG modeling standards enable visual design, execution and maintenance of software and other processes. Originally aimed at standardizing distributed object-oriented systems, the company now focuses on modeling (programs, systems and business processes) and model-based standards. OMG evolved towards modeling standards by creating the standard for the Unified Modeling Language (UML) followed by related standards for Model Driven Architecture (MDA).

Specifically in the area of Robotics, in 2005 the OMG launched the Robotics Domain Task Force (RTF) with the purpose of fostering the integration of robotics systems from modular components through the adoption of OMG standards. To realize this purpose, the RTF has been promoting important actions and in the last years has released a set of specifications: Robotic Technology Component (RTC) [35], Robotic Interaction Service

(ROIs) [36], Dynamic Deployment and Configuration for Robotic Technology Component (DDC4RTC), Unified Component Model for Distributed, Real-time and Embedded Systems (UCM), Finite State Machine Component for RTC (FSM4RTC) [33], Hardware Abstraction Layer for Robots (HAL4RT) [34], among others.

Let's slightly describe some of these standards:

The RTC proposal specifies a component model that meets the requirements of robotic systems. A component in RTC is a logical representation of a hardware and/or software entity that provides well-known functionality and services. So, the developers can combine RTCs from multiple vendors into a single application, allowing them to create more flexible designs more quickly than before. It includes a Platform-Independent Model (PIM) expressed in UML and three Platform-Specific Models (PSMs) expressed in OMG IDL: Local, Lightweight CMM and CORBA. In the Local PSM, the components reside on the same network node and communicate over direct object references without the mediation of a network or network-centric middleware such as CORBA. In the Lightweight CMM, most components are assumed to be distributed relative to one another and they communicate using a CMM-based middleware. And in CORBA, components are also assumed to be distributed and they communicate using a CORBA-based middleware.

The RoIS Framework abstracts the hardware in the service robot (sensors and actuators) and the Human-Robot Interaction (HRI) functions provided by the robot. It provides a uniform interface between the service robot and the application. Using the RoIS Framework as an intermediary, a service application selects and uses only necessary functions and leaves hardware-related matters, such as which sensor to use, to the HRI engine.

The DDC4RTC specification defines data models and service interfaces of deployment and configuration for RTC based dynamic applications as an extension to DEPL (OMG Deployment and Configuration of Component-based Distributed Applications Specification) specification. Generally speaking, since system structure and configuration are frequently affected by robot movement and application or scenario state, it is important to be able to represent and realize dynamic component deployment and runtime re-configuration requirements.

The HAL4RT specification defines the Platform-Independent Model (PIM) of a Hardware Abstraction Layer for robotic systems that is capable to support at least the following devices: Sensors (sensor kind and unit of measure should be provided) and Actuators (commands to perform motions, and motion feedback information should be provided). In addition this specification defines the Platform specific Model (PSM) in language C based on the HAL PIM. This specification aims to enable engineers such as device makers, device users, and software users to build robotic software without any concern about the differences among the targeted devices, by standardizing the API of these devices.

All these standards interact with each other to provide a higher level of abstraction that facilitates the task of programming robots.

4   A Case Study: Applying MDA with the OMG Robotic Standards

In this section we describe the development of a robotic system applying the MDA approach. The code is automatically derived from models compliant with the OMG robotic standards. For implementing this case study we use the modeling tool Papyrus [37], an Eclipse graphical editing tool for UML2. In accordance with its primary goal of implementing the complete UML2 standard specification, Papyrus provides an extensive support for UML profiles. It includes facilities for defining and applying UML profiles in a very rich and efficient manner. But, it also provides powerful tool customization capabilities similar to DSML-like meta-tools. In this way, Papyrus is a tool that brings together the advantages of using a general purpose language such as UML2, and those of DSML-based approaches. In particular, the SOA and RTC profiles are smoothly incorporated to Papyrus. On the other hand, for implementing the transformations we use Acceleo [19], an open source code generator implementing the OMG's MOF Model to Text Language (MTL) standard that uses any EMF based models (e.g., UML, SysML) to generate any kind of code (e.g., Java, C, PHP) while keeping the traceability of the generated text.

4.1   Using the RTC Standard

The purpose of the RTC specification is to manage the lifecycle of all components in a uniform way. This specification does not attempt to replace the existing UML

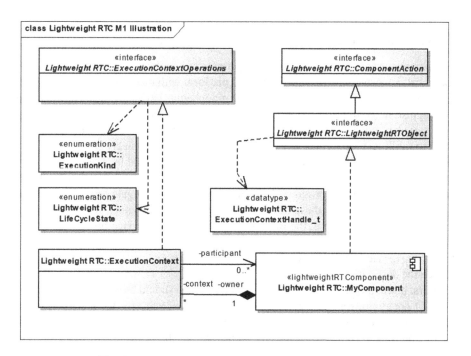

Fig. 1. Simplified LightweightRTC metamodel definition

component models, but focuses on structural and behavioral characteristics required by robotic applications that are not covered by other UML models. It also separates functional specification and execution control. By extending the general-purpose component functionality of UML with direct support for domain-specific structural and behavioral design patterns, RTC elements can serve as powerful building blocks in a robotics system.

The RTC PIM consists of three parts: The Lightweight RTC, the Execution semantics and the Introspection, as follows,

The Lightweight RTC describes a simple model containing definitions of concepts such as component, port and similar ones.

The Execution semantics are extensions to Lightweight RTC to directly support critical design patterns used in robotics applications such as periodic sampled data processing, discrete event/stimulus response processing and modes of operation.

And finally, the Introspection is an API allowing for the examination of elements at runtime. It is useful for dynamic component networks.

The Lightweight RTC specification (see Fig. 1) defines the stereotype lightweightRTComponent extending UML basic component, and describes some interfaces which enable communication between components. When the stereotype is applied, the component must implement all the methods that were defined in the required interfaces. On the other hand, a RTC component may participate in any number of execution contexts. These contexts shall be represented to a RTC component as instances of ExecutionContext class. The ExecutionContext manages the behavior of each RTC component that participates in it.

4.2   The Robot Firefighter

To illustrate our approach, we use a small example of a mobile robot to fight fires. This robot must move and navigate itself around a platform with random obstacles and must find fire sources. Once a flame is detected, the robot begins navigating towards the flame to extinguish it. To improve the efficiency of the robot in the fire extinction, the robot interacts with pre-existing systems. These systems are not part of the robot, but cooperate with it to fulfill its purpose. On one side there are fire detectors placed physically in the environment at strategic locations. Also a Map Service is available. These devices are accessible as external services on the web. All of these services work together for determining if there is a fire in progress. If so, the robot should navigate towards the flame and extinguish it. Each of these devices covers a monitoring zone. When the device indicates the presence of fire, the robot should ask the Map Service how to get to that area. For this, the robot must provide its own position - which it knows through its GPS - to the Map Service. The Map Service then returns a trajectory that the robot must follow to reach the destination.

In first place, the PIM models for this robotic system should be created. By applying the CBD paradigm, robotic elements, such as actuators and sensors, are modeled as components. Thus, the following components were identified: ObstacleDetector, MotionController, NearByFireDetector, FireExtinguisher, GPS, FireDetector and MapService.

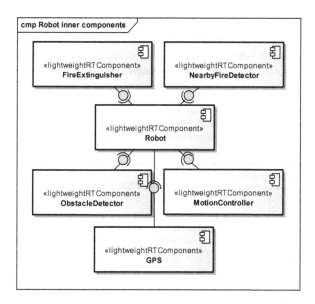

Fig. 2. PIM of the robot firefighter: inner component model.

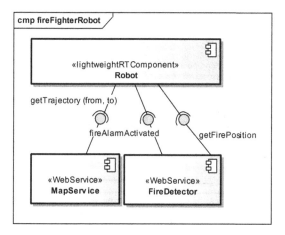

Fig. 3. PIM of the robot firefighter: component and service model.

The first five components are inner components, physically allocated into the robot, while the last two are external components that do not form part of the robot, but collaborate with it by providing helpful services. All of the components provide ports to communicate with each other and they are connected to the robot with their respective glue code. Figure 2 shows the composition of the robot, describing its inner components: ObstacleDetector, MotionController, NearByFireDetector, FireExtinguisher and GPS.

These PIM models are expressed in the UML language enriched with the RTC stereotypes. Figure 3 presents the PIM models specifying the external services (i.e., FireDetector and MapService) as components. In our specific case, the service model is reduced
to two elements, but in more complex systems, several services can be smoothly
modeled.

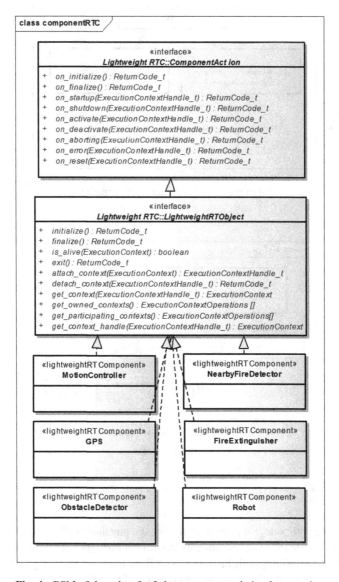

Fig. 4. PSM of the robot firefighter: component's implementation.

These PIM models are expressed in UML language enriched with the RTC stereotypes. Figure 4 shows the PSM model that is automatically derived from the PIM model in Fig. 2. This PSM describes the design of the system complying with the RTC specification. The interface LightweightRTObject defines a lifecycle standard, specifying the states and transitions through which all RTCs will pass from the time they are created until the time they are destroyed. The ComponentAction interface provides callbacks corresponding to the execution of the lifecycle operations of LightweightRTObject. A RTC developer may implement these callback operations in order to execute application-specific logic pointing response to those transitions.

Once the structural models are stable, the behavioral models describing the interaction among components are created. Figure 5 shows a UML state machine describing the overall behavior of the robot. The state machine specifies the four states which the robot can go through: walkAround, navigatingTowardsTheFirePosition, approachingTheFlame and fireExtinguish. Immediately after starting its workflow the robot enters to the state walkAround, and remains in the same state while no fire is detected. When the fire detector triggers an alarm the robot switches to the state navigatingTowardsTheFirePosition. Then, the robot keeps in the same state, moving in the direction of the fire, until the fire is reached.

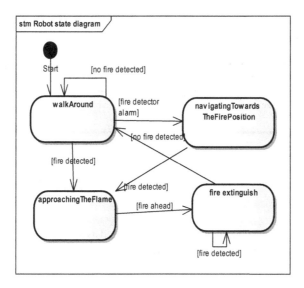

Fig. 5. PIM of the robot firefighter: overall behavioral model

Once the robot reaches the fire it enters to the state approachingTheFlame. In such state the robot approaches the fire as close as possible. When the fire is very close the robot switches to state fireExtinguish where it triggers mechanisms to extinguish the fire.

Other behavioral models are created for the remaining behaviors of the robot, but are not presented in this paper for space limitations.

Then, similarly to what was done with the structural models, PSM behavioral models are automatically derived. For example, Fig. 6 shows a PSM of the robot´s behavior that was automatically derived from the State machine in Fig. 5 by applying the state pattern as prescribed by the RTC.

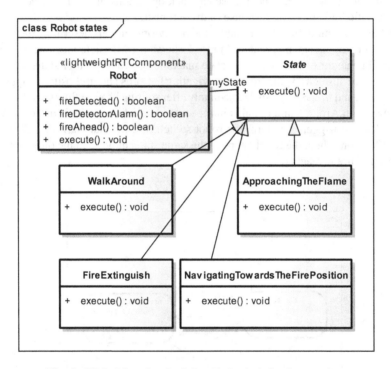

Fig. 6. PIM of the robot firefighter: behavior's implementation.

For each state in the state machine, a class is created as subclass of the abstract class State. Each transition trigger in the state machine is mapped to a Boolean operation in the main class Robot. A method named execute() is defined in the class Robot; according to the State Pattern this method just delegates its behavior to the execute() method in the corresponding State.

The next step of the development process consists in the transformation of structural as well as behavioral PSM models to a specific programming language. The following listing shows the transformation program written in Acceleo that takes as input the robot structural models and produces Java code as output.

```
[module generateRTCCustomComponents
('http://www.eclipse.org/uml2/5.0.0/UML')]

[template public generateElement(aComponent : Component)]
[comment @main/]
[file ('myRTC/' +aComponent.name+'.java',false, 'UTF-8')]

package myRTC;
import java.util.List;
import java.util.ArrayList;
import lightweightRTC.ExecutionContext;
import lightweightRTC.ExecutionContextHandle_t;
import lightweightRTC.ExecutionContextOperations;
import lightweightRTC.LightweightRTObject;
import lightweightRTC.ReturnCode_t;

public class [aComponent.name/] implements LightweightRTObject {

private List<ExecutionContext> contexts= new ArrayList();
  /*
   * @generated
   */
  public ReturnCode_t finalize_() {
    return this.on_finalize();
  }
```

The acceleo program above generates the following Java code as output,

```
package myRTC;

import java.util.List;
import java.util.ArrayList;
import lightweightRTC.ExecutionContext;
import lightweightRTC.ExecutionContextHandle_t;
import lightweightRTC.ExecutionContextOperations;
import lightweightRTC.LifeCycleState;
import lightweightRTC.LightweightRTObject;
import lightweightRTC.ReturnCode_t;

public class Robot implements LightweightRTObject {
  private List<ExecutionContext> contexts = new ArrayList();
  /*
   * @generated
   */
  public ReturnCode_t finalize_() {
    return this.on_finalize();
  }
```

The rationale for building this Java program was the following, for each component in the PIM, a Java class was created as an implementation of the LightweightRTObject standard interface. Additionally all the Lightweight RTC resources were imported in the program.

4.3   Lessons Learned from the Case Study

In this case study we have identified the different models that can be created to specify both the structure and the behavior of the robot. These models were represented using the OMG robotic standard, which is basically the well-known UML language enriched with appropriate stereotypes to describe structural and behavioral characteristics required by robotic applications that are not covered by other UML models. This standard specification manages the lifecycle of all robotic components in a uniform way. Additionally, the case study shows how the models are gradually defined at different abstraction levels, starting with the more abstract models, completely independent of the platform, from which other less abstract models could be automatically derived, to finally get to the executable code.

5   Related Work

It is broadly recognized that there is a need to incorporate software engineering principles within the development of future robot platforms. This has lead in the last years to the conception of a set of activities with the objective of assembling researchers from both fields, Model-Driven Software Development on one hand and Robotics on the other hand. Examples of these activities are the International Workshop on Domain-Specific Languages and Models for Robotic Systems (DSLRob) [42] launched in 2009, and the Workshop on Model-Driven Robot Software Engineering(MORSE) [3] initiated in 2013, both with the goal of incentivizing the interaction of these areas. As a result, in recent years several software frameworks have been developed to provide simple and intuitive ways of writing software applications for robot platforms. This includes academic research as well as industrial products.

On the industrial side one of the most well known is Lego Mindstorms Evolution 3 [26], developed especially for the Lego robots which can be built out of the Lego model kits. This is an extremely flexible and powerful system which allows anyone to build a robot using a few standard parts like motors, color sensors, touch sensors, infrared sensors and other Lego elements. Afterwards, the user can graphically implement a program by choosing the desired activities from the pallet of available blocks. Because of this target group, the software only has a limited set of functions and cannot be extended in any way. Evolution 3 only supports the creation of software for Lego robots, and thus cannot be regarded as a general robot modeling framework.

Other industrial tool is Choregraphe [1], an environment developed by Aldebaran Robotics, the manufacturer of the NAO humanoid robot, to allow robots to be programmed by graphical applications. It also supports code reuse and debugging capabilities and makes it possible to monitor and control NAO robots manually. The program uses an intuitive drag-and-drop interface in which a program is created using boxes that can be combined into a kind of flow diagram. In summary, although it is easy to use, Choregraphe allows the creation of complex programs. Like Lego Mindstorms Evolution 3, Choregraphe can only be used in combination with the NAO robot and thus cannot be regarded as a general robot modeling framework.

Another example of industrial product is Robotino View 2, a visual development environment provided by Festo Didactic exclusively for Robotino robots. Robotino View 2 shares the same limitation as the two previously mentioned frameworks — it is proprietary and can only be used with one kind of robot.

Finally, Microsoft Robotics Developer Studio 4 (MRDS4) [27] is another programming environment for building robotics applications. It provides a Visual Programming Language with an intuitive drag-and-drop interface for hobbyists and support for Microsoft Visual Studio for professional developers. It has several significant advantages. First, numerous robots are supported. Second, a high-fidelity simulation environment is provided by Visual Simulation Environment (VSE), and the functionality of MRDS4 can be extended by providing additional libraries and services. Also, extensive documentation, samples and tutorials are available.

On the academic side, many works [8, 11, 12, 23, 25, 28, 49] has taken advantage of CBD for developing robotic systems whilst other proposals [4, 16, 18, 49] have applied SOA to building robotic systems. Promising proposals were found for applying model-driven development to robotics [2, 5, 6, 9, 13, 17, 21, 22, 24, 25, 39–41, 46, 48], while only one work combined all three technologies [47]. Let us examine the most representative ones:

Atkinson and colleagues in [2] introduce a prototype domain-specific modeling framework designed to support the quick, simple and reliable creation of control software for standard robot platforms. In this paper they have presented a prototype framework, known as the Deep Robot Modeling Framework (DRMF). The current version of the prototype supports a rudimentary implementation of all of these features in the context of the NAO robot platform developed by Alderbaran Robots, although the basic framework is platform independent. Applications developed using the NAO-specific languages are automatically mapped into C++ code that can be loaded onto, and used to drive, individual NAO robots.

Dhouib and colleagues in [17] define the language RobotML as an extension to the Eclipse-based UML modeling tool Papyrus. Papyrus puts strong emphasis on UML's profile mechanism, which allows domain-specific adaptations. RobotML aims to provide model-driven engineering capabilities for the domain of robot programming, implementing code generators for different target platforms.

In [15] a small and declarative domain-specific language for pick and place applications was elaborated for demonstrating the feasibility of the model driven approach. Configurable code generation for C++ is provided.

These related works focus on defining specific modeling languages that enable the designer to create abstract models of the robotic system and to automatically generate code from them. Although these different languages and platforms are superficially very different, at a high enough level of abstraction they all contain the same basic constructs

– predefined types representing the components and actions from which the structure and behavior of individual robots are constructed. In principle, therefore, they could all be brought together under the umbrella of a single, unified robot modeling framework. We believe that our approach makes a contribution towards the application of standard instead of developing new concepts which are then difficult to integrate.

6   Conclusions

Programming robots is a complicated and time-consuming task. Often, control and communication paths within the system are tightly coupled to the actual physical configuration of the robot. Robotic researchers have been mainly concentrated on creating hardware/software solutions for specialized tasks, leading to an extensive land-scape of comparable but isolated solutions which cannot be reused and combined easily. Furthermore, these approaches lack comprehensive software engineering methodolo-gies and abstractions to handle the increased heterogeneity and complexity of robotic software systems.

The contribution of this research consists in delineating guidelines for the construc-tion of robotic software systems, taking advantage of the application of the OMG standard robotic specifications which adhere to the model-driven approach MDA. Model-driven approaches further simplify the reuse of already implemented and tested modules by enabling developers to model their applications on a higher abstraction level incorporating existing modules, managing the complexity and facilitating the reusability of robot code.

We observed that the CBD and SOA paradigms provide a starting point for a MDA approach in robotics where the differences between various software platforms and middleware systems can be completely hidden from the user due to the definition of intermediate abstraction level. In particular, the proposed methodology takes advantages of the standards defined by the Robotics Domain Task Force (RTF) which promotes the integration of modular robotic systems components under the umbrella of MDA.

The approach captures the fundamental concepts of the robotic software develop-ment process, its relationships and properties. This modeling approach includes concepts to represent services and components as primary elements in the robotic system in a higher abstraction level.

The proposed methodology has been prototyped using Papyrus and Acceleo that are tools provided by the Eclipse Modeling Project that focuses on the evolution of model-based development technologies within the Eclipse community.

At the moment, there are few proposals taking advantage of the combined application of CBD, SOA and MDA to robotic software system development as reviewed in [38] and more recently in [30], and there is a lack of proposals towards the application of the OMG robotic standard.

References

1. Aldebaran Robotics: Choreographe overview (2014). http://doc.aldebaran.com/2-1/software/choregraphe/index.html
2. Atkinson, C., Gerbig, R., Markert, K., Zrianina, M., Egurnov, A., Kajzar, F.: Towards a deep, domain-specific modeling framework for robot applications. In: Workshop on Model-Driven Robot Software Engineering, MORSE 2014 (2014)
3. Aßmann, U., Atkinson, C., Burger, E., Goldschmidt, T., Reussner, R. (eds.): Proceedings of MORSE/VAO 2015, Workshop on Model-Driven Robot Software Engineering and View-based Software-Engineering, Italy. ACM, New York (2015)
4. Amoretti, M., Zanichelli, F., Conte, G.: A service-oriented approach for building autonomic peer-to-peer robot systems In: 16th IEEE International Workshops on, WETICE 2007 (2007)
5. Arney, D., Fischmeister, S., Lee, I., Takashima, Y., Yim, M.: Model-based programming of modular robots. In: 13th IEEE International Symposium on Object/Component/Service-Oriented Real-Time Distributed Computing (ISORC), pp. 66–74 (2010)
6. Baer, P.A., Reichle, R., Zapf, M., Weise, T., Geihs, K.: A generative approach to the development of autonomous robot software. In: Fourth IEEE International Workshop on Engineering of Autonomic and Autonomous Systems, EASe 2007 (2007)
7. Barner, S., Geisinger, M., Buckl, C., Knoll, A.: EasyLab: model-based development of software for mechatronic systems. In: IEEE/ASME International Conference on Mechatronic and Embedded Systems and Applications, Beijing, China (2008)
8. Basu, A., Bensalem, B., Bozga, M., Combaz, J., Jaber, M., Nguyen, T., Sifakis, J.: Rigorous component-based system design using the BIP framework. IEEE Softw. **28**(3), 41–48 (2011)
9. Baumgartl, J., Buchmann, T., Henrich, D., Westfechtel, B.: Towards easy robot programming: using DSLs, code generators and software product lines. In: Proceedings of the 8th International Joint Conference on Software Technologies, ICSOFT 2013 pp. 548–554 (2013)
10. Bell, M.: Introduction to Service-Oriented Modeling. Service-Oriented Modeling: Service Analysis, Design, and Architecture. Wiley, Hoboken (2008)
11. Biggs, G.: Flexible, adaptable utility components for component-based robot software. In: 2010 IEEE International Conference on Robotics and Automation (ICRA), pp. 4615–4620 (2010)
12. Brooks, A., Kaupp, T., Makarenko, A., Oreback, A., Williams, S.: Towards component-based robotics. In: Proceedings of IEEE/RSJ International Conference on Intelligent Robots and Systems (IROS 2005) (2005)
13. Brugali, D., Shakhimardanov, A.: Component-based robotic engineering (Part II). IEEE Robot. Autom. Mag. **17**(1), 100–112 (2010)
14. Bruyninckx, H.: Open robot control software: the OROCOS project. In: Proceedings of 2001 IEEE International Conference on Robotics and Automation (ICRA 2001), Korea, vol. 3 (2001)
15. Buchmann, T., Baumgartl, J., Henrich, D., Westfechtel, B.: Towards a domain-specific language for pick-and-place applications (2014). arXiv:1401.1376
16. Cesetti, A., Scotti, C.P., Di Buo, G., Longhi, S.: A service oriented architecture supporting an autonomous mobile robot for industrial applications. In: 18th Mediterranean Conference on Control and Automation (MED), pp. 604–609 (2010)
17. Dhouib, S., Kchir, S., Stinckwich, S., Ziadi, T., Ziane, M.: RobotML, a domain-specific language to design, simulate and deploy robotic applications. In: Noda, I., Ando, N., Brugali, D., Kuffner, J.J. (eds.) SIMPAR 2012. LNCS, vol. 7628, pp. 149–160. Springer, Heidelberg (2012)

18. Ebenhofer, G., Bauer, H., Plasch, M., Zambal, S.: A system integration approach for service-oriented robotics. In: 2013 IEEE 18th International Conference on Emerging Technologies and Factory Automation, ETFA 2013, Italy, September 2013
19. Eclipse Acceleo Project. http://www.eclipse.org/acceleo/
20. Gerkey, B.P., Vaughan, R.T., Howard, A.: Most valuable player: a robot device server for distributed control. In: IEEE/RSJ International Conference on Intelligent Robots and Systems (2001)
21. Son, H.S., Kim, W.Y., Kim, R.: Semi-automatic software development based on MDE for heterogeneous multi-joint robots. In Future Generation Communication and Networking Symposia, FGCNS 2008, pp. 93–98 (2008)
22. Iborra, A., Caceres, D., Ortiz, F., Franco, J., Palma, P., Alvarez, B.: Design of Service Robots. Experiences Using Software Engineering. IEEE Robotics and Automation Magazine 1070-9932/09/, pp. 24–33. IEEE, March 2009
23. Jawawi, D.N.A., Deris, S., Mamat, R.: Early-life cycle reuse approach for component-based software of autonomous mobile robot system. In: Software Engineering, Artificial Intelligence, Networking, and Parallel/Distributed Computing Conference (2008)
24. Jorges, S., Kubczak, C., Pageau, F., Margaria, T.: Model driven design of reliable robot control programs using the jABC. In: Fourth IEEE International Workshop on Engineering of Autonomic and Autonomous Systems, EASe 2007, pp. 137–148 (2007)
25. Jung, E., Kapoor, C., Batory, D.: Automatic code generation for actuator interfacing from a declarative specification. In: IEEE/RSJ International Conference on Intelligent Robots and Systems, (IROS 2005), pp. 2839–2844 (2005)
26. LEGO. http://shop.lego.com/en-US/ LEGO-MINDSTORMS-EV3-31313; Visited April 2014
27. Microsoft Robotics Group: Robotics Developer Studio: Reference Platform Design (2012)
28. Jung, M.Y., Deguet, A., Kazanzides, P.: A component-based architecture for flexible integration of robotic systems. In: IEEE/International Conference on Intelligent Robots and Systems (2010)
29. Nesnas, I., Wright, A., Bajracharya, M., Simmons, R., Estlin, T.: CLARAty and challenges of developing interoperable robotic software. In: Proceedings of 2003 IEEE/RSJ International Conference on Intelligent Robots and Systems (IROS 2003), vol. 3, pp. 2428–2435 (2003)
30. Nordmann, A., Hochgeschwender, N., Wigand, D.L., Wrede, S.: A survey on domain-specific modeling and languages in robotics. J. Softw. Eng. Robot. 7(1), 75–99 (2016)
31. OMG MDA Guide 2.0. http://www.omg.org/mda. Edited in Boston on 18 June 2014
32. OMG Robotics Domain Task Force (DTF). http://robotics.omg.org/. Accessed 3 Mar 2016
33. OMG Finite State Machine Component for RTC™ Formal Version Of FSM4RTC™ (2016). http://www.omg.org/spec/FSM4RTC/Current
34. OMG Hardware Abstraction Layer for Robotic Technology™ (HAL4RT™), January 2016. http://www.omg.org/spec/HAL4RT/Current
35. OMG Robotic Technology Component™ (RTC) (2012). http://www.omg.org/spec/RTC/
36. OMG Robotic Interaction Service™ (RoIS™) (2016). http://www.omg.org/spec/RoIS/
37. Papyrus Eclipse project (2015). http://www.eclipse.org/papyrus/
38. Pons, C., Giandini, R., Arévalo, G.: A systematic review of applying modern software engineering techniques to developing robotic systems. Ingeniería e Investigación 32(1), 58–63 (2012)
39. Poppa, F., Zimmer, U.: RobotUI - a software architecture for modular robotics user interface frameworks. In: 25th IEEE/RSJ International Conference on Robotics and Intelligent Systems, IROS 2012, Algarve, Portugal, pp. 2571–2576, October 2012

40. Sanchez, P., Alonso, D., Rosique, F., Alvarez, B., Pastor, J.: Introducing safety requirements traceability support in model-driven development of robotic applications. IEEE Trans. Comput. **60**, 1059–1071 (2010)
41. Schlegel, C., Steck, A., Lotz, A.: Robotic software systems: from code-driven to model-driven software development (Chapter 23). In: Robotic Systems - Applications, Control and Programming (2012). ISBN 978-953-307-941-7
42. Schlegel, C., Schultz, U., Stinckwich, S., Wrede, S.: Proceedings of the Sixth International Workshop on Domain-Specific Languages and Models for Robotic Systems (DSLRob 2015) (2015). arXiv:1601.00877
43. SmartSoft, July 2013. http://smart-robotics.sourceforge.net/
44. Stahl, T., Voelter, M.: Model Driven Software Development. Wiley, Hoboken (2006). ISBN 0470025700
45. Szyperski, C.: Component Software: Beyond Object-Oriented Programming, 2nd edn. Addison-Wesley Professional, Boston (2002). ISBN 0-201-74572-0
46. Thomas, U., Hirzinger, G., Rumpe, B., Schulze, C., Wortmann, A.: A new skill based robot programming language using UML/P Statecharts. In: Proceedings - IEEE International Conference on Robotics and Automation, ICRA 2013, Germany, pp. 461–466, May 2013
47. Tsai, W.T., Huang, Q., Sun, X.: A collaborative service-oriented simulation framework with microsoft robotic studio®. In: 41st Annual Simulation Symposium, ANSS 2008 (2008)
48. Wei, H., Duan, X., Li, S., Tong, G., Wang, T.: A component based design framework for robot software architecture. In: IEEE/RSJ International Conference on Intelligent Robots and Systems, pp. 3429–3434 (2009)
49. Yang, T.-H., Lee, W.-P.: A service-oriented framework for the development of home robots. Int. J. Adv. Robot. Syst. **10**(122) (2013)

Domain Model Optimized Deployment and Execution of Cloud Applications with TOSCA

Fabian Glaser[(✉)]

Institute of Computer Science, University of Göttingen, Göttingen, Germany
fglaser@cs.uni-goettingen.de
http://swe.informatik.uni-goettingen.de

Abstract. Cloud computing promises to provide computing power as a utility and the adaptability to application requirements is one of its key benefits. However, using cloud infrastructures still requires a lot of technical expertise, which becomes a burden especially for non-computer scientists. Therefore, using model-driven approaches seems promising and can help to lower this burden by raising the level of abstraction. To achieve the correct scale of the cloud resources, a mechanism is required to map the computational requirements of the users domain model to parameters of the cloud infrastructure. In this paper, we present a framework, which scales the required infrastructure according to the demands of the users domain model. The framework utilizes a metamodel based on the Topology and Orchestration Specification for Cloud Applications (TOSCA) for modelling the cloud applications. Additionally, we introduce a domain-specific language to define a mapping between domain model parameters and parameters of the cloud infrastructure to achieve an appropriate scale.

Keywords: Model driven engineering · Cloud orchestration · TOSCA

1 Introduction

Due to its elasticity and on-demand self-service characteristics, cloud computing [1] is a great solution for users with varying computational requirements. However, setting up, running and scaling applications and the required infrastructure in the cloud is a cumbersome and error-prone task. Therefore, methods and tools are needed that simplify the process and lower the entry-barrier especially for non computer-scientists. With help of *model driven engineering* (MDE), the level of abstraction is raised and *domain specific languages* (DSLs) help to simplify tasks by focusing on the vocabulary of a certain domain. With MDE also the problem of API-heterogeneity of different cloud providers, often called *cloud-provider lock-in*, can be tackled [2], and graphical tools for modelling cloud infrastructures can be provided [3,4]. In combination with the templates and scripts used

© Springer International Publishing AG 2016
J. Grabowski and S. Herbold (Eds.): SAM 2016, LNCS 9959, pp. 68–83, 2016.
DOI: 10.1007/978-3-319-46613-2_5

by cloud orchestration and configuration management tools, fully automated, model driven deployment of cloud applications becomes possible.

These methods can be used for example to provide preconfigured computational resources to simulations scientists on demand. However, the appropriate scale of the infrastructure largely depends on what the scientist wants to compute. For example, an algorithm might require a certain amount of RAM in the deployed *virtual machines* (VMs), or the number of entities in a simulation might require a certain number of cores to be computed efficiently. These parameters are encoded in the *domain model* of the scientist, which comprise all digital artefacts, the scientist created to solve a certain research problem. We argue that the scale of the provided infrastructure should be able to adapt to the computational requirements of the domain model of the scientist automatically.

To tackle this problem, we defined a framework [5] to be able to scale the cloud infrastructure with the help of parametrized *deployment models* of the users application based on the *Topology and Orchestration Specification for Cloud Applications* (TOSCA) [7]. In this paper, we introduce a DSL for the mapping between the domain model of the user and the deployment model to define its correct scale.

The remainder of this paper is structured as follows. After providing the foundations of this work in Sect. 2, we provide a driving example in Sect. 3. We discuss our framework in Sect. 4 and introduce the DSL for the mapping in Sect. 5. We evaluate the approach with help of a case study on the driving example in Sect. 6. Related work is given in Sect. 7. Finally, we draw our conclusions and give an outlook on future work in Sect. 8.

2   Automated Cloud Application Deployment

To define cloud computing, we refer to the definition given by the *National Institute of Standards and Technology* (NIST) [1]: "Cloud computing is a model for enabling ubiquitous, convenient, on-demand network access to a shared pool of configurable computing resources (e.g., networks, servers, storage, applications, and services) that can be rapidly provisioned and released with minimal management effort or service provider interaction." Thereby, NIST defines three service models for cloud computing, which operate on different levels of abstraction. On the highest level of abstraction is *Software-as-a-Service* (SaaS), where fully fledged applications are delivered to the user e.g., via a web-browser. Below that, *Platform-as-a-Service* (PaaS) offers programming environments or platforms such as pre-configured databases as services. On the lowest level of abstraction the user is able to directly acquire computing resources (e.g., virtual machines, virtual network, and virtual storage) on demand via *Infrastructure-as-a-Service* (IaaS). To offer higher level services such as PaaS and SaaS on top of IaaS, cloud providers can rely on automation achieved with *cloud orchestration* and *configuration management* tools, which we will discuss in the following.

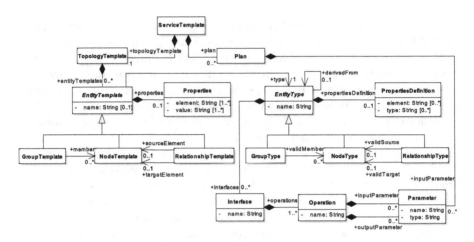

Fig. 1. TOSCA metamodel (adapted from Bergmayr et al. [4]).

2.1 Cloud Orchestration

To be able to manage and reuse configured resources in the cloud, *cloud orchestration* tools have emerged. Since many different cloud-provider dependent definitions of the term exist and it lacks of widely accepted definition, we will use the following definition in the scope of this paper:

Cloud Orchestration refers to the automated launch and life-cycle management of resources e.g., VMs, virtual storage, or virtual networks in the cloud. It also assigns software configurations to the defined resources, without defining the installation process or the configuration of the software itself. Cloud orchestration tools often provide additional functionality for automatic (event-based) scaling of the deployed infrastructure.

Cloud Orchestration tools use template languages that allow to define the topology and also the life-cycle operations on the topology in a reusable manner. Examples include the language of Amazons CloudFormation [6] and the *Heat Orchestration Template* (HOT) language of OpenStacks Heat orchestrator. The *Organization for the Advancement of Structured Information Standards* (OASIS) aims to standardize such a template language with the *Topology and Orchestration Specification for Cloud Applications* (TOSCA) [7]. The first version of the standard based on the *Extensible Markup Language* (XML) was originally published in 2013, while a draft of a simplified rendering based on *YAML Ain't Markup Language* (YAML) [8] was first published in 2015 and is still under development.

A simplified metamodel of TOSCA is depicted in Fig. 1. A *ServiceTemplate* captures the structure and the life-cycle operations of the application. It consists of a *TopologyTemplate* and a *Plan*. Plans define how the cloud application is managed and deployed. TopologyTemplates contain *EntityTemplates*, which are either *NodeTemplates* that define e.g., the virtual machines or application components, *RelationshipTemplates* that encode the relationships between the Node-Templates, e.g., that a certain application component is deployed on a certain virtual machine, or *GroupTemplates*[1] that allow to define groups of NodeTemplates, which e.g. should be scaled together. EntityTemplates have *Properties*, e.g., the IP address of a virtual machine, and a certain *type* that references an *EntityType*. The *EntityType* defines the allowed Properties through *PropertyDefintions*, and have *Interfaces*, which define the *Operations* that can be executed on the type, e.g., the termination of a certain application component, or the restart of a virtual machine. Operations have *Parameters* that define their input and output. In addition to parameters for operations, TOSCA also allows to define input parameters for Plans. These parameters can be used to parameterize the deployment workflow of the model and can e.g., include the virtual machine type to use or the number of instances of a certain type to launch.

2.2 Configuration Management

To enforce a certain software configuration on the resources defined above, *Configuration Management* tools are used. We use the following definition of the term in scope of this paper:

Configuration Management refers to the automated and reusable enforcement of a certain software configuration on several machines. It comprises the configuration of the operating system, the installation and configuration of software and the configuration, launch, and termination of services.

Configuration Management tools became popular with the rise of the DevOps movement [9] in recent years. They use declarative domain specific languages to define the desired software configuration in a reusable manner. Examples are the language used in Puppets [10] *manifests* or the language that defines Ansibles [11] *playbooks*. In Ansible, playbooks are based on YAML and define *tasks* that should be executed on a group of hosts. The following listing shows the definition of the software configuration for a webserver with Ansible:

```
1 - hosts: webservers
2   vars:
3     http_port: 80
4   tasks:
5   - name: ensure apache is at the latest version
6     yum: name=httpd state=latest
7   - name: write the apache config file
8     template: src=/srv/httpd.j2 dest=/etc/httpd.conf
```

---

[1] GroupTemplates and GroupTypes are currently part of the TOSCA YAML specification, but not part of the TOSCA XML specification. We included them in the metamodel, because we need their functionality to for modeling scalability in our deployments.

The configuration is enforced on the hosts in the group `webservers` (Line 1), the http port is set with help of a variable (Line 3). In the first task (Line 5), an Apache webserver is installed with help of the package manager `yum`, and in the second task (Line 7) a template for the server configuration is copied to the hosts. Additionally, tasks can be encapsulated to form *roles*, and several roles can be assigned to a host or a group of hosts.

3 Driving Example

Our driving example originates from material science and uses the *Open Field Operation and Manipulation* (OpenFOAM) [14] software package. It exemplifies a case where the domain model of the scientist has an influence on the required scale of the cloud resources. OpenFOAM is a extensible C++ toolbox for solving systems of numerical equations, primary from the domain of computational fluid dynamics on a predefined environment. It has a large user base both from industry and academia and can be executed across large-scale *High Performance Computing* (HPC) clusters using the *Message Passing Interface* (MPI). Typically, using OpenFOAM involves three steps. In the *Pre-processing* step, the mathematical model, the description of the domain, on which the model should be solved, and a mesh, which describes the decomposition of the domain for computation is defined. In the *Solving* step, user-defined or predefined solvers are used to solve the mathematical model on the domain, and in the *Post-Processing* step additional tools can be used to visualize and analyse the created solutions. We will refer to the artefacts created by the scientist as the *domain model*, which in case of OpenFOAM consists of the following parts:

1. The *geometry* of the domain on which the mathematical model should be solved and how the mesh on this domain is created.
2. The *initial and boundary conditions* for the problem for each parameter.
3. The *physical properties* for the system of partial differential equations (PDEs) to be solved.
4. The *control* of the simulation, such as the simulation time and the reading and writing of the solution.
5. A *domain decomposition* that describes how the domain should be decomposed for parallel computation.

Regarding a suitable scale of the infrastructure, information on how many worker nodes can be utilized are encoded in the domain decomposition. Information on how much storage is needed is influenced by the total length of the simulation and the frequency with witch simulation data is written do disk.

We use OpenFOAM to exemplify the usage of our framework, which uses a combination of MDE, cloud orchestration and configuration management to automatically provision and scale the cloud infrastructure.

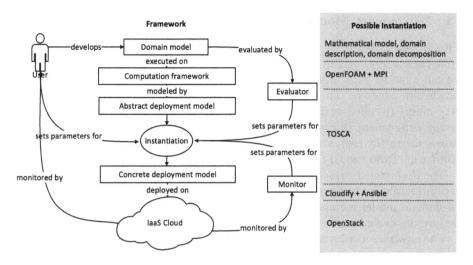

Fig. 2. A framework for adapting application deployments according to domain model demands.

4   The Framework

An overview of our framework and a possible instantiation for our driving example is depicted in Fig. 2. We will discuss its components in the following. In this paper we focus on the role of the evaluator and the static evaluation of the domain model.

4.1   Domain Model

Domain models come in very different formats, they even might consist of code that is later on compiled and linked to external libraries. In most cases, no formal metamodel for the domain is available. In case of OpenFOAM, the parts of the domain model described in Sect. 3 are encoded in text files that have a OpenFOAM specific format.

4.2   Computation Framework

The *computation framework* (CF) represents the required software for executing the domain model and its dependencies. It is the most restrictive component for the cloud deployment, since it encodes how the computational load is distributed on the underlying infrastructure and defines the needed soft- and hardware configuration. In the driving example, OpenFOAM and its dependencies represent the CF. OpenFOAM uses MPI for distributed computation, hence it requires a MPI cluster to run and distribute the computational load.

4.3   Deployment Models with TOSCA

With the given template/type of mechanism TOSCA and its ability to define input parameters, we can distinguish between two types of deployment models: We call a model with unset parameters *abstract* and a model with instantiated parameters *concrete*. The transformation from an abstract model into a concrete model is called *instantiation*. The appropriate setting of the parameters for the deployment during the instantiation process, is done with the help of three sources: the user, static information from the domain model, and runtime information from the CF.

The *deployment model* for the CF comprises three elements: a cloud orchestration template, configuration management scripts and a description on how the domain model parameters are mapped to parameters of the infrastructure used by the *evaluator*. We introduce the language for the mapping in Sect. 5.

The abstract deployment model for the OpenFOAM cluster is shown in Fig. 3. Since there is no standardized graphical syntax for TOSCA available, we use the following notation: NodeTemplates are depicted by boxes with solid lines, RelationshipTemplates are visualized by connections between the boxes, and GroupTemplates are depicted with boxes with dashed lines. For the Node-Templates and the Groups we additionally list the type and a subset of the Properties. One virtual machine serves as a gateway node. This node gets a public IP address (*floating IP*) assigned and is reachable from the outside of the cloud. The gateway node is connected to an extra volume which provides the storage for the simulation data. An arbitrary number of virtual machines is deployed to serve as worker nodes in the cluster to do the calculations. The gateway node exports its volume via a *Network File System* (NFS), which is then mounted and shared by the worker nodes. The software configuration for the gateway and mpiworker nodes is modeled with help of a NodeTemplate of type ansible.nodes.Application. With help of these NodeTemplates the corresponding Ansible roles for the software configuration are associated to the host in which the NodeTemplate is contained. Since the software configuration for the worker nodes is dependent on the software configuration of the gateway, we use an additional *depence_on* relationship between the Ansible nodes. In the abstract deployment model, several parameters can be adjusted to provide an appropriate scale for the required computational power. Hence, the following parameters are kept as input parameters of the model:

P1: The size S of the NFS.
P2: The virtual machine type T of the gateway and worker nodes. The virtual machine *type* or virtual machine *flavor* is the common way of IaaS providers to encode the hardware configuration of a virtual machine. This includes RAM size, number of compute cores, and disk space.
P3: The number of worker nodes N. MPI can be used to distribute computation across a single machine with multiple cores, or across multiple machines.

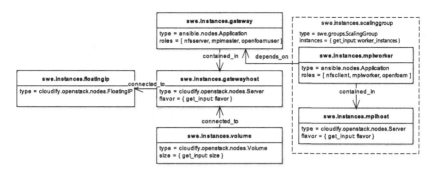

Fig. 3. Abstract deployment model for OpenFOAM.

4.4   Evaluator and Monitor

To find suitable parameter settings that match the requirements of a domain model, we distinguish between *static evaluation*, whereby the CF is not executed in the cloud, and *dynamic evaluation*, whereby the CF is executed and monitored. The static evaluation is performed before the CF is deployed on the cloud infrastructure and to derive its initial appropriate scale. We implement the static evaluation with help of the *evaluator*. This evaluator maps values of parameters of the domain model to suitable parameter settings for the concrete deployment model. This mapping is domain specific and needs to be defined for each domain separately. For this purpose, we defined a small DSL, which will be presented in Sect. 5.

Dynamic evaluations are done by monitoring the execution of the CF with help of a *monitor*. According to the outcome of the deployment evaluation, the parameters that have been used for the initial deployment are readjusted and a new instantiation of the abstract deployment model is initiated. Hereby, either a new concrete deployment model is created and deployed, or the existing concrete deployment model and its instantiation is adjusted. Dynamic evaluation and adjustments of a deployed infrastructure is nowadays implemented by many cloud orchestrators with their ability to process scaling policies that define under which conditions certain actions are automatically triggered on the infrastructure. For example, if the number of accesses on a webserver exceeds a certain threshold (condition), deploy an additional webserver (action). While it is worthwhile to investigate, if parts of these scaling policies can be derived from the domain model and the abstract deployment model of the CF, we focus on the determination of the appropriate scale for the infrastructure before the CF is deployed in scope of this paper.

4.5   Automated Deployment

The deployment of the CF is fully automated to avoid manual interaction with the cloud and enable transparent deployment of the CF for the user. A cloud orchestration framework is used for the orchestrated launch of the infrastructure

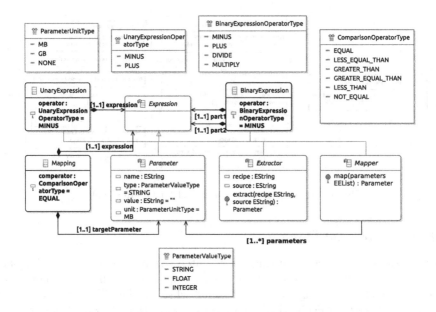

Fig. 4. Metamodel of the mapping language.

and a configuration management tool is utilized to automatically configure the launched infrastructure. As depicted on the right hand side in Fig. 2, we use the cloud orchestrator Cloudify and the configuration management tool Ansible to automatically deploy the CF on a private OpenStack [15] cloud.

5 Mapping Domain Model Parameters to Infrastructure Parameters

Since the domain models come in very heterogeneous formats and in most cases lack of a formal metamodel, it is not possible to define a formal model transformation from the domain model to a model that is executable on the infrastructure. Instead, our approach is to provide a mapping mechanism, that is able to describe how parameters of the deployment model can be computed from extracted parameters of the domain model.

To be able to define the mapping for the evaluator, we developed a DSL which we will discuss in the following. The metamodel for the mapping language is depicted in Fig. 4. A *Mapping* consists of a *TargetParameter* and an *Expression*. Hereby, the *TargetParameter* represents a parameter of the abstract deployment model and the *Expression* describes how the value for this parameter can be extracted from the domain model. The *Comperator* describes the relationship between the *TargetParameter* and the *Expression*. It can be e.g., of type *EQUAL*, to define that the *TargetParameter* must match the outcome of the *Expression*. *Expressions* can be unary, binary, simple parameters, of type *Extractor*, or *Mapper*. *Extractors* encode how parameters are extracted from *Sources* of the domain model, which can either be files or folders. *Extractors* contain a *recipe*, which define additional information on how a parameter is extracted from a *source*. *Mappers* define how the extracted values are mapped to target parameters. They implement logic, where parameters of the domain model require a setting of the deployment model, which can not be derived automatically from the extracted value, e.g., a certain number of cores might be required for computation, but the deployment model does only allow to set the flavor of the VMs, and not the number of cores directly.

For the time being, we defined basic Extractors, that extract information from the structure of the domain model e.g., the number of files the model consists of, and their size. We also defined Extractors that extract file content, e.g., the number of lines in a file, and the ability to extract information with help of a regular expression (*FileContentExtractor*). Since our target IaaS system OpenStack does not allow to determine a fitting VM flavor for a given number of cores automatically, we defined a Mapper that maps compute cores to the VM flavor (*FlavorMapper*) and the other way around (*CoreMapper*). Additional domain-specific Extractors and Mappers can be defined and implemented that inherit from the corresponding base classes. We exemplify the usage of the language in Sect. 6.3.

6 Evaluation

We prototypically implemented the evaluator based on the language introduced above and the instantiation process to evaluate the framework. We now investigate if we are able to derive an appropriate scale of the deployed infrastructure with the introduced framework. To evaluate the mapping mechanism on our driving example, we require different domain models for OpenFOAM. The tutorial data for OpenFOAM 2.4.0[2] comprise around 200 domain models. For the evaluation of our framework and the mapping we picked six domain models with different computational requirements. The selected domain models and the number of compute cores they require are given in Table 1. Even if these tutorial domain models are small in comparison with realistic OpenFOAM simulations that require large-scale HPC clusters to be computed, they are suitable to test our framework.

6.1 Implementation

We prototypically implemented our framework with help of the *Eclipse Modeling Framework* (EMF) [16]. We used the *XML Schema Definition* (XSD) of TOSCA to generate an Ecore-metamodel. This metamodel served as a basis for code generation for the implementation of the evaluator and the instantiation process. EMF was also used for the definition and implementation of the mapping language. The utilized cloud orchestrator Cloudify currently supports only a subset

---

[2] Available online at https://github.com/OpenFOAM/OpenFOAM-2.4.x/tree/master/tutorials.

of the functionality of TOSCA and is additionally not completely compliant with the standard. We used the Eclipse *Epsilon Generation Language* (EGL) [17] to generate Cloudify compliant YAML templates from our TOSCA metamodel. TOSCA is still subject to change and the development of the TOSCA YAML version is a little ahead of the TOSCA XML version. Since the TOSCA YAML version introduces some new features that are not yet reflected in the TOSCA XML schema, we added the desired features to our generated Ecore-metamodel manually. Hereby, we added *GroupTypes* and *GroupTemplates*, that allow to group NodeTemplates and the ability to set concrete values for Parameters.

Table 1. Selected cases from OpenFOAM tutorial data.

	Domain model	Req. Cores
1	multiphase/twoPhaseEulerFoam/laminar/mixerVessel2D/	1
2	heatTransfer/buoyantBoussinesqSimpleFoam/iglooWithFridges/	2
3	multiphase/multiphaseInterFoam/laminar/damBreak4phaseFine/	4
4	combustion/fireFoam/les/oppositeBurningPanels/	6
5	multiphase/interDyMFoam/ras/DTCHull/	8
6	multiphase/interDyMFoam/ras/testTubeMixer/	16

6.2 Metrics

We aim to produce deployments that are *efficient*. We call a deployment *efficient* if it neither utilizes more nor less resources than actually needed. To measure the efficiency of the deployment, we use the following metrics to detect if too many or to few resources were provisioned:

M1: Average load on the provisioned cluster during the execution of the domain model. This number should be close to the number of provisioned cores in the cluster, indicating that all cores are utilized for computation.

M2: Utilized portion of the NFS [%]. To detect over-provisioning of the storage size, we measure how much of the storage has been actually used to store the resulting data of the simulation.

6.3 Selection and Mapping of Domain Model Parameters

A suitable size for the NFS S depends on the expected size of the simulation outcome. This in turn depends on the total simulation time T_{total} and on the frequency f_{write} with which partial results are written do disk. Both are parameters of the domain model. Given an estimate for the size S_{part} of the partial results, the size for the distributed file system can be calculated as

$$S = \frac{T_{total}}{f_{write}} \times S_{part}. \tag{1}$$

To pick a suitable virtual machine type T for the gateway and worker nodes from the types $TYPES$ offered by the IaaS provider, we need the number of cores N_{core}, we can utilize. The number of cores we can utilize, depends on the number of subdomains N_{sub} of the domain decomposition of the domain model as described in Sect. 3. Hence, we pick the virtual machine type as

$$T = \min_{t \in TYPES,\ t.cores \leq N_{sub}} |t.cores - N_{sub}|. \tag{2}$$

The suitable number of worker nodes N, we can use for distributed computation depends on the number of subdomains N_{sub} in the domain model, but also on the virtual machine type T we picked in the last step. We can than calculate a suitable number of worker nodes as

$$N = \lceil \frac{N_{sub}}{T.cores} \rceil - 1. \tag{3}$$

We subtract one, since the gateway node is also used for computation.

The following listing shows how the setting of parameter S is defined with help of the XML serialization of the mapping language:

```
1 <mapping>
2    <targetParameter xsi:type=''mapping:TargetParameter''
3     name=''size'' type=''INTEGER'' unit=''GB''/>
4    <expression xsi:type=''mapping:BinaryExpression''
5     operator=''MULTIPLY''>
6    <part1 xsi:type=''mapping:BinaryExpression''
7      operator=''DIVIDE''>
8      <part1 xsi:type=''mapping:FileContentExtractor''
9        recipe=''endTime((\s+)(\d+(.\d+)?))#3''
10       source=''system/controlDict''/>
11     <part2 xsi:type=''mapping:FileContentExtractor''
12       recipe=''writeInterval((\s+)(\d+(.\d+)?))#3''
13       source=''system/controlDict''/>
14   </part1>
15   <part2 xsi:type=''mapping:FileContentExtractor''
16     recipe=''partSize((\s+)(\d+(.\d+)?))#3''
17     source="system/partSizeDict"/>
18   </expression>
19 </mapping>
```

The TargetParameter size is set with help of a BinaryExpression that implements the multiplication of Eq. 1 (Line 4–18). It itself contains a second Binary-Expression (Line 6–14) that implements the division of the equation. The simulation time T_{Total} is extracted from the domain model with help of a *FileContentExtractor* defined in the lines 8–10, and the write interval f_{write} is extracted from the domain model with help of a FileContentExtractor defined in the lines 11–13. The expected size of the partial results can not be automatically derived

Table 2. Results for the evaluated and deployed OpenFOAM cases.

	Domain model	Deployed cluster			Metrics	
		#VMs	#Cores	NFS Size	M1	M2
1	multiphase/twoPhaseEulerFoam/ laminar/mixerVessel2D/	1	1	1 GB	0.94	32 %
2	heatTransfer/buoyantBoussinesq SimpleFoam/iglooWithFridges/	1	2	1 GB	1.57	55 %
3	multiphase/multiphaseInterFoam/ laminar/damBreak4phaseFine/	1	4	3 GB	3.79	92 %
4	combustion/fireFoam/les/ oppositeBurningPanels/	2	8	9 GB	5.91	84 %
5	multiphase/interDyMFoam/ ras/DTCHull/	2	8	3 GB	7.88	100 %
6	multiphase/interDyMFoam/ ras/testTubeMixer/	4	16	1 GB	15.92	26 %

from the domain model. It is a good example for a parameter that needs to be provided by the user or with help of runtime information from executing the CF. Since we are not able to utilize runtime information yet, we provided the expected size of the partial results as part of the domain model. It is read with a FileContentExtractor from a file defined in the lines 15–17. Together with the domain model itself, the parameters mapping is passed to the evaluator, which evaluates the domain model and returns a list of initialized parameters for the deployment model. These parameters are then used in the instantiation process.

6.4   Results and Discussion

We executed the mapping on the OpenFOAM cases which are provided by Table 1, and deployed the CF and the corresponding infrastructure automatically in a small IaaS cloud based on OpenStack [15]. Then we executed the domain model and collected the metrics defined in Sect. 6.2 with help of the cluster monitoring tool Ganglia [18].

The results are summarized in Table 2. The number of deployed virtual machines (#VMs), the total number of provisioned cores (#Cores) and the size of the provisioned NFS is given. The total cluster size is automatically adjusted to each domain model. The average load on the cluster (**M1**) indicates that except for domain model 4 all provisioned cores were used for computation. In Case 4 only 6 of the 8 provisioned compute cores were utilized. Since the abstract model of our OpenFOAM cluster only allows the same virtual machine type for all nodes in the cluster, and no virtual machine type with 6 compute cores is available, 2 cores were over-provisioned. The framework was also able to adjust the size of the NFS. Since the size of the provisioned NFS is rounded to full GB and the required size for the partial results is only a rough estimate, in most cases not 100 % of the NFS was utilized (**M2**).

While the presented evaluation only considers fairly small tutorial domain models, it shows that we are able to automatically adjust the scale of the provisioned resources to the computational requirements of the domain model. In case of the size for the NFS, additional user input was required to provide an estimate for the size of the partial results. However, this information could also be automatically derived during runtime. We are going to extend our work to use runtime information of the CF in the future.

7   Related Work

Besides TOSCA, other cloud-related standardization attempts exist. In the MDE community, the *Open Cloud Computing Interface* (OCCI) [12] received the most attention. Merle et al. [13] defined a metamodel for OCCI with help of EMF to provide a common basis for the generation and conformance testing of OCCI tools. This metamodel is used by Paraiso et al. [19] to model the deployment of applications with help of containers. Several works extend the *Unified Modeling Language* (UML) to be able to capture cloud-specifics [20–22]. Bergmayr et al. [4] show how to convert refined UML models to TOSCA templates. Their approach is also based on an Ecore metamodel generated from the TOSCA XSD. With the Cloud Application Management Framework (CAMF) [3], Loulloudes et al. attempt to build a whole IDE to manage cloud applications with the help of TOSCA.

Other approaches developed completely new cloud-specific modelling languages. Brandtzaeg et al. introduce CloudML [23], Silva et al. define the CloudDSL [24], and Hamdaqa et al. present the StratusML [25]. All of theses languages are specifiably tailored for the modeling of cloud applications. Bunch et al. define Neptune [26], a domain specific language especially to deploy scientific applications in the cloud. While our approach in modeling the CF is similar to the works introduced above, the definition of the mapping between the domain of the user and the deployment model is new.

Similar to the concept we defined for the dynamic update of the deployment during runtime, Ferry et al. [27] define a Models@Runtime approach for the deployment of cloud applications. We will evaluate the work of Ferry et al. when we extend our implementation to be able to utilize runtime information of the CF.

8   Conclusion and Outlook

Cloud orchestration and configuration management enable fully automated deployment of applications in the cloud. In our work, we combine the two technologies with MDE and a mapping mechanism to bridge the gap between the domain model to be computed and the required cloud infrastructure to enable appropriate scaling according to the domain model demands. The introduced mechanism determines an appropriate scale of the infrastructure before it is deployed in the cloud. In this paper we presented an initial evaluation of the concept with help of a prototypical implementation and an example from the domain of simulation science. Our initial experiences show that it is possible to scale the infrastructure appropriately with information extracted from the domain model. However, some information on the runtime behaviour of the domain model can not be predicted by static evaluations. As future work, we will move towards the automated modification and adaptation of our deployment models during runtime. The evaluation, we presented in this paper only covers an initial case study. To fully show the validity of our approach, we will conduct more case studies with software stacks from different domains.

Acknowledgements. The work of Fabian Glaser is partially funded by the Joint Centre of Simulation Technology (https://www.simzentrum.de/) of the University of Göttingen and the Technical University of Clausthal (Project 11.4.1).

References

1. Mell, P., Grance, T.: The NIST definition of cloud computing. Technical report 800-145, National Institute of Standards and Technology (NIST), Gaithersburg, MD, September 2011.http://csrc.nist.gov/publications/nistpubs/800-145/SP800-145.pdf

2. Ardagna, D., Di Nitto, E., Mohagheghi, P., Mosser, S., Ballagny, C., D'Andria, F., Casale, G., Matthews, P., Nechifor, C.-S. Petcu, D., et al.: MODAClouds: a model driven approach for the design and execution of applications on multiple clouds. In: 2012 ICSE Workshop on Modeling in Software Engineering (MISE), pp. 50–56. IEEE (2012)

3. Loulloudes, N., Sofokleous, C., Trihinas, D., Dikaiakos, M.D., Pallis, G.: Enabling interoperable cloud application management through an open source ecosystem. IEEE Internet Comput. **19**(3), 54–59 (2015)

4. Bergmayr, A., Breitenbücher, U., Kopp, O., Wimmer, M., Kappel, G., Leymann, F.: From architecture modeling to application provisioning for the cloud by combining UML and TOSCA. In: 6th International Conference on Cloud Computing and Services Science (CLOSER) (2016)

5. Glaser, F.: Towards domain-model optimized deployment and execution of scientific applications in cloud environments. In: Doctoral Symposium at the 5th Conference on Cloud Computing and Services Sciences (DCCLOSER 2015), Lisbon, Portugal, May 2015

6. Amazon Web Services: AWS CloudFormation - Infrastructure as Code & AWS Resource Provisioning. https://aws.amazon.com/cloudformation. Accessed 12 Jun 2016

7. OASIS: Topology and Orchestration Specification for Cloud Applications (TOSCA) 1.0, November 2013. http://docs.oasis-open.org/tosca/TOSCA/v1.0/os/TOSCA-v1.0-os.html. Accessed 03 Dec 2015

8. OASIS: TOSCA Simple Profile in YAML Version 1.0, February 2016. http://docs.oasis-open.org/tosca/TOSCA-Simple-Profile-YAML/v1.0/TOSCA-Simple-Profile-YAML-v1.0.html. Accessed 12 Jun 2016

9. Hüttermann, M.: DevOps for developers. Apress (2012)

10. Puppet - The shortest path to better software. https://puppet.com. Accessed 12 Jun 2016
11. Red Hat, Ansible is Simple IT Automation. https://www.ansible.com/. Accessed 12 Jun 2016
12. Nyren, R., Edmonds,A., Papaspyrou, A., Metsch, T.: Open Cloud Computing Interface - Core, April 2011. http://ogf.org/documents/GDF.183.pdf
13. Merle, P., Barais, O., Parpaillon, J., Plouzeau, N., Tata, S.: A precise metamodel for open cloud computing interface. In: 8th IEEE International Conference on Cloud Computing (CLOUD), pp. 852–859. IEEE (2015)
14. OpenCFD: OpenFOAM - The Open Source Computational Fluid Dynamics (CFD) Toolbox. http://www.openfoam.com/. Accessed 12 Jun 2016
15. OpenStack Open Source Cloud Computing Software. https://www.openstack.org/. Accessed 12 Jun 2016
16. The Eclipse Foundation, Eclipse Modeling Project. https://eclipse.org/modeling/emf/. Accessed 12 Jun 2016
17. The Eclipse Foundation, Epsilon Generation Language – Code Generation Language. http://www.eclipse.org/epsilon/doc/egl/. Accessed 12 Jun 2016
18. Ganglia Monitoring System. http://ganglia.info/. Accessed 12 Jun 2016
19. Paraiso, F., Challita, S., Al-Dhuraibi, Y., Merle, P.: Model-driven management of docker containers. In: 9th IEEE International Conference on Cloud Computing (CLOUD), San Francisco, United States, June 2016. https://hal.inria.fr/hal-01314827
20. Bergmayr, A., Troya, J., Neubauer, P., Wimmer, M., Kappel, G.: UML-based cloud application modeling with libraries, profiles, and templates. In: 3rd International Workshop on Model-Driven Engineering on and for the Cloud (CloudMDE), pp. 56–65 (2014)
21. Kamali, A., Mohammadi, S., Barforoush, A.A.: UCC: UML profile to cloud computing modeling: using stereotypes and tag values. In: 7th International Symposium on Telecommunications (IST), pp. 689–694. IEEE (2014)
22. Guillén, J., Miranda, J., Murillo, J.M., Canal, C.: A UML profile for modeling multicloud applications. In: Lau, K.-K., Lamersdorf, W., Pimentel, E. (eds.) ESOCC 2013. LNCS, vol. 8135, pp. 180–187. Springer, Heidelberg (2013). doi:10.1007/978-3-642-40651-5_15
23. Brandtzæg, E., Mosser, S., Mohagheghi, P.: Towards CloudML, a model-based approach to provision resources in the clouds. In: 8th European Conference on Modelling Foundations and Applications (ECMFA), pp. 18–27 (2012)
24. Silva, G.C., Rose, L.M., Calinescu, R.: Cloud DSL: a language for supporting cloud portability by describing cloud entities. In: CloudMDE 2014, p. 36 (2014)
25. Hamdaqa, M., Tahvildari, L.: Stratus ML: a layered cloud modeling framework. In: 2015 IEEE International Conference on Cloud Engineering (IC2E), pp. 96–105, March 2015
26. Bunch, C., Drawert, B., Chohan, N., Krintz, C., Petzold, L., Shams, K.: Language and runtime support for automatic configuration and deployment of scientific computing software over cloud fabrics. J. Grid Comput. 10(1), 23–46 (2012)
27. Ferry, N., Brataas, G., Rossini, A., Chauvel, F., Solberg, A.: Towards bridging the gap between scalability and elasticity. In: 4th International Conference on Cloud Computing and Services Science (CLOSER), pp. 746–751 (2014)

Representativeness and Descriptiveness of Task Trees Generated from Website Usage Traces

Patrick Harms[(✉)]

Institute of Computer Science, University of Göttingen, Göttingen, Germany
patrick.harms@informatik.uni-goettingen.de
http://swe.informatik.uni-goettingen.de

Abstract. Task trees are often used to define the actions on a software as well as their order which is required to accomplish a certain task. With an increasing task complexity, their creation can be laborious and error-prone. Hence, there was work done to generate them automatically from recordings of user actions. In this paper, we assess for one of these approaches if the generated task trees are representative and descriptive for recorded and also unrecorded user actions. This characteristic is important as it allows for subsequent valid analyses of the software usage based on these task trees. For our evaluations, we transform the task trees generated from one set of recorded actions into grammars for the language spoken between the user and the software. From these grammars, we generate parsers with which we try to parse action combinations in other usage recordings. Our results show, that the approach under analysis produces partially representative task trees, which are also descriptive for unrecorded user behavior.

Keywords: Usage-based · Task tree generation · Task model analysis

1 Introduction

With task models, system designers have a powerful tool for defining the interaction of users with a website or any other software. A concrete variant of these models are task trees, which define the detailed actions to be done for performing a certain task as well as their required order [1]. Task trees can be an important source for the analysis of user behaviour [2]. But with an increasing task complexity, as well as with different variants of performing the same task, the manual creation of a task tree can become laborious and error-prone. Hence, task trees should be generated automatically from recordings of user behavior. In this way, they can form the basis of subsequent usage analyses, e.g., usability evaluations [3,4]. In addition, they can be the source for automated user-centered system adaptions [5,6].

In previous work, we defined a process for automatic generation of task trees from recorded user behavior [4,7,8]. For a subsequent analysis and usage of task trees generated with this approach, it is important that they are a valid model

© Springer International Publishing AG 2016
J. Grabowski and S. Herbold (Eds.): SAM 2016, LNCS 9959, pp. 84–99, 2016.
DOI: 10.1007/978-3-319-46613-2_6

for the user behavior. As such, the task trees should not only describe the user behavior from which they were generated, but also unrecorded user behavior. In one of our previous publications [9], we already compared task trees generated for separate recordings of user behavior on the same software and checked if the same or similar task trees are generated. That work showed, that our approach produces similar task trees. But we did not check, if the generated task trees are really a valid model for unrecorded user behavior. Therefore, the goal of this paper is to answer the following research questions:

RQ1, Representativeness: How representative are the task trees generated by our approach described in [4,7,8] for the recorded user behavior from which they were created?

RQ2, Descriptiveness: To what extent do the task trees generated from recorded user behavior describe also unrecorded user behavior?

To answer these research questions, we performed several analyses of the task trees. Their description in this paper is structured as follows. First, we briefly describe our notion of task trees and their generation in Sect. 2. Then, we describe in Sect. 3 the approach that we use in this paper to check their descriptiveness using their grammatical nature. In Sect. 4, we describe one of our case studies that we performed to answer our research questions which is followed by a discussion of the results in Sect. 5. We refer to related work in Sect. 6 and summarize the paper in Sect. 7.

2   Task Trees and Trace-Based Task Tree Generation

In this section, we introduce our concepts of task trees as required for the remainder of this paper. Furthermore, we provide a brief description of our approach for the automated generation from recorded user behavior. The section is based on our previous work described in [4,7–9].

When users utilize a software, they perform individual *actions*. An action is, e.g., entering text on the keyboard into a certain text field or clicking with a mouse button on some element of the user interface. Users combine multiple actions to perform a certain *task*. For example, to perform the task of logging in on a website, they may perform the actions of clicking into the user name field, entering the user name, clicking on the password field, entering the password, and submitting the form using a click on a login button.

Tasks and actions may be combined to higher level tasks. For example, for ordering a product in an online shop, users may perform the described task for logging in, then some actions for the checkout process, and finally a task for logging out again. As such, actions and tasks form a tree structure called a *task tree*. In our work, we define that task trees consist of nodes where the leaf nodes are the actions that users can perform on a software and the parent nodes represent tasks. A task can never be directly or indirectly its own child.

Parent nodes in a task tree define the order in which their children, actions or other tasks, can be executed. For this, parent nodes have one of four different types. Those types are sequence, iteration, optional, or selection. A *sequence* has two or more children which are executed in the given order. An *iteration* has only one child, which can be executed one or more times. An *optional* also has only one child, which can be left out. Finally, a *selection* has two or more children, of which only one is executed. An example of a task tree utilizing these types is shown in Fig. 1. In the figure, the leaf nodes (hatched boxes) represent the actions required for a login process on a website. The parent nodes (grey boxes) define through their given types the allowed order of execution of their respective children. For example, the children of *Sequence 2*, which are clicking on the user name field and entering the user name, are executed in their given order as the type of their parent node is a sequence. *Selection 1* defines, that the user can either enter the user name (represented by *Sequence 2*) or the password (represented by *Sequence 3*). *Iteration 1* defines, that the user may repeat this selection multiple times. This allows the user, e.g., to first enter the user name, then enter the password, and then correct the user name again. The user finishes the login process by clicking on the login button. Optionally, the user may check a check box before to stay logged in (defined by *Optional 1*). Van Welie et al. provide a more formal definition of task trees in [1].

Our process to generate this kind of task trees [4,7,8] works as follows. We first record the individual actions that users perform on a software. The results are lists of actions in the order in which they were performed. On these lists, we perform an alternating detection of iterations and sequences. An iteration is detected if the lists contain subsequent identical elements. Those are replaced by a corresponding iteration. A sequence is detected if the lists contain subsequent element combinations that occur multiple times. Those are replaced by corresponding sequences. Through the alternation of the iteration and sequence

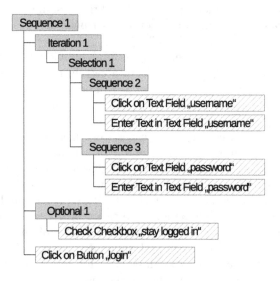

Fig. 1. Example for a task tree of a login process on a website (adapted from [4]).

detection, the iteration detection may also detect repetitions of sequences and the sequence detection may detect sequences with iterations and other sequences as their children.

After the alternating iteration and sequence detection, our approach may have detected similar tasks. For example, there may be two tasks t_1 and t_2 representing a login process, but for navigating to the password field, t_1 includes a click on the password field and t_2 the usage of the tabulator key, instead. The other actions of both tasks would be identical. Hence, we defined a further process that allows the detection and merging of similar tasks [4,8]. This process is based on the comparison of the actions that are used in two similar tasks t_1 and t_2 and may detect two things. Either, t_1 includes an action a that is left out in t_2. Then the process merges t_1 and t_2, but makes a optional using a corresponding parent node. Or t_1 and t_2 differ in a certain action where t_1 contains action a_1 and t_2 contains action a_2 at the same logical position. Then t_1 and t_2 are merged and the possibility of using either of a_1 and a_2 is reflected by a new parent node of type selection having a_1 and a_2 as its children.

The alternating iteration and sequence detection as well as the detection and merging of similar tasks may run into further complex situations. As the focus of this paper is not the description of all details of our process, we leave them for our other publications [4,7,8]. Not all recorded actions may be assigned to a detected task. The reason is, that some action combinations are executed only once and are, therefore, not detected by our approach. We consider them as noise in the data.

3   Transformation of Task Trees into Grammars

To evaluate the representativeness of task trees, we use a visualization which we describe together with the case study in Sect. 4. For evaluating the descriptiveness of the task trees for unrecorded user behavior, we use a more complex approach based on [4], that we introduce in this section. The actions users perform on a software can be considered as the words of a language that users "speak" with a software. Task trees define the order in which these words are used. As such, they represent the grammar of this language [10]. To evaluate the descriptiveness of our automatically generated task trees, we generate them for a set of recorded actions A_1^s. Then we check, if they are also a valid model for another set of recorded actions A_2^s. For this, we transform the task trees generated based on A_1^s into grammars. Then we generate parsers from these grammars. Using these parsers, we try to parse the recorded actions in A_2^s. The more actions we can parse through this, the higher we consider the representativeness of the task trees. To transform a task tree t into a grammar g, we define the following rules which we already published in [4]:

- The leaf nodes of t become the terminal symbols in g.
- The sequences, iterations, and selections of t become non-terminals in g.
- For an iteration i with child c, we generate two production rules of the form $i \rightarrow i\ c$ and $i \rightarrow c$ in g.

- For a selection z with children $c_1 \ldots c_n$, we create n production rules of the form $z \to c_i$ in g.
- For a sequence s with children $c_1 \ldots c_n$, we create one production rule of the form $s \to c_1 \ldots c_n$ in g.
- For a sequence s with children $c_1 \ldots c_i \ldots c_n$ where c_i can be left out, we generate a further production rule $s \to c_1 \ldots c_{(i-1)} c_{(i+1)} \ldots c_n$ in g.

In the last rule, a child can be left out in various ways. For example, it can be an optional or an iteration having an optional as its child. We consider all these variants as defined by the rule. In addition, there may be multiple children of a sequence that can be left out. In this case, we create as many production rules as required to represent all possible permutations of leaving out one or several of these children.

In Fig. 2, we show an example of applying the above rules on a task tree. On the left, we display a task tree. The actions are identified by single letters for simplification. On the right side, we show the corresponding grammar. Each action in the task tree indicated through hatched boxes becomes a terminal symbol in the grammar. For each parent node in the task tree indicated through grey boxes there are non-terminals and corresponding production rules in the grammar. The production rules are grouped to show which rules were generated for which parent node in the task tree. For example, for *Sequence 2*, we generated one production rule having the children of *Sequence 2* (*a*, *Selection 1*, and *b*) as the right hand side of the production rule. For *Sequence 1*, we generated two productions rules as the second child of *Sequence 1* can be left out.

From such a grammar, we generate a simple LR (SLR) parser as described by Aho et al. [11]. The details of this generation and the implementation of this type of parsers are not important for this paper. Hence, we do not describe them in

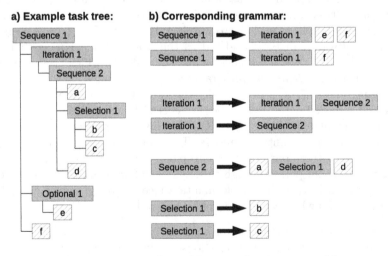

Fig. 2. Example of a grammar transformed from a task tree generated by our approach.

more detail, but refer to the corresponding literature. Due to the nature of SLR parsers, not all grammars generated by our approach can be used to generate such a parser. An example is the following grammar from [4]:

$$A \to BC$$
$$B \to BD$$
$$B \to D \tag{1}$$
$$D \to ab$$
$$C \to ac$$

When parsing a sentence of a language, SLR parsers only read the next word of the sentence. For the above grammar, the action combination $abac$ would be a valid sentence. When parsing this input, an SLR parser would parse over the first two actions ab and detect this as a representation of the non-terminal D, and, due to the third production rule, as the non-terminal B. It can only be a representation of B as the initial rule of the grammar indicates that a sentence always starts with a representation of B. The next action to parse is the action a. Due to the first and the second rule of the grammar, this can now either start a second representation of D or a representation of C. For the parser, it cannot be decided which of these alternatives is the case. The parser could only decide if it read a further symbol ahead. But this is not done by SLR parsers.

Unfortunately, our above transformation rules may result in structures of the above grammar. For example, the non-terminal B may represent an iteration and D and C may represent two sequences. In such a case, we cannot generate a valid parser for A. But in our approach, we generate separate parsers for any detected task tree. This includes parsers not only for A, but also for tasks being children of A, i.e., for B and C. Through this, the action combination $abac$ will be split up. The first two actions will be parsed by the parser representing B and the second two actions by the second parser representing C. Hence, it is not required to have a parser for A as the other parsers would also parse any action combination described by A. Only in situations, where A has production rules with a terminal node on the right side, this does not work anymore.

4   Case Study

To evaluate the representativeness and descriptiveness of the generated task trees, we performed several case studies of which we describe due to paper size restrictions only one in this paper. The other case studies and their results, as well as more details on the case study at hand, are described in [4]. All case studies follow the same setup which is described in the following. For the implementation of the case studies, we utilized the framework AutoQUEST (Automatic Quality Engineering of Event-driven Software). AutoQUEST provides functionality for quality assurance of event driven software [12]. In addition to others, it can be used to record user actions on websites. Afterwards, the recorded data can be analyzed for assessing the websites usability or to generate usage-based test cases. AutoQUEST implements the task tree generation as described in [4,7,8] resulting in task trees of the form described in Sect. 2.

. In the case studies, we first recorded the actions users took on a website. Then we generated task trees for the recorded data set. In addition, we subdivided the data set into subsets of identical size. For each of these subsets we also generated tasks trees. Then we created plots of the task trees showing the relationship between the coverage of detected sequences and the number of all covered actions. Finally, we transformed the task trees generated for a specific subset into grammars, generated parsers for the grammars, and evaluated how many actions of another subset or the full data set are matched by these parsers as described in Sect. 3. In the following subsections, we describe these steps in detail and provide corresponding results.

4.1 Recorded User Actions

In the case study at hand, we analyzed recordings of a web-based application portal. Via this portal, prospective students can apply for their master studies in computer science at our university. For this, the applicants provide personal information, e.g., their name, date of birth, and address, as well as information about their previous studies and other education. The interaction style is mainly wizard based. This means, the applicants are guided through the individual application steps. One page of the wizard requesting the personal information of the applicants is shown in Fig. 3. Overall, the portal consists of 107 web pages including, in addition to the wizard, administrative pages, login masks, registration forms, description pages, and others.

We recorded the users of the portal over a period of 18 months. This resulted in about 656,100 actions distributed over 14,811 sessions. A session in our recording begins with the opening of the website and either the closing of the website or the occurrence of a timeout. The details of the recorded data can be found in the upper part of Table 1.

4.2 Generation of Task Trees

After recording the actions, we generated task trees from them. The resulting number of sequences, iterations, selections, and optionals are listed in the lower part of Table 1. For example, we generated 20,508 sequences.

Then, we created subsets $A_1^s \ldots A_n^s \subset A$ of the recorded actions A. These subsets were of a predefined size s being a percentage of all recorded actions belonging to the full data set. The considered subset sizes were 1 %, 2.5 %, 5 %, 10 %, 20 %, 30 %, and 50 %. Depending on the intended subset size, we generated different amounts of subsets. Depending on these amounts and the mathematical possibility, the subsets of a certain size were created disjunctive to each other or not. Details on the generated subsets of a certain size and the number of actions contained in a subset can be found in the first three rows of Table 2. For example, we created 50 subsets of size 1 %, which were disjunctive to each other

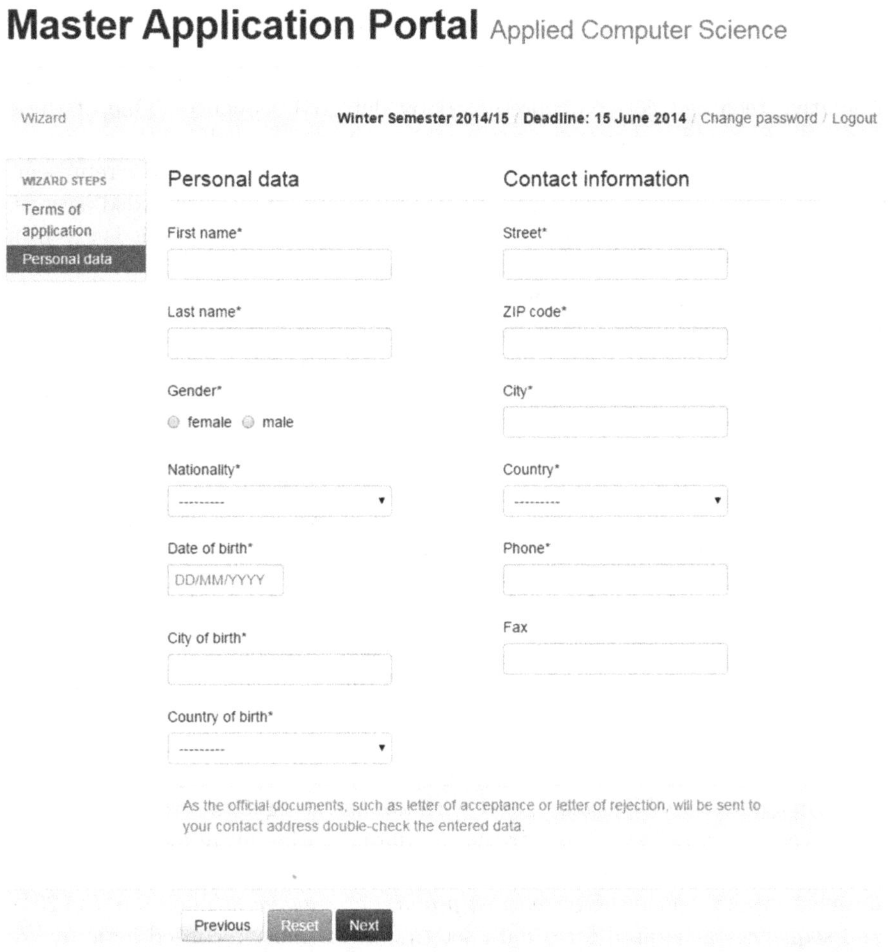

Master Application Portal Applied Computer Science

Wizard   **Winter Semester 2014/15 Deadline: 15 June 2014** / Change password / Logout

| WIZARD STEPS | Personal data | Contact information |

Terms of application

Personal data

First name*

Last name*

Gender*
○ female ○ male

Nationality*
---------- ▼

Date of birth*
DD/MM/YYYY

City of birth*

Country of birth*
---------- ▼

Street*

ZIP code*

City*

Country*
---------- ▼

Phone*

Fax

As the official documents, such as letter of acceptance or letter of rejection, will be sent to your contact address double-check the entered data.

Previous Reset Next

Fig. 3. Screenshot of one wizard page requesting for the personal data of an applicant in the application portal used for the case study.

and contained 6,561 actions. The division of the data set into subsets was done on session level to ensure that task execution were not split. The assignment of sessions to subsets was done randomly. Hence, we did not consider all possible permutations of this division.

For each of the subsets, we also generated task trees. We list the average numbers (μ) and standard deviations (σ) of detected sequences, iterations, selections, and optionals in the lowest four rows of Table 2. For example, for subsets of size 1 % (first column), we detected on average 523 sequences with a standard deviation of 15.

4.3   Assessment of the Task Tree Representativeness

For the assessment of the task tree representativeness, we created plots of the cumulative recorded actions represented by detected sequences. One of these plots is shown in Fig. 4. For the creation of the plot, we first ordered the sequences S generated for a data set by the number of recorded actions they represent. We started this ordering with the sequence representing most recorded actions. These ordered sequences represent the x-axis of the plot. The x-axis is given in percentage of all detected sequences S. A certain point on the x-axis represents the subset $S' \subset S$ of a data set that contains only those sequences covering most recorded actions. On the y-axis, we then plot the cumulative ratio of actions covered by the subset S' represented by the corresponding point on the x-axis. This ratio is given in percentage of the actions contained in the respective data set. In Fig. 4, we created plots for several data sets. The black line shows the actions covered by sequences detected on the full applicants portal data set. Here, e.g., those 20 % of sequences that cover most recorded actions already cover 86.3 % of all actions in the data set. All sequences detected on the data set cover 95.1 % of the actions in the data set. The cyan lines represent the plots for five randomly chosen subsets of size 40 %. The red lines represent the plots for five randomly chosen subsets of size 10 %. The grey lines represent the plots for five randomly chosen subsets of size 2.5 %. In the plots, we only focused on sequences, as these define the major ordering of a task tree. In contrast, iterations, optionals, and selections only define executions variants [4].

The figure shows, that all plots follow a similar shape. A small amount of detected sequences (less than or equal 20 %) covers already a large amount of the actions in a data set. We also see, that with an increasing data set size, the effect becomes stronger. For example, for the full data set, the initial increasing of the plot is stronger than for the plots generated for the different subsets. Because of this effect, we introduce the term *most prominent sequences*. Those are the 20 % of all sequences generated for a data set that cover most recorded actions. We will use this separation of sequences in the following section.

Table 1. Facts of the case study including recorded actions and detected tasks.

	Applicants portal
Recorded data	
Recording period	10/2013 – 02/2015 (18 months)
Actions	656,100
Sessions	14,811
Generated tasks	
Sequences	20,508
Iterations	2,199
Optionals	161
Selections	119

Table 2. Information about created subsets, generated task trees, and the comparisons done for the case study.

Subsets	1 %		2.5 %		5 %		10 %		20 %		30 %		40 %		50 %	
Statistics																
Count	50		30		20		10		5		9		6		6	
Disjunctive	yes		yes		yes		yes		yes		no		no		no	
Actions	6,561		16,402		32,805		65,610		131,220		196,830		262,440		328,050	
Parsing attempts																
Same size	20		20		15		15		15		15		15		15	
Full set	20		20		15		10		5		5		5		5	
Generated tasks	μ	σ	μ	σ	μ	σ	μ	σ	μ	σ	μ	σ	μ	σ	μ	σ
Sequences	523	15	1,124	22	1,967	33	3,380	30	5,830	57	8,012	95	10,066	181	11,898	36
Iterations	189	14	334	20	502	18	731	22	1,043	20	1,267	28	1,448	11	1,606	22
Selections	2	1	5	2	8	2	13	3	24	6	28	13	28	20	52	17
Optionals	1	1	4	2	10	3	21	5	41	4	53	14	50	21	85	13

4.4   Assessment of the Task Tree Descriptiveness

In the next step of our evaluation, we assessed the descriptiveness of the generated task trees. For this, we transformed the task trees generated for a certain subset $A_i^s \subset A$ of the full data set A into grammars. From these grammars, we generated parsers. With these parsers, we then checked, which actions of a another subset $A_j^s \subset A | j \neq i$ or of the full data set A are described by these grammars. We call this a *parsing attempt*. For a parsing attempt, we subdivided the other data set (A_j^s or A) into sublists $a_i \ldots a_j$ of recorded actions with a minimum length of two. For each of these sublists, we checked if any of the parsers generated for A_i^s accepts the sublist as a valid input. If so, the corresponding grammar, and hence the corresponding task tree, is a valid model for this sublist. We considered all actions of a subset A_j^s or of the full data set A that can be described with task trees generated for an A_i^s as so called *matches*. To get representative results, we performed not only one parsing attempt between subsets, but for multiple subsets of a certain size. The number of parsing attempts we performed are listed in the rows four and five of Table 2. For example, for subsets of size 1 %, we performed 20 parsing attempts in other subsets of the same size and additionally 20 parsing attempts in the full data set.

For each of the parsing attempts, we recorded the ratio of matches, i.e., the percentage of actions in a subset A_j^s or in A that are described by the task trees generated from A_i^s. Then we calculated the average of this ratio for the different parsing attempts listed in Table 2. We compiled the resulting average ratios for the applicants portal into the bar charts in Fig. 5. The left bar chart represents the average matches between subsets of the same size, the right bar chart the average matches of subset task trees in A. The x-axis of both charts show

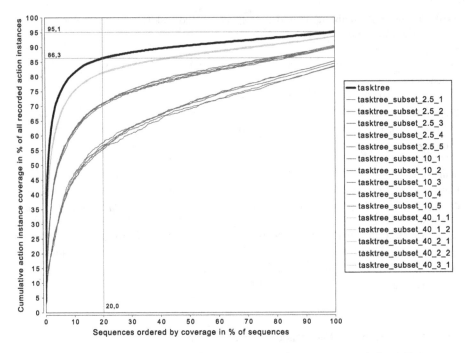

Fig. 4. Plot for the cumulative action coverage of the sequences of the full data set (black) and five subsets for the subset sizes 2.5 % (grey), 10 % (red), and 40 % (cyan) (from [4]). (Color figure online)

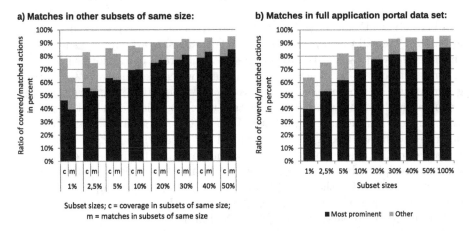

Fig. 5. Plot for the actions matched by parsers, which were generated from merged task trees for a specific subset size of the full data set in the case study.

the subset sizes from 1 % to 50 %. In the left bar chart, there are two bars per subset size. The left bar, called c, shows the average ratio of actions in a subset covered by the sequences generated from them. The right bar shows the average ratio of matches in another subset of the same size. Each bar is subdivided into a black and a grey part. The black part represents the covered actions or matches of the most prominent sequences only (see previous subsection). The grey part adds the actions covered or matched by the remaining sequences. For example, the sequences generated on a subset of size 5 % (third bars in left bar chart) cover on average 86 % of the actions in this set (left bar) and cause matches of 81 % of the actions in another subset of the same size (right bar). The most prominent sequences generated on this subset size cover already 62 % in the subset from which they were generated and match 61 % of actions in subsets of the same size.

In the right chart of Fig. 5, each bar, except the most right, represents the matches of task trees generated for a subset in the full applicants portal data set. The most right bar is equivalent to the left bars of the bar pairs in the left plot and shows the ratio of actions covered by the sequences generated for the full application portal data set. Also here, the bars are separated into a black and a grey part where the black part shows the matches of the most prominent sequences only and the grey part the matches of the other remaining sequences. For example, the sequences generated for subsets of size 5 % (third bar) cover 81 % of the actions in the full data set. The most prominent sequences here already cover 61 %. All sequences generated for the full data set (right most bar) cover 95 %, where the most prominent sequences cover 87 %.

In the left bar chart, we see that with increasing subset size, the task trees generated for one subset cover more and more actions in another subset of the same size. Even more, we see that for smaller subset sizes, the matches in another subset are smaller than the actions covered in the subset from which the task trees were generated (the left bars of the bar pairs are higher than the right bars), but for larger subsets this switches (the right bars or the bar pairs are higher than the left bars). This effect is due to the differences between our task tree generation and our descriptiveness check. Consider the actions aba which were performed in the given order. Our task tree generation may detect a sequence s_1 representing ab and a further sequence s_2 representing ba. Only one of these sequences will cover two of the three actions aba. Either s_1 will cover the first two actions or s_2 will cover the last two actions. But when considering the same action combination and the two parsers generated for s_1 and s_2, then in our descriptiveness check, both parser will report matches. Hence, although not all three actions can be covered by the tasks generated from them, the parsers of these tasks would match all three actions.

In the right bar chart, we see that the task trees generated from smaller subset sizes already match a high number of actions in the full data set. The higher the subset size, the more actions are matched. Considering both charts, we derive that the most prominent sequences also cover most actions and that the difference between their coverage and the coverage of all generated sequences becomes smaller with an increasing subset size.

5   Discussion

Considering the effects shown in Fig. 4, we conclude that already a small amount of detected sequences covers a large amount of actions in the data set from which they were detected. Hence, we can answer our first research question, **RQ1**, with the statement, that the representativeness of the task trees generated by our approach differs. Some task trees represent more recorded users actions and are, therefore, more representative than others. This is a helpful information for subsequent analyses based on these models. As we generate typically a large number of task trees for a data set, this information allows us to decide, which generated task trees are worth a further analysis and which may be considered as describing noise in the data. In addition, this information can be used to adapt our task tree generation so that only representative task trees are detected.

The results in Fig. 5 show, that the task trees generated for a data set are also descriptive for user behavior not being part of the data set and, hence, also for unrecorded user behavior. This is the first part of the answer for our second research question, **RQ2**. The second part of the answer is, that with an increasing data set size, the descriptiveness of the task trees also increases. But considering Fig. 5b in more detail, we also see that after a certain data set size is reached, the descriptiveness cannot be increased significantly anymore. For example, considering the differences between the bars for subset sizes 5 % and 10 % as well as between 50 % and 100 %, we see that with a doubling of the input data, the descriptiveness may be increased, but that this increase is less for the larger two subset sizes. Most important, the descriptiveness itself cannot be doubled by doubling the sample size. Based on this, we conclude that it may not be required to record always all users of a website to get representative and descriptive models.

In our extended description of the case study at hand, as well as of the other case studies [4], we show the same types of plots as we show here for other data sets. In these plots, we see the same effects but on different coverage levels. Anyway, comparing these plots, we additionally see that the representativeness and descriptiveness of the generated task trees depends on the number of different actions that users can perform on a website. This can be derived from the fact that more recordings are required when more actions are available to ensure that any action and any possible action combination is recorded often enough to result in a representative task tree. This is also an important information for subsequent analyses done based on our task trees.

There are two threats to the validity or our results. First of all, we do not generate grammars and parser for all detected task trees, if the grammars would be invalid as described in Sect. 3. Through this, we may not find all possible matches. On the other hand, due to the fact that our parsing attempts may find more matches than recorded actions they represent (see previous section), our results may include a certain amount of matches, which do not correspond correctly to the descriptiveness. As such, our results underlie a failure rate which may influence our results. But considering the differences between the bar pairs in Fig. 5a, which is rather small, we consider that the effect of the failure rate is also rather small. This means we do not match significantly less or more actions than our task trees cover.

6 Related Work

Task models can be used to describe a task decomposition, actions, and their execution order. Additionally, they include the user goals that can be achieved with a task and the objects that are required for the task execution [1]. They may also include actions, which are not only done by the user but by the systems with which the users interact [13,14]. There are multiple approaches for task modeling that utilize tree structures. Examples are TaskMODL [15], GOMS (Goals, Operators, Methods, and Selection Rules) [16], and ConcurTaskTrees [13,14]. Depending on their concrete usage, they are focused on individual application areas. For example, ConcurTaskTrees allow modeling system behavior in addition to user behavior which is not possible with Goals, Operators, Methods, and Selection Rules (GOMS). The task trees generated by our approach [4,7,8] are a tree based type of task model and describe only the actions and their execution order. As other approaches, they are trimmed to a certain application area which is a subsequent usability evaluation [3,4].

There are approaches for detecting tasks in recorded users actions, e.g., ACT-R [17] and Convenient, Rapid, Interactive Tool for Integrating Quick Usability Evaluations (CRITIQUE) [5]. In addition, as the actions of users on a software are similar to words of a language spoken between the user and the software [10], techniques for grammatical inference based on language examples seem to be an alternative for our task tree generation. But both, the mentioned examples and grammatical inference, required labeled input data indicating the beginning and end of a task [18], respectively a sentence of the language [19], which is not required by our approach. It is also possible to derive statistical models of the usage of a system from recorded user actions [20]. In contrast to our approach, these define only probabilities of user interactions but not actually happening action combinations.

Regarding the evaluation of the representativeness and descriptiveness of our task trees as done in this paper, to the best of our knowledge, there is no related work that evaluates the same aspects. In one of our previous works, we evaluated if similar task trees are generated for different sets of recorded user action on the same software [9]. But this work is not as far reaching as the one described in this paper, as it neither focuses on representativeness of these tasks nor on descriptiveness. But both information is important to allow for reliable subsequent analyses of the generated models. More detailed results of the evaluation in this paper, also on other case studies, are described in the PhD Thesis in [4].

7 Conclusion and Outlook

In this paper, we evaluated the representativeness and descriptiveness of task trees generated automatically from recorded user actions as described in [4,7,8].

Both aspects are a required prerequisite for reliable subsequent usage analysis based on these task trees as described in [3,4]. Our results show, that the task trees are representative and descriptive for recorded and unrecorded user behavior. The representativeness of the task trees varies and allows for subdividing the task trees into more and less representative. This eases subsequent analyses as only more representative task trees need to be considered.

In future work, we will use the results of this paper in various ways. For example, we will adapt the task tree generation process, so that it detects only highly representative task trees and less noise. In addition, we will adapt our subsequent analysis of the task trees to focus only on the representative ones. Finally, we will define an estimation heuristics from which we can determine, based on the number of available actions on a software, how many user recordings we require to get representative task trees and subsequent analysis results.

References

1. Van Welie, M., Van Der Veer, G.C., Eliëns, A.: An ontology for task world models. In: Proceedings of DSV-IS98, Abingdon (1998). http://citeseerx.ist.psu.edu/viewdoc/summary?doi=10.1.1.13.4415
2. Paternò, F.: Model-based tools for pervasive usability. Interact. Comput. **17**(3), 291–315 (2005)
3. Harms, P., Grabowski, J.: Usage-based automatic detection of usability smells. In: Sauer, S., Bogdan, C., Forbrig, P., Bernhaupt, R., Winckler, M. (eds.) HCSE 2014. LNCS, vol. 8742, pp. 217–234. Springer, Heidelberg (2014). doi:10.1007/978-3-662-44811-3_13
4. Harms, P.: Automated field usability evaluation using generated task trees, Ph.D. dissertation, January 2016. http://hdl.handle.net/11858/00-1735-0000-0028-8684-1
5. Hudson, S.E., John, B.E., Knudsen, K., Byrne, M.D.: A tool for creating predictive performance models from user interface demonstrations. In: Proceedings of the 12th Annual ACM Symposium on User Interface Software and Technology, UIST 1999, New York, NY, USA, pp. 93–102. ACM (1999)
6. Gomez, S., Laidlaw, D.: Modeling task performance for a crowd of users from interaction histories. In: Proceedings of the SIGCHI Conference on Human Factors in Computing Systems, CHI 2012. New York, NY, USA, pp. 2465–2468. ACM (2012). http://doi.acm.org/10.1145/2207676.2208412
7. Harms, P., Herbold, S., Grabowski, J.: Trace-based task tree generation. In: Proceedings of the Seventh International Conference on Advances in Computer-Human Interactions (ACHI 2014). XPS - Xpert Publishing Services (2014)
8. Harms, P., Herbold, S., Grabowski, J.: Extended trace-based task tree generation. Int. J. Adv. Intell. Syst. **7**(3 and 4), 450–467 (2014). http://www.iariajournals.org/intelligent_systems/
9. Harms, P., Grabowski, J.: Consistency of task trees generated from website usage traces. In: Fischer, J., Scheidgen, M., Schieferdecker, I., Reed, R. (eds.) SDL 2015. LNCS, vol. 9369, pp. 106–121. Springer, Heidelberg (2015). doi:10.1007/978-3-319-24912-4_9
10. Hilbert, D.M., Redmiles, D.F.: Extracting usability information from user interface events. ACM Comput. Surv. **32**(4), 384–421 (2000). http://doi.acm.org/10.1145/371578.371593

11. Aho, A.V., Sethi, R., Ullmann, J.D.: Compilerbau Teil 1. Oldenburg Verlag München, Wien (1999)
12. Herbold, S., Harms, P.: AutoQUEST - automated quality engineering of event-driven software, March 2013
13. Paternò, F., Mancini, C., Meniconi, S.: ConcurTaskTrees: a diagrammatic notation for specifying task models. In: Proceedings of the IFIP TC13 Interantional Conference on Human-Computer Interaction, INTERACT 1997, London, UK, UK, pp. 362–369. Chapman & Hall Ltd. (1997)
14. Paternò, F.: ConcurTaskTrees: an engineered approach to model-based design of interactive systems. In: The Handbook of Analysis for Human Computer Interaction, pp. 1–18 (1999)
15. Trætteberg, H.: Model-based user interface design, Ph.D. dissertation, May 2002
16. Limbourg, Q., Vanderdonckt, J., Michotte, B., Bouillon, L., Florins, M., Trevisan, D.: Usixml: a user interface description language for context-sensitive user interfaces. In: Proceedings of the ACM AVI–2004 Workshop "Developing User Interfaces with XML: Advances on User Interface Description Languages", pp. 55–62 (2004). ACM Press
17. John, B.E., Prevas, K., Salvucci, D.D., Koedinger, K.: Predictive human performance modeling made easy. In: Proceedings of the SIGCHI Conference on Human Factors in Computing Systems, CHI 2004, New York, NY, USA, pp. 455–462. ACM (2004)
18. Norman, K.L., Panizzi, E.: Levels of automation and user participation in usability testing. Interact. Comput. **18**(2), 246–264 (2006). http://dx.doi.org/10.1016/j.intcom.2005.06.002
19. D'Ulizia, A., Ferri, F., Grifoni, P.: A survey of grammatical inference methods for natural language learning. Artif. Intell. Rev. **36**(1), 1–27 (2011). http://dx.doi.org/10.1007/s10462-010-9199-1
20. Siochi, A.C., Hix, D.: A study of computer-supported user interface evaluation using maximal repeating pattern analysis. In: Proceedings of the SIGCHI Conference on Human Factors in Computing Systems, CHI 1991, New York, NY, USA, pp. 301–305. ACM (1991). http://doi.acm.org/10.1145/108844.108926

Optimizing Performance of SDL Systems

Mihal Brumbulli[✉] and Emmanuel Gaudin

PragmaDev, Paris, France
{mihal.brumbulli,emmanuel.gaudin}@pragmadev.com

Abstract. The interest in pragmatic analysis methods is constantly fueled by the increasing complexity of software systems. Although the methods are not scarce, to apply them successfully an additional expertise is required, which often deviates from the development process or the domain the system is intended for. The model-driven paradigm facilitates the development and analysis by means of automation. It can address the issue at a certain extent by raising the level of abstraction closer to the domain. The inherent complexity is shifted from the model towards the automation process. This has been quite effective in handling functional aspects, but non-functional aspects like performance have proven to be challenging in this regard. In this paper we present a model-driven approach for performance analysis based on standardized languages. SDL is used to capture the functional aspects of the system, which are further enriched with performance annotations. Deployment diagrams allow for the available resources to be assigned to system components, and model execution is driven by real test cases in TTCN-3. Automatic execution of different scenarios and graphical presentation of the results can aid the user to optimize performance by choosing the best allocation of resources in terms of execution time and payload.

Keywords: Performance · SDL · TTCN-3 · Architecture · Simulation

1 Introduction

It is an established fact that the complexity of software systems is characterized by a trend to grow. This trend is not expected to change in the future considering the interest in the internet of things [12] where billions of interconnected objects will provide many services to the end users. The Specification and Description Language (SDL) [20] is an international standard that provides many advantages for modeling communicating systems [32]. Models are seen as effective means to deal with system complexity. They can speed up and facilitate the development process by raising the abstraction level. As complexity cannot be eliminated, the best way to deal with it is to let software tools handle it (automatically) and focus on the higher level of abstraction provided by models. This is indeed a core feature of any pragmatic model-driven approach [31]. It enables the use of the same model for different purposes, e.g., generation of the target code or a representation for analyzing relevant aspects. One of the challenges is to ensure

© Springer International Publishing AG 2016
J. Grabowski and S. Herbold (Eds.): SAM 2016, LNCS 9959, pp. 100–115, 2016.
DOI: 10.1007/978-3-319-46613-2_7

that the automation process does produce a valid representation for analysis. Extensive discussions exist regarding functional aspects, and pragmatic solutions have been proposed [3].

The problem becomes more complex with the introduction of non-functional aspects. This is reflected in both parts of the model-driven approach, i.e., the model and the automation process. The modeling language requires additional notations to capture non-functional aspects, and the automation process must be aware of such notations. Performance is a typical non-functional aspect whose analysis requires additional expertise at both levels. A common approach is to annotate existing models and/or to extend them with new diagrams. An automation process transforms these annotated models into some other notation for analysis. It is important for the analysis to consider also functional aspects, e.g., if execution time is relevant for performance analysis, then the time spent carrying out a certain action may affect the behavior of the system, hence the need to consider behavior during analysis.

In [26] it is argued that, in order for the analysis models to be concise and efficient, only functional aspects that influence performance should be captured in the model. This is a sound claim when put in the context of the formalism used for analysis (e.g., Markov chain, Petri net, etc.), where a complete functional model may indeed increase the complexity. However, this approach can widen the gap between functional and performance model, and there is a risk for performance to become an "afterthought" in the process, which is not a good idea as discussed in [25].

In this paper we present a model-driven approach for performance analysis based on standardized languages. SDL is used to capture the functional aspects of the system. State machines are enriched with performance aspects in terms of execution time and payload via a simple interface. System components (SDL block agents) are mapped to processing resources using deployment diagrams [30]. Model execution is driven by real test cases described in Testing and Test Control Notation Version 3 (TTCN-3) [11,17].

The approach for performance modeling is introduced in Sect. 2 and analysis via simulation in Sect. 3. In Sect. 4 we give an overview of related work and position our approach in respect to existing state of the art. We conclude in Sect. 5 with a discussion around the approach and future work.

2   Performance Modeling

Two performance aspects are introduced into the model: the *time* spent during execution, and *payload* as total resources utilized during execution. These apply on SDL state machines (behavior diagram) by means of annotations and deployment diagrams via properties. Their syntax and semantics are as described in the following paragraphs.

2.1   Structure and Behavior

In SDL the overall design is called the *system*, and everything outside of it is defined as the *environment*. The system can be composed of *agents* and *communication constructs*. There are two kinds of agents: *blocks* and *processes*. Agents have an *extended finite state machine* (hereafter state machine) and can contain other agents and communication constructs. In a process agent only, one contained state machine can be in a transition at any given time. In traditional usage (before SDL-2000) and in this paper, a state machine is not specified for a block, and a block can contain only other blocks or processes. A state machine has an implicit queue for *signals*. Each kind of signal has a name and parameters; signal instances go through *channels* that connect agents and end up in the implicit queues of processes. Figure 1 illustrates these concepts in a simple example.

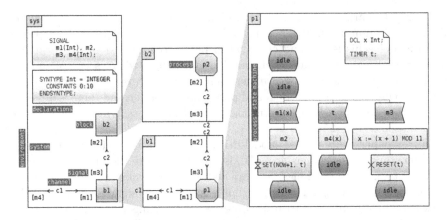

Fig. 1. Example of an SDL system.

The system is composed of two blocks, namely *b1* and *b2*; each containing a single process, *p1* and *p2* respectively. The behavior of the system is triggered by the external signal of kind *m1*, whose single parameter (x in Fig. 1) is an integer between 0 and 10. Upon receiving *m1*, process *p1* sends *m2* to *p2* and starts the timer *t* which is supposed to fire after 1 unit of time. Process *p2* (not shown in the figure) replies back with *m3*, and *p1* signals the environment with *m4*. The parameter of *m4* is also an integer whose value is determined by *m3*, i.e., if the signal is received before the timer *t* fires, then the value will be $x + 1$, otherwise the value of x will not change. If it is assumed the time taken for transitions is insignificant,[1] the way the system behaves always follows the former scenario, thus *m3* will always arrive before the timer fires.

Graphical symbols in the state machine can be annotated with performance aspects as shown in Fig. 2 in the *Behavior Diagram* of the process *p2*.

---

[1] In SDL-2010 [19] an undefined amount of time passes while an action is executed, and it is valid for the time taken to be zero.

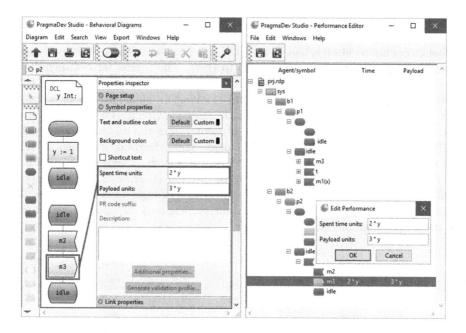

Fig. 2. Performance editor for SDL state machines.

The annotations can be attached to any symbol in a transition (from its start to its terminator), e.g., from an input symbol down to a next-state. It should be noted that annotations to symbols outside a transition (e.g., state, text, etc.) will be ignored during execution of the state machine. To further aid the user in this regard we introduce the *Performance Editor*, which generates a tree-like representation of the SDL model as shown in Fig. 2. The leaves are the symbols that appear in transitions, and performance annotations can be edited only at this level of the tree.

The annotations can be any valid SDL expression that results in a positive integer representing *units* of time and payload. The actual values are determined based on the available resources or processing speed of the machine where the process is being executed. For example, for two machines *M1* and *M2* with the later being twice as fast as the former, we could say that a time unit in *M1* has a weight of 2 and that of *M2* a weight of 1. These weights are multiplied to the values derived from the expressions in Fig. 2, and as a result the execution will take 4 units of time in *M1* and 2 units in *M2*. To note here is that if process *p2* is executed in either machine, then the behavior of the system will be different from what was described above, because the timer will fire before the arrival of the signal *m3*.

2.2   Communication and Architecture

Although communication is handled in SDL via channels, nothing was mentioned regarding performance aspects attached to them. The reason for not introducing further annotations at the SDL level is that channels propagate through the hierarchical structure of the system, and tracking all signal routes in a complex system is not a sound choice from the user viewpoint. These aspects are introduced together with the allocation of resources in the *architectural* model.

The architecture is modeled using the deployment diagram as defined in [30]. The choice was motivated by past experience where such a diagram was used for simulation modeling [4,6] and testing [5] of distributed systems. Although not formalized, the diagram is descriptive and flexible enough to accommodate all additional information for performance analysis. Figure 3 shows an architecture for the simple example introduced above.

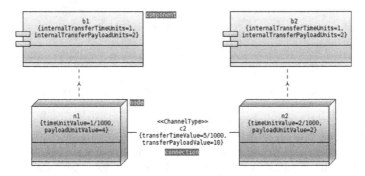

Fig. 3. Example architecture for the SDL system in Fig. 1.

Each *component* is named after the SDL agent (block) it represents, e.g., *b1* and *b2* represent the SDL blocks with the same name in Fig. 1. A component can have two properties, namely *internalTransferTimeUnits* and *internalTransferPayloadUnits*. As the names suggest, these are the performance aspects associated to internal communication, and they apply to all SDL channels whose endpoints are inside the SDL block represented by the component. If we look at the hierarchical structure of an SDL system like a tree,[2] and the sender and receiver process of a signal are both in the sub-tree of the block represented by the component, then the component's properties are associated to the communication path. The values are positive integers representing units of time and payload. This pair of values coupled with the pair attached to the signal output in the state machine (as shown in Fig. 2) enable fine-grained performance annotation of potentially every signal in the system.

The *nodes* represent computation resources and every component in the diagram should be linked to exactly one of them. The resources are expressed in

---

[2] The system is the root, blocks are internal nodes, and processes are leaves.

terms of time and payload via the node's properties *timeUnitValue* and *payload-UnitValue*. These are the *weights* that apply to all annotated values in the SDL state machines and components for communication. Accepted values for *payloadUnitValue* are positive integers, while for *timeUnitValue* are positive integers divided by a power of 10 (e.g., 2/1000).[3] The purpose of the divisor is to differentiate between time values used in the model (SDL timers) and execution time in terms of performance. This is very important considering that execution time is usually orders of magnitude smaller than values used in timers. In the example shown in Fig. 3 every signal exchange inside *b2* will take *internalTransferTimeUnits* * *timeUnitValue* = 0.002 units of time as opposed to 0.001 in *b1*. In general every process inside components attached to *n1* will run twice as fast compared to those attached to *n2* due to the *timeUnitValue*. The same logic can be applied for the payload, where *n1* consumes twice the amount of resources compared to *n2*.

A *connection* (as shown in Fig. 3) is used to introduce performance aspects associated to communication between components attached to different nodes. This means that, for a communication path between *b1* and *b2*, the properties of the connection apply instead of the properties of the components. For example, every signal sent from *b1* will take 0.005 units of time to arrive in *b2*.

2.3   Stimuli

System stimuli for performance analysis is provided by real test cases described in TTCN-3. The abstract definition of test cases in TTCN-3 makes it possible to specify test systems which are independent of the platform. The abstract definitions can be either compiled or interpreted. The former can be used to test target code while the later enables execution of the test cases together with the SDL system for the purpose of analysis. Figure 4 shows a TTCN-3 module definition with a single test case, where the system under test is the SDL example introduced in Fig. 1.

The purpose of the test case *tc* is to trigger the behavior previously described in Sect. 2.1, i.e., it sends an *m1* signal with parameter value set to 5 and expects an *m4* signal with parameter value 6. This is defined as the "desired" behavior in the example, because it will result in a *pass* verdict for the test case (alternative behaviors will result in a *fail*).

TTCN-3 test cases interact with the SDL system via the channels connected to the environment. The main advantage over generic (stochastic or deterministic) stimuli is that it allows to check whether functional aspects of the system are affected during performance analysis.

It should be noted that the execution of a test case itself and communication with the SDL system have no impact in the performance, i.e., time and payload values associated with the test case are 0 (zero). This is the same as having an implicit node and a component in the architecture that represent all test cases, where the "test" node is connected to all other nodes in the architecture, and

---

[3] A divisor of 1 can be omitted, thus only a positive integer is enough.

```
 1: module test {
 2:    // Signals
 3:    type record m1 { integer param1 }
 4:    type record m4 { integer param1 }
 5:    // Port
 6:    type port c1_type message {
 7:       out m1
 8:       in m4
 9:    }
10:    // Component
11:    type component sys {
12:       port c1_type c1
13:    }
14:    // Templates
15:    template m1 stimuli := { param1 := 5 }
16:    template m4 result := { param1 := 6 }
17:    // Test-case
18:    testcase tc() runs on sys {
19:       c1.send(stimuli)
20:       alt {
21:          [] c1.receive(result) { setverdict(pass) }
22:          [] c1.receive { setverdict(fail) }
23:       }
24:    }
25: }
```

Fig. 4. Example of a TTCN-3 module definition with a single test case.

all performance related properties of the node, component, and connections are set to 0 (zero). The "test" node and component are transparent to the user, and they are automatically added to any given architecture. This is illustrated in Fig. 5 with the *test* node, *tc* component, and *test2n1* and *test2n2* connections.

2.4   Semantics of Time and Payload

The execution of SDL processes attached on the same node in the architecture is sequential, and execution on different nodes is parallel.

Time. Each node in the architecture is considered to have an internal *clock* which advances based on the time spent by the processes executing on that node. Sequential execution (only one node) is straightforward because there is only one clock. If two (or more) nodes are involved, their respective clocks are synchronized based on signal exchange. For example, let's suppose that the internal clock of $n1$ is 100 units and that of $n2$ is 80 units. If the $m2$ signal is sent from $n1$ to $n2$, then its estimated time of arrival will be $100 + 5/1000$ units. The value is obtained by adding to the clock $n1$ the time delay associated with the signal transfer represented by the *transferTimeValue* property of the $c2$ connection in Fig. 3. Because the clock of $n2$ is less than the estimated time, upon receiving the signal $n2$ will:

- advance its clock to the estimated time of arrival of the signal $m2$,
- handle any events (e.g., SDL timers) that may have been triggered because of the clock change,
- handle the received signal.

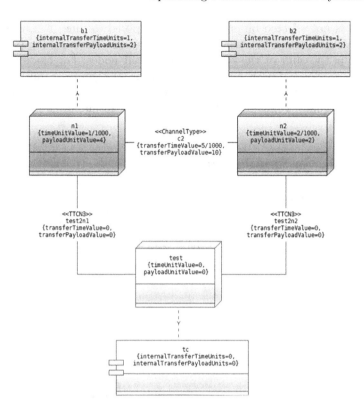

Fig. 5. Implicit test case representation in the architecture.

On the other hand, sending the *m3* signal from *n2* to *n1* requires no changes to the clock, because the clock of *n1* is greater than the estimated time of arrival of the signal. In this case the signal is handled immediately, unless the queue of the receiver has still signals whose time of arrival is less than that of the signal in question.

If the system time needs to be queried for some purpose, then the node's clock with the highest value is returned. However, this should not be confused with the time in the model (e.g., the *NOW* keyword of SDL). In this case the time is that of the node's clock on which the process is executing. The purpose of querying system time would be as performance analysis result at the end of the execution.

Payload. Each node in the architecture is considered to have an internal payload *accumulator* which is incremented based on the payload associated to the symbols in the processes' state machines and signal exchange within the node. The payload associated to communication between nodes (e.g., *transferPayloadValue* property of the *c2* connection in Fig. 3) is added to the accumulator of the receiver.

Payload is not affected by parallelism (as opposed to time), i.e., there is no need for synchronization between node accumulators. The resulting payload of the system is the sum of the accumulators of all nodes. For example, if the accumulated payload of *n1* is 40 and that of *n2* is 30, then the resulting system payload will be 70. The value of system payload is also meant to be queried at the end of execution together with system time as results of the performance analysis.

3   Analysis via Simulation

The PragmaDev Co-Simulator allows execution of TTCN-3 test cases against an SDL system. SDL and TTCN-3 descriptions are translated into an internal representation (byte code) to be interpreted by the *Executor*, which in turn forwards the scheduling of events to the *Scheduler* as shown in Fig. 6.

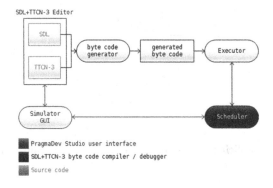

Fig. 6. Architecture of the PragmaDev Co-Simulator.

We extend the existing scheduler for the time and payload semantics described in Sect. 2.4. The new performance-aware scheduler introduces an additional step in the execution flow of Fig. 6. After the byte code of an SDL symbol in the state machine has been interpreted by the executor, and before it is scheduled for execution, the tool checks whether there are performance annotations associated to it. If this is the case, then the SDL expressions in the performance annotations are interpreted and the internal clock and payload accumulator are updated. As the change in the clock may trigger other events, they are scheduled first for execution followed by the execution of the byte code of the SDL symbol in question.

As simulation is based on deterministic stimuli and behavior following the TTCN-3 and SDL semantics, the potential of the performance-aware scheduler and the approach itself lies in the comparison of different architectures rather than the actual result of the analysis for a single architecture. However, it is worth mentioning that there are also benefits in simulating a single architecture. These are the cases where the analysis is aimed at the investigation of the impact

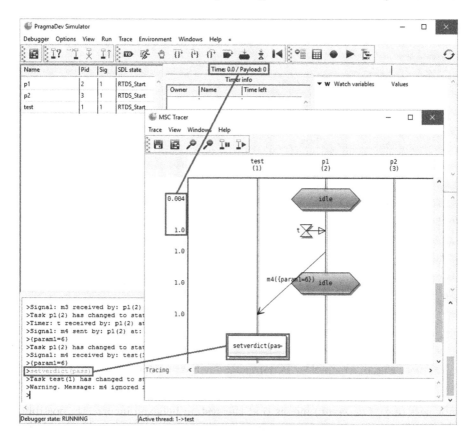

Fig. 7. PragmaDev Simulator user interface and live execution trace in MSC.

that performance aspects may have in the functional behavior of the system. For this purpose we have extended the interface of the existing simulator so that performance results can be displayed when using the new scheduler. Time, payload, and the verdict of the test case are shown in the simulator interface and the live execution trace (using MSC) as illustrated in Fig. 7.

We introduce the *Performance Analyzer* shown in Fig. 8 to facilitate the comparison of different architectures for a set of test cases (stimuli). The user is only concerned with the input of architectures and test cases intended for analysis. The tool computes automatically all possible pairs (architecture, test case), and for each of them launches a simulator instance (with the performance-aware scheduler) in the background. When the simulation is done, it retrieves the result in a tuple (verdict, time, payload) and displays it in tabular and graphical form. The result shown for a given pair depends on the verdict of the test case:

– *pass* implies that the behavior of the system was conform to the correct behavior described in the test case, thus the values of time and payload can be displayed;

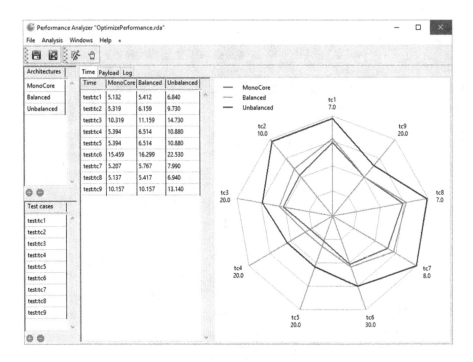

Fig. 8. PragmaDev Performance Analyzer user interface.

- not *pass* (e.g., *fail, error*) means that the system behaved incorrectly possibly due to the performance aspects, thus it makes sense to display the verdict in the table of results instead of the values of time and payload, and a zero value is shown in the graph.

In cases where the second scenario is manifested, and if the cause of such result needs to be further investigated, then the "stand-alone" simulation (as shown in Fig. 7) of the corresponding pair should be the next step as it enables an in-depth analysis of the case.

The results are displayed graphically via a radar graph, where each architecture is shown with a different color. This representation better aids the decision on the best architecture for a given test case or best architecture overall. An architecture is better than another in terms of performance (time or payload) if the surface covered by its line in the graph is smaller.

4   Related Work

Valuable work has been done for the performance analysis of systems described in SDL. Several methods have been proposed to capture performance aspects, describe system stimuli, and perform the analysis.

Some solutions bring modifications to the language that enable quantitative analysis of the model. However, these are restricted to a small subset of the language, which can pose limitations on the functional aspects that can be captured. A typical example in this category is TSDL [1], where Markovian type algorithms are used for performance analysis. SDL-net [2] does not suffer from such limitations because the performance aspects are introduced in the Petri net (used for analysis) rather than in the SDL description. However, the original SDL model may differ from the SDL-net model, and the usage of data types is very restricted due to the Petri net method.

Another category of approach is based on the principle of syntactically unchanged SDL models. SPECS [7] uses annotated SDL specifications, where performance aspects are added separately via a graphical user interface. The models are simulated on a virtual machine that is derived from the SDL description and performance annotations. Simulation is also used in SPEET [33], where system stimuli is provided by traffic load generators, and probes can be defined within the formal description. HIT [14] uses a set of templates that enable transformation of the SDL description into a quantitatively assessable model. QUEST [9] uses time consuming machines for modeling resources: workload models are mapped to machines, and a simulation model is automatically generated.

The advantage of simulation over other methods (analytic and/or numeric) is that it can deal better with complexity. However, simulation models need to be validated to ensure conformance to the original SDL description, and they can produce a vast amount of data if system stimuli is modeled by stochastic traffic generators. Easy-Sim [29] tries to address the first issue via tool coupling. Functional aspects of the system are modeled in SDL whereas performance related aspects are modeled by the SES/workbench. The coupling is implemented by routing SDL events through the SES workbench. For example, a timer can be set in the SES/workbench with the purpose of delaying an SDL signal. What is interesting about the approach is that it introduces also extensions to Message Sequence Charts (MSC) [15] to specify performance requirements of SDL systems. This idea is also employed by the DO-IT toolbox [24], which follows the SDL+ methodology [18] but in the context of non-functional requirements.

A different approach is presented in [34], where the Unified Modeling Language (UML) [28] is used to capture performance aspects and the UML profile of SDL [16] for the behavior of the system. So, it is possible to exploit the flexibility of UML notations and the formal nature of SDL in the same description, which is then translated into a simulation model for analysis.

It should be noted that a lot of work has been done using UML for performance analysis, which is backed-up by the existence of the standard UML profile MARTE [27]. However, there is no substantial difference in the methodology (compared to SDL) and how the analysis is actually performed, i.e., Pertri net [23], Markovian type [21], or simulation [10,22].

The approach presented in this paper aims at seamless integration of performance analysis in the development of SDL systems. SDL state machines can be enriched with performance aspects at any time during development via a simple graphical interface, and afterwards they can be mapped to available resources using a deployment diagram. Compared to the existing state-of-the-art introduced in this section, a pragmatic and deterministic approach was used to describe system stimuli. Instead of stochastic stimuli described in some external notation, we used real test cases in TTCN-3 (user defined or automatically generated [8]). This enabled testing of the system for functional and performance aspects, and what is also of interest, checking whether performance has an impact on the functional behavior of the system. As the approach is based on ITU-T standard languages with formal semantics, it can exploit the full set of existing features of tools including the SDL+TTCN-3 co-simulator (model executor). To make the simulator performance-aware without touching the functional execution semantics, a "coupling-like" solution was adopted where SDL events were routed through the performance scheduler before execution. However, this should not be confused with the coupling employed in [29] because the performance-aware scheduler is integral part of the simulator and not an external tool.

5   Conclusions

The complexity of software systems is characterized by a trend to grow which is expected to continue in the future. The model-driven paradigm provides means to effectively deal with system complexity as it raises the abstraction level during the development process. This has proven to be an effective choice in handling functional aspects, however, the introduction of non-functional aspects like performance in the model suffers from the inherent complexity of the underlying mechanism used for analysis.

The model-driven approach presented in this paper aims at the seamless integration of performance analysis in the development process. SDL was used to capture the functional aspects of the system via state machines, which were further enriched with performance aspects in terms of execution time and payload, and mapped to available resources in the architectural description via deployment diagrams. Compared to the existing state-of-the-art, a pragmatic and deterministic approach was used to describe system stimuli, where real test cases in TTCN-3 were used instead of stochastic stimuli described in some external notation. This enabled testing of both functional and performance aspects, and also checking whether the later had an impact on the former. The existing simulator was extended with a performance-aware scheduler, and the new Performance Analyzer enabled automation of performance analysis on a set of architectures and test cases and graphical representation of results to facilitate comparison.

Considering the above mentioned benefits of the approach and tool support, there are certain aspects that we plan to address in the future. First and foremost we plan to introduce consumable resources by means of additional annotations in the SDL model and properties in the deployment diagram. As these can potentially have an impact on functional aspects of the system, their impact should be assessed during analysis. This can be the waiting time for a resource to be available, possible deadlocks due to unavailable resources, peak usage of resources, etc. Equally important is the graphical presentation of the results in a comparative way in the Performance Analyzer. Whether the current presentation format (table and radar graph) is adequate also for consumable resources is to be further investigated. Supporting user defined performance aspects would be the next step., i.e., provide means to add custom annotations in the model with their corresponding properties in the architecture. Last but not least, following the ideas presented in [13], we are also thinking about the possibility of extending the approach (and tool support) with means for automatic performance properties verification.

References

1. Bause, F., Buchholz, P.: Qualitative and quantitative analysis of timed SDL specifications. In: Gerner, N., Hegering, H.G., Swoboda, J. (eds.) Kommunikation in Verteilten Systemen, pp. 486–500. Springer, Heidelberg (1993)
2. Bause, F., Kabutz, H., Kemper, P., Kritzinger, P.S.: SDL and Petri Net performance analysis of communicating systems. In: Dembinski, P., Sredniawa, M. (eds.) Protocol Specification, Testing and Verification XV, pp. 269–282. Chapman & Hall, New York (1995)
3. Brumbulli, M.: Model-driven development and simulation of distributed communication systems. Ph.D. thesis, Humboldt Universität zu Berlin (2015)
4. Brumbulli, M., Fischer, J.: Simulation configuration modeling of distributed communication systems. In: Haugen, Ø., Reed, R., Gotzhein, R. (eds.) SAM 2012. LNCS, vol. 7744, pp. 198–211. Springer, Heidelberg (2013)
5. Brumbulli, M., Gaudin, E.: Automatic interleaving for testing distributed systems. In: 8th European Congress on Embedded Real Time Software and Systems (ERTS 2016) (2016)
6. Brumbulli, M., Gaudin, E.: Towards model-driven simulation of the internet of things, advances in intelligent systems and computing. In: Cardin, M.-L., Fong, S.H., Krob, D., Lui, P.C., Tan, Y.H. (eds.) Complex Systems Design & Management Asia, vol. 426, pp. 17–29. Springer International Publishing, Switzerland (2016)
7. Bütow, M., Mestern, M., Schapiro, C., Kritzinger, P.S.: Performance modelling with the formal specification language SDL. In: Gotzhein, R., Bredereke, J. (eds.) Formal Description Techniques IX: Theory, Application and Tools, pp. 213–228. Chapman & Hall, New York (1996)
8. Deltour, J., Faivre, A., Gaudin, E., Lapitre, A.: Model-based testing: an approach with SDL/RTDS and DIVERSITY. In: Amyot, D., Fonseca i Casas, P., Mussbacher, G. (eds.) SAM 2014. LNCS, vol. 8769, pp. 198–206. Springer, Heidelberg (2014)
9. Diefenbruch, M., Hintelmann, J., Müller-Clostermann, B.: The QUEST approach for the performance evaluation of SDL-systems. In: Gotzhein, R., Bredereke, J. (eds.) Formal Description Techniques IX: Theory, Application and Tools, pp. 229–244. Chapman & Hall, New York (1996)
10. Dietrich, I., Dressler, F., Schmitt, V., German, R.: Syntony: network protocol simulation based on standard-conform UML 2 models. In: Glynn, P. (ed.) Proceedings of the 2nd International Conference on Performance Evaluation Methodologies and Tools, ValueTools 2007, pp. 21: 1–21: 11. ICST, Brussels (2007)

11. ETSI: TTCN-3 Core Language. ETSI Standard ES 201 873-1, European Telecommunications Standards Institute (2014). http://www.ttcn-3.org/index.php/downloads/standards

12. Gartner Inc.: Gartner says the Internet of Things installed base will grow to 26 billion units by 2020 (2013). http://www.gartner.com/newsroom/id/2636073

13. Gaudin, E., Brunel, E.: Property verification with MSC. In: Khendek, F., Toeroe, M., Gherbi, A., Reed, R. (eds.) SDL 2013. LNCS, vol. 7916, pp. 19–35. Springer, Heidelberg (2013)

14. Heck, E., Hogrefe, D., Muller-Clostermann, B.: Hierarchical performance evaluation based on formally specified communication protocols. IEEE Trans. Comput. **40**(4), 500–513 (1991)

15. ITU-T: Message Sequence Chart (MSC). ITU-T Recommendation Z.120, International Telecommunication Union - Telecommunication Standardization Sector (2011). http://handle.itu.int/11.1002/1000/11063

16. ITU-T: Specification and Description Language - Unified modeling language profile for SDL-2010. ITU-T Recommendation Z.109, International Telecommunication Union - Telecommunication Standardization Sector (2013). http://handle.itu.int/11.1002/1000/12035

17. ITU-T: Testing and Test Control Notation version 3: TTCN-3 core language. ITU-T Recommendation Z.161, International Telecommunication Union - Telecommunication Standardization Sector (2014). http://handle.itu.int/11.1002/1000/12617

18. ITU-T: ITU-T Z.100-series - Supplement on SDL+ methodology: Use of ITU System Design Languages. ITU-T Recommendation Z Suppl. 1, International Telecommunication Union - Telecommunication Standardization Sector (2015). http://handle.itu.int/11.1002/1000/12447

19. ITU-T: Specification and Description Language - Basic SDL-2010. ITU-T Recommendation Z.101, International Telecommunication Union - Telecommunication Standardization Sector (2016). http://handle.itu.int/11.1002/1000/12847

20. ITU-T: Specification and Description Language - Overview of SDL-2010. ITU-T Recommendation Z.100, International Telecommunication Union - Telecommunication Standardization Sector (2016). http://handle.itu.int/11.1002/1000/12846

21. Lindemann, C., Thümmler, A., Klemm, A., Lohmann, M., Waldhorst, O.P.: Performance analysis of time-enhanced UML diagrams based on stochastic processes. In: Proceedings of the 3rd International Workshop on Software and Performance, WOSP 2002, New York, NY, USA, pp. 25–34. ACM (2002)

22. Marzolla, M., Balsamo, S.: UML-PSI: the UML performance simulator. In: Proceedings of the 1st International Conference on the Quantitative Evaluation of Systems, QEST 2004, pp. 340–341. IEEE Computer Society (2004)

23. Merseguer, J., Campos, J.: Software performance modeling using UML and Petri Nets. In: Calzarossa, M.C., Gelenbe, E. (eds.) MASCOTS 2003. LNCS, vol. 2965, pp. 265–289. Springer, Heidelberg (2004)

24. Mitschele-Thiel, A., Langendörfer, P., Henke, R.: Design and optimization of high-performance protocols with the DO-IT toolbox. In: Gotzhein, R., Bredereke, J. (eds.) Formal Description Techniques IX: Theory, Application and Tools, pp. 45–60. Chapman & Hall, New York (1996)

25. Mitschele-Thiel, A., Müller-Clostermann, B.: Performance engineering of SDL/MSC systems. Comput. Netw. **31**(17), 1801–1815 (1999)

26. Monin, W., Dubois, F., Vincent, D., Combes, P.: Looking for better integration of design and performance engineering. In: Reed, R., Reed, J. (eds.) SDL 2003. LNCS, vol. 2708, pp. 1–17. Springer, Heidelberg (2003)

27. OMG: UML Profile for MARTE: Modeling and Analysis of Real-Time Embedded Systems. Version 1.1. OMG Standard, Object Management Group (2011). http://www.omg.org/spec/MARTE/1.1

28. OMG: OMG Unified Modeling Language (OMG UML). Version 2.5. OMG Standard, Object Management Group (2015). http://www.omg.org/spec/UML/2.5

29. Schaffer, C., Raschhofer, R.J., Simma, A.: EaSy-Sim: a tool environment for the design of complex, real-time systems. In: Pichler, F., Díaz, R.M., Albrecht, R. (eds.) EUROCAST 1995. LNCS, vol. 1030, pp. 358–374. Springer, Heidelberg (1996)

30. SDL-RT Consortium: Specification and Description Language - Real Time. SDL-RT Standard V2.3, SDL-RT Consortium (2013). http://www.sdl-rt.org/standard/V2.3/html/index.htm

31. Selic, B.: The pragmatics of model-driven development. IEEE Softw. **20**(5), 19–25 (2003)

32. Sherratt, E., Ober, I., Gaudin, E., Fonseca i Casas, P., Kristoffersen, F.: SDL - the IoT language. In: Fischer, J., Scheidgen, M., Schieferdecker, I., Reed, R. (eds.) SDL 2015. LNCS, vol. 9369, pp. 27–41. Springer, Heidelberg (2015)

33. Steppler, M., Lott, M.: SPEET - SDL performance evaluation tool. In: Cavalli, A., Sarma, A. (eds.) SDL 1997 Time for Testing, SDL, MSC and Trends, pp. 53–68. Elsevier, Amsterdam (1997)

34. de Wet, N., Kritzinger, P.: Using UML models for the performance analysis of network systems. Comput. Netw. **49**(5), 627–642 (2005)

Evolving the ETSI Test Description Language

Philip Makedonski[1(✉)], Gusztáv Adamis[2], Martti Käärik[3], Finn Kristoffersen[4], and Xavier Zeitoun[5]

[1] Institute of Computer Science, University of Göttingen, Göttingen, Germany
makedonski@cs.uni-goettingen.de
[2] Test Competence Center, Ericsson Hungary Ltd., Budapest, Hungary
gusztav.adamis@ericsson.com
[3] Elvior OU, Talinn, Estonia
martti.kaarik@elvior.com
[4] Cinderella ApS, Copenhagen, Denmark
finn@cinderella.dk
[5] CEA, LIST, Gif-sur-yvette, France
xavier.zeitoun@cea.fr

Abstract. Increasing software and system complexity due to the integration of more and more diverse sub-systems presents new testing challenges. Standardisation and certification requirements in certain domains such as telecommunication, automotive, aerospace, and health-care contribute further challenges for testing systems operating in these domains. Consequently, there is a need for suitable methodologies, processes, languages, and tools to address these testing challenges. To address some of these challenges, the Test Description Language (TDL) has been developed at the European Telecommunications Standards Institute (ETSI) over the past three years. TDL bridges the gap between declarative test purposes and imperative test cases by offering a standardised language for the specification of test descriptions. TDL started as a standardised meta-model, subsequently enriched with a graphical syntax, exchange format, and a UML profile. A reference implementation of TDL has been developed as a common platform to accelerate the adoption of TDL and lower the barrier to entry for both end-users and tool-vendors. This article tells the story of the evolution of TDL from its conception.

Keywords: Model-based testing · Test description language · Domain-specific modeling

1 Introduction

Increasing software and system complexity due to the integration of more and more diverse sub-systems presents new testing challenges. Standardisation and certification requirements in certain domains such as telecommunication, automotive, aerospace, and health-care contribute further testing challenges for systems operating in these domains, especially as they need to evolve and operate

J. Grabowski and S. Herbold (Eds.): SAM 2016, LNCS 9959, pp. 116–131, 2016.
DOI: 10.1007/978-3-319-46613-2_8

over long periods of time. Consequently, there is a need for suitable methodologies, processes, languages, and tools to address these testing challenges. The European Telecommunications Standards Institute (ETSI) has a long experience with the development of test specifications for standardised systems. To facilitate the efficient development of standardised test specifications and address some of the continuously evolving challenges, the Technical Committee Methods for Testing and Specification (TC-MTS) at ETSI has been active in developing methodologies, processes, and languages for testing, and in particular in the context of standardisation. The ETSI test development process [17] follows a stepwise approach based on the ISO/IEC 9646-1 [25] norm. Each step on the way from base standard to executable test cases results in intermediate artifacts at different levels of abstraction, which are intended for particular stakeholders such as standardisation experts, technology experts, and test engineers.

With strong emphasis on test automation, TC-MTS lead the work on the development and maintenance and evolution of the Testing and Test Control Notation version 3 (TTCN-3) [10] over the past 15 years. While TTCN-3 has been established as the language of choice for the implementation of test cases at ETSI, on the higher levels of abstraction there was a distinctive lack of well-established notations. Even with overall agreement on the basic structure and content of test purposes and test descriptions, there was a proliferation of dialects and customised notations for different standards. The Test Purpose Notation (TPLan) [11] sought to provide a notation for the standardised specification of test purposes. This left a gap between the declarative test purposes and the imperative test cases. Without a suitable and standardised language for this purpose, the development of test descriptions by means of different notations and dialects lead to significant overhead and frequent inconsistencies that needed to be checked and fixed manually. The consequences are particularly severe for test descriptions related to technologies and standards that continue to evolve over decades. More recently, TC-MTS has also explored the requirements for the application of Model-Based Testing (MBT) in standardisation [12] with MBT technologies becoming more mature and finding wider acceptance in the industry.

The Test Description Language (TDL) [13] seeks to bridge the methodological gap between declarative test purposes and executable test cases by providing a formalised model-based solution for the specification of test descriptions. At the core of TDL there is a common meta-model with well-defined semantics, which can be represented by means of different concrete notations. A TDL test description created in one notation can be reviewed and approved in other notations, customized to suit the preferred level of abstraction and notational conventions of the different users. TDL can also serve as an exchange and visualisation platform for generated tests, contributing to the ongoing activities within TC-MTS to establish MBT technologies within standardisation at ETSI [9,12,17].

TC-MTS laid down the foundation of TDL with Specialist Task Force (STF) 454 in 2013 in terms of the basic concepts of the language and their semantics. In 2014, STF 476 added language functionality for the integration of TDL test descriptions into test automation frameworks as well as a standardised graphical syntax for end-users. STF 476 also contributed an exchange format in order to foster tool interoperability, as well as an extension to TDL enabling refined test objective specification. In 2015, STF 492 developed an open reference implementation intended to serve as a common platform to accelerate the adoption of TDL and lower the barrier to entry for both end-users and tool-vendors. The work on the reference implementation contributed to the public launch of TDL at User Conference on Advanced Automated Testing (UCAAT) 2015 sharing the work on TDL with a broader audience. The discussions during the launch event generated feedback from numerous stakeholders from different domains that will influence the future development of the language.

This article is structured as follows: Sect. 2 showcases the different parts of the TDL standard in their current form. Section 3 contains a technical overview of the reference implementation of TDL. Section 4 discusses related work. Finally, Sect. 5 provides a summary and an outlook on the future of TDL.

2   The TDL Standard

The TDL specification evolved into a multi-part standard. In this section, we first provide a broad overview of the core principles behind the design of TDL and then take a closer look at the different parts and illustrate some of the features of the language with examples.

2.1   Core Design Principles

The TDL is intended for the design, documentation, and representation of formal test descriptions for black-box testing following a scenario-based approach describing interactions with the System Under Test (SUT). Test objectives derived from requirements may be attached to different scenarios or even to parts of a scenario. The scenarios are then used as basis for deriving and automating tests. TDL can also be used for the representation of test sequences derived from MBT tools, system simulators, or traces from test execution runs.

At the core of TDL is the Meta-model (MM) [13] standard specifying the abstract syntax including the concepts of the language, the relationships among them, their properties, and their intended semantics. The Exchange Format (XF) [15] serves as basis for the interoperability of tools. Concrete syntax notations may be mapped to the abstract syntax making the elements of the meta-model accessible to users by means of different representations, such as graphical, textual, tabular, tree-based, possibly targeting different levels of abstraction. The Graphical Representation (GR) [14] provides a standardised concrete syntax for the graphical representation of TDL elements as a common ground. The Structured Test Objective Specification (TO) [16] provides an extension of TDL that introduces additional concepts to the MM, as well as corresponding representations in the GR and the XF.

The decomposition of TDL into a multipart standard has the advantage that tool vendors and users can decide which parts they want to conform to.

For example, tools providing customised syntax representations for a specific group of users may opt to support only the MM and XF parts, rather than supporting the GR which may be unnecessary for the targeted user group.

2.2   The Meta-Model

Part 1 of the TDL standard defines the abstract syntax, static and dynamic semantics of TDL. The abstract syntax is specified in terms of a Meta-Object Facility (MOF) [33] meta-model describing the concepts of the language and the relations between them. Constraints on the concepts and their relationships are formalized by means of the Object Constraint Language (OCL) [30]. The meta-model concepts are defined in packages covering different aspects of TDL.

The *Foundation* package defines the basic structural concepts of a TDL specification. These include the abstract notion of an element as the common ancestor of all other concepts of the language, packages for grouping elements together, concepts for importing elements from packages, annotations, and comments.

The *Data* package contains concepts for data definition and data use. The data definition concepts cover abstract data type definitions, data instance specifications, actions, functions, parameters, and variables. Members and member assignments may be used to specify the internal structure of data type and data instance definitions, respectively. The data concepts in TDL are abstract symbols that can be related by means of data element mappings to concrete data representations stored in external resources, such as TTCN-3 or Extensible Markup Language (XML) documents, which are referenced by means of data resource mappings. The defined data elements can be referenced in various contexts, such as parameters, interactions, timers, etc. by means of data use concepts. The data use concepts also include wildcards such as any value of a given type.

The *Test Configuration* package defines the concepts related to the test architectures for TDL test descriptions. Test configurations in TDL are composed of at least two component instances, one in the role of *Tester* and one in the role of *SUT*, with at least one connection between their gate instances. A component instance inherits the gate instances, timers and variables of the component type it conforms to. A gate instance conforms to a gate type which specifies the data that can be used in interactions over gate instances of that gate type.

The *Test Behaviour* package defines the concepts necessary for the specification of behaviour. These include atomic behaviours, such as interactions for exchanging data between gates of component instances, local or global actions, references to other test descriptions, as well as explicit verdict assignments. Compound behaviours, including conditional, alternative, repeated, interrupt, and default behaviour, are used to group atomic behaviours.

The *Time* package in TDL contains concepts for the specification time operations, time constraints, and timers. Time in TDL is global and progresses monotonically in discrete quantities. TDL offers time operations including *Wait* and *Quiescence*, which are used to delay the execution or ensure that no interactions occur in the gates of a component instance in the role of *Tester*. Timer operations (*Start, Stop, Timeout*) operate on component instance timers.

Finally, *Annex B* of Part 1 contains an example text-based notation for illustrative purposes in order to showcase some concrete examples of the use of the TDL MM. It can serve as the basis for a textual concrete syntax for TDL, however, the notation itself is only informative at this point in time.

2.3   The Graphical Representation

Part 2 of the TDL standard defines the default, general-purpose graphical representation format for TDL meta-model elements. One of the key design requirements was that the graphical representation of TDL shall resemble the graphical format of the most frequently used modeling notations in order to preserve familiarity and ensure that it is easy to learn for users. Considering that Unified Modeling Language (UML) is widely used in the industry and also gaining momentum in standardisation, the graphical representation of TDL was aligned with UML to the extent to which the corresponding TDL elements have (almost) direct equivalents in UML. Elements of the TDL meta-model that have no direct equivalent or have different semantics are represented in a different way in order to avoid confusion.

The specification of a TDL test description typically requires three major parts—data and data type specification, test configuration specification, test behaviour specification. An example of a data type and a data instance specification is shown in the bottom part of Fig. 1. In this case, the definition of a data type **Message** and a data instance **Request** of data type **Message** is illustrated. In TDL, the type definition symbols have double borders. As noted in Sect. 2.2, TDL only provides abstract symbols for data that can be mapped to external data. A data mapping specification is shown in the upper part of Fig. 1. In this example, it is assumed that there is a file **data.ttcn3** containing some concrete data specifications in TTCN-3, which is made accessible as a mapping target in TDL by means of a data resource mapping. The data element mappings then specify how the abstract data type and data instance symbols specified in TDL are related to the corresponding concrete data specifications. In the example shown in Fig. 1, the **Request** data instance is mapped to a template **m_rq** defined in **data.ttcn3**. Similarly, the abstract **Message** data type defined in TDL is mapped to the concrete **t_msg** data type defined in **data.ttcn3**. The resolution and validation of the correctness and consistency of such mappings is left to tool implementations.

The definition of a test configuration is illustrated in Fig. 2. In order to define a test configuration, first one or more gate types need to be defined. The gate type **defaultGT** which can send and receive data instances of type **Message** is shown in the top left part of Fig. 2. Next, one or more component types need to be defined. The component type **defaultCT** which has a gate **g** of type **defaultGT**, as well as a variable **v** of type **Message**, is shown in the top center part of Fig. 2. Finally, a simple test configuration **defaultTC** containing two component instances of type **defaultCT** (SS in the role **TESTER** and UE in the role **SUT**), as well as a connection between their gates, is shown in the bottom part of Fig. 2.

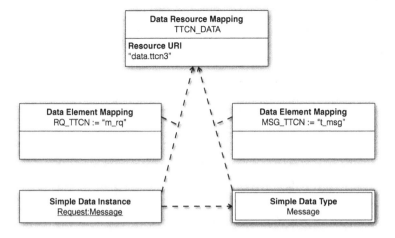

Fig. 1. Data definition and mapping specification

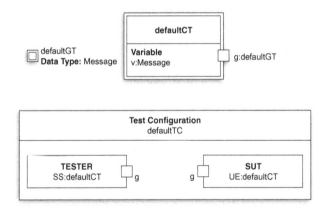

Fig. 2. Gate type, component type, and test configuration

The specification of behaviour is exemplified in Fig. 3. The example features a simple interaction sequence between the previously defined component instances. The SS in the role of TESTER sends a Request message. The UE in the role of SUT may respond to the SS by either an Accept or a Reject message. The verdict in the first case will be PASS, while in the second case it will be FAIL.

2.4   The Exchange Format

Part 3 of the TDL standard defines the exchange format for TDL models. The exchange format describes the rules for serialization and de-serialisation of TDL models which enables interchange of TDL models between tools. The TDL XF is based on the XML Metadata Interchange (XMI) specification [34]. The TDL XF

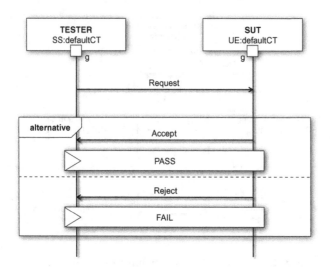

Fig. 3. Behaviour specification

specifies production rules for deriving a TDL XMI Schema covering the complete definition of the TDL MM, including the MM extensions defined in the TDL TO, as well as production rules for TDL XMI documents for the serialization of TDL models. However, the semantic correctness of a TDL model represented in the form of an XMI document cannot be validated based on the exchange format rules alone. After de-serialisation, the resulting TDL model still needs to be checked with respect to the rules defined in the MM.

2.5   Extending TDL: Structured Test Objectives

Part 4 of the TDL standard defines an extension of TDL to support the specification of structured test objectives in a formalised manner within TDL. In Part 1 of TDL, the description of a test objective can be specified only as informal text. In Part 4, additional concepts are introduced as extensions to the meta-model in order to capture additional features of test objectives. These include:

- domain specification concepts such as abstract events and entities, as well as reusable event occurrence templates,
- structured test objectives containing event occurrence sequences for initial conditions, expected behaviour, and final conditions,
- event occurrence specifications containing entity references, event references, event occurrence arguments, and time constraints,
- extended data specification for literal data used as event occurrence arguments that do not require the definition of data types and data instances.

The concrete syntax notation is related to the TPLan notation used within ETSI in order to align it with existing procedures and capitalise on user familiarity. An example is shown in Fig. 4. While the notation for the structured test

TP Id	TP_1
Test Objective	Ensure that a request is accepted
Reference	SAM 2016 Examples
PICS Selection	

Initial Conditions

```
with {
    the SS entity connected to the UE entity
}
```

Expected Behaviour

```
ensure that {
  when {
      the UE entity receives a Request message
  }
  then {
      the UE entity sends an Accept message
  }
}
```

Final Conditions

Fig. 4. Structured test objective specification

objectives as a whole is graphical in nature, its contents describing the event occurrences are in the form of structured natural language, where entity and event references are surrounded by keywords and free text in the form of comments. This adds sufficient formalisation to the specification of test objectives in order to enable tool support for the validation of test objectives and for mapping them to test descriptions, while still retaining a natural language feel. Similar to Part 1, Part 4 contains an informative text-based notation in its *Annex B* focusing on the concepts introduced as extensions to the meta-model.

2.6 The UML Profile for TDL

To enable the application of TDL in UML based working environments, a UML Profile for TDL (UP4TDL) was developed. Profiling in UML is a way to adapt the UML meta-model with domain-specific concerns. In simplified terms, domain-specific concepts are represented in a UML profile by means of *stereotypes*. A stereotype enables the extension of a UML meta-class with additional properties, relations, or constraints in order to address domain-specific concerns.

The overall architecture of UP4TDL is similar to the package structure of TDL. The top-level package of the UP4TDL contains stereotypes that enable binding annotations to any TDL elements. The test objective concept is also declared there. For structuring TDL models in packages and importing TDL elements from other packages, the UP4TDL relies on already existing concepts in UML (*UML::Package* and *UML::ElementImport* respectively). The *DataDefinition* package contains the equivalents of the concepts from the *TDL:Data* package, most of which are already present in UML. One major addition is related to the data element mapping which allows the binding of abstract mappable data elements to concrete data specifications stored in a data resource. The *DataUse* package contains an almost independent meta-model that is used as the basis for integrating data-related expressions in TDL models. These expressions are used in the specification of arguments of inter-actions. The *Behaviour* package contains two kinds of stereotypes. A set of stereotypes that extend *UML::CombinedFragment* represents the set of elements defined in *TDL::CombinedBehaviour*. The other stereotypes mostly extend *UML::OccurenceSpecification* and represent corresponding elements defined in *TDL::AtomicBehaviour*. Finally, the *Time* package contains stereotypes repre-senting elements related to the management of time in TDL. Currently, they are specific to TDL. In future work, linking these concepts with the Modeling and Analysis of Real-Time Embedded Systems (MARTE) profile [29] may help to refine the embedding of UP4TDL into the UML environment.

The UML Testing Profile (UTP) [31] is published by the Object Manage-ment Group (OMG) and is also providing high level test-related concepts for use within UML-based working environments. UTP and UP4TDL share similar global choices for representing various aspects of both languages. The arrange-ment of test components in a test configuration may be described by a composite-like diagram. Test behaviours can be described by sequence-like diagrams. The data types and data instances may be presented in a class-like diagram. However, there are also a number of differences between UP4TDL and UTP. Since TDL and UTP evolved independently, UP4TDL also follows some design decisions that keep it closer to TDL. While behaviour specifications in UTP may have different kinds of representations, the behaviour-related stereotypes in UP4TDL are also intended to be directly mapped to corresponding behaviour-related con-cepts in TDL (e.g. *ExceptionalBehaviour, PeriodicBehaviour*).

In TDL, a global synchronization mechanism is assumed. Consider the two communication events shown in Fig. 5. In UTP, these communication events are represented by means of *UML::Message*. Without additional constraints (such as *GlobalOrdering*) they are only locally ordered. Consequently, the fol-lowing event sequence <*Tunnel* sent, *Request* sent, *Request* received, *Tunnel* received> would be considered valid. In TDL, such a communication sequence is

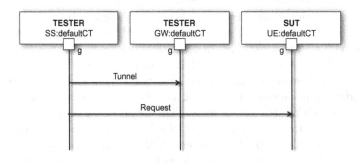

Fig. 5. Communication event ordering

represented by means of *TDL::Interactions* which are assumed to be atomic (no distinction between the send event and the receive event) and globally ordered. Consequently, the only acceptable event sequence would be <*Tunnel occurred, Request occurred*>. This simplification choice is compatible with the way test cases are implemented in many test management tools.

3   An Implementation of TDL

A reference implementation of TDL is essential for validating the TDL standards by enabling the application of the specified concepts in practice and checking their applicability, consistency, and usability. The reference implementation can also help tool vendors to accelerate the adoption of TDL in their existing solutions by using it as an import and/or export facility for TDL models, by adding custom features on top of it, or by integrating it with existing products.

3.1   Requirements

A basic TDL implementation shall be able to read and write models serialized according to the XF. It shall also allow users to check static semantics of models to verify their compliance with TDL. The specific means of creating and editing TDL models is beyond the scope of the standard. TDL users may apply domain-specific textual notations mapped to the TDL MM, such as the notation described in *Annex B* of Part 1. Users may also utilize existing general purpose modeling tools or other customized combined notations. The TDL MM specifies constraints on the elements of the language, which are formalised by means of OCL expressions. In order to evaluate these expressions against TDL models, they also need to be integrated in the reference implementation.

One of the use cases for TDL from the very start was visualising tests generated from MBT tools as well as visualising test execution traces. The reference implementation focused on providing such facilities by implementing means for the visualisation of TDL models according to the TDL GR as the graphical representations are also better suited for use in (standards-related) documents and during high-level discussions, as well as for instructional purposes.

Due to the peculiarities and intended use of structured test objectives, it was determined that instead of graphical shapes that can be exported as images, the graphical representations of structured test objectives shall be realised as tables exported in a Word document according to user-defined templates, which can then be manipulated further in order to fit in within an existing document.

For the use of the UP4TDL, the profile itself needed to be implemented first. However, using the facilities provided within modeling environments for manipulating features provided by UML profiles can be rather cumbersome. Hence, customised editing facilities for UML models using the UP4TDL were also necessary in order to improve the usability of the UP4TDL implementation.

The availability of necessary tools and technologies for implementing model-based domain-specific languages is an important factor influencing the choice of platform for the reference implementation of TDL.

3.2 Realisation

Eclipse and associated technologies were chosen as the base platform for the implementation as it is the most widely used modeling platform today. At the core of Eclipse modeling platform is the Eclipse Modeling Framework (EMF) which provides an implementation of MOF (named *Ecore*) which was used to for the implementation of the TDL meta-model. The meta-model specification in the form of a UML model was done in the Papyrus modeling environment [2]. The resulting UML meta-model for TDL was transformed into an Ecore meta-model for implementation purposes. The EMF provides the necessary facilities for model serialisation and de-serialisation based on XMI. These facilities were configured to work with XMI documents that are compliant with the TDL XF.

The semantic rules that are defined in the TDL standard as OCL constraints can be integrated into the meta-model by means of annotations, which can be used for automated validation of model instances. However, any modifications to the constraints would require changing the meta-model and related generated resources. Alternatively, the constraints can be specified as an add-on which can be applied to the model instances as needed. This allows add-on constraints to be modified, maintained, and extended independently from the meta-model. The Epsilon Validation Language (EVL) [27] provides means for the implementation of add-on constraints. The EVL also extends the capabilities of OCL by providing additional facilities for the specification of guards on constraints which are used to specify under which conditions the evaluation of a constraint shall be skipped.

The Eclipse Graphical Modeling Framework (GMF) links EMF modeling capabilities with graphical editing. Diagram editors can be implemented by creating mappings between meta-model elements and diagram shapes, from which the code for graphical editors is generated. This separation facilitates the inclusion of custom shape and layout implementations. The Sirius project [4] utilizes GMF and allows the declarative definition of diagram viewers and editors as opposed to code generation. Sirius was chosen as an implementation platform to avoid the maintenance overhead that comes with code generation as the application matures. In addition, while the reference implementation focuses on the visualisation of TDL models, facilities provided by the Sirius platform can be extended with the specification of editing capabilities thus enabling an easy transition from a viewer to an editor in the future.

The labels related to data use in the GR specification exhibit a more complex structure than most other labels. For the realisation of these labels, an Xtext-based serialisation relying on a partial grammar specification mapped to the TDL MM was used. Xtext [6] is a framework for developing textual languages on top of EMF. Xtext was also used for the realisation of the syntax specified in the informative *Annex B* of Part 1 as part of the reference implementation enabling the quick creation and manipulation of TDL models. Apart from the grammar specification, it also includes further customisations in the scoping and linking facilities, as well as enhanced semantic syntax highlighting which provides customisable styles for identifiers based on their type and usage context. Similarly, a Xtext-based realisation of the syntax specified in the informative

Annex B of Part 4 is also included for users relying on TDL mainly for the specification of structured test objectives.

The export of structured test objectives into tables in Word documents relies on facilities from Docx4j [1] library providing Application Programming Interface (API) for manipulating Word documents. A set of predefined templates, including a template according to the concrete syntax defined in Part 4, are included in the implementation. Users may define additional templates. The templates describe the overall structure of the representation and contain a set of placeholders for the different labels. Xtext is then used to substitute the label placeholders with serialisation of the corresponding model elements and their contents, in a similar manner as the labels in the GR viewer.

The implementation of the UP4TDL as well as supporting editing facilities was realised on top of Papyrus. Papyrus provides a graphical editor and an extensible framework for working with UML models. It was customised in order to allow users to create graphical representations of UML models applying UP4TDL with dedicated editing facilities. The customisations are shared among three new kinds of diagrams—the *DataDefinition* diagram, the *TestDescription* diagram, and the *TestConfiguration* diagram. Using the TDL *TestConfiguration* diagram, the user can declare component types, component instances, gates, and connections. To specify the types of data that are exchanged through gates, the user may need to open a *DataDefinition* diagram to specify the data types and data instances. In the *DataDefinition* diagram, the user can also map these data elements to a data resource containing concrete data representations. Finally, the user can start creating test descriptions that use the specified test configuration by means of the *TestDescription* diagram. Additional editing facilities are provided to streamline the work with UML models applying the UP4TDL. These include a customised property editor that shows only the TDL-related properties of stereotypes and an Xtext-based editor for the arguments of interactions.

The public availability of the implementation will be announced on the TDL website [5], once licensing questions have been addressed at ETSI.

4 Related Work

Domain-specific testing languages offer a convenient solution, as they allow domain experts to use familiar concepts to express and describe the system behaviour for the purposes of testing. For example, automotive engineers may rely on dedicated concepts, such as Electronic Control Unit (ECU), bus, power port, etc., from the automotive domain in a domain-specific testing language tailored for testing automotive systems.

The Check Case Definition Language (CCDL) [32] provides a high-level approach for requirements-based black-box system level testing embedded in its own testing process. Test simulations and expected results specified in human readable form in CCDL can be compiled into executable test scripts. However, due to lack of standardisation, high-level test descriptions in CCDL are heavily tool-dependent. High-level keyword-based test languages, using frameworks such as the Robot Framework [3], have also been integrated with MBT [35]. Beyond textual keyword-based languages, graphical domain-specific testing languages, such as one built on top of TTCN-3 [26], have also been developed.

There have been efforts to address the lack of standardisation in some application domains, such as the standardised meta-model for testing avionics embedded systems [19], and the Automotive Test Exchange Format (ATX) [7] and TestML [18] focusing on automotive systems. Additionally, the Open Test Sequence Exchange Format (OTX) [22–24] standardised at the International Organization for Standardization (ISO) aims to provide tool-independent XML-based data exchange format for the formal description and documentation of executable test sequences for automobile diagnostics. These efforts have focused primarily on enabling the exchange of test specifications between involved stake-holders and tools, and are hardly concerned with precise semantics. The domain and purpose specialisation of these languages limits their applicability outside of the originally intended domain and testing activity.

The Message Sequence Chart (MSC) [21] standardised at the International Telecommunication Union (ITU) was one of the first languages for the specification of scenarios, not focusing strictly on testing. In addition to the main specification, Annex B [20] provides a formal specification of the semantics of MSC. Some of the features of MSC were subsequently adopted in OMG's UML in the form of *Sequence Diagram*. While allowing specialisation of the sequence diagram for different situations and domains, the loose semantics of UML and the different potential usages and interpretations of sequence diagrams [28] are a limiting factor for its use as a universal and consistent test description language.

The UTP [31] adds domain-specifics concepts related to testing thus enabling test modeling with UML. While it maintains the wide scope of UML, it also inherits the disadvantages associated with UML. The UP4TDL transfers the concepts of TDL in the UML world providing a more specialised and integrated means for test modeling with UML and inheriting the semantics from TDL.

The Precise UML [8] introduces a subset of UML and OCL for MBT seeking to address the open-ended interpretations of the semantics of different diagrams focusing on the specification of a behavioural model of the SUT. Its scope is narrowed down the generation of test cases out of an SUT model.

Approaches based on a concrete executable language with strict semantics, such as TTCN-3, enable the exchange of executable tests between partners. However, such languages are not well suited for review and high-level discussions due to the level of detail and the need to be able to understand the programming language-like syntax.

While various domain-specific testing languages have been developed, they all share a common set of challenges, including imprecise, informal, or no semantics, lack of standardisation, lack of comprehensive tool support, and poor interoperability with other tools. A common standardised meta-model for testing with associated well-defined semantics can help in consolidating approaches and providing a solid foundation for interoperability between tools.

5   Conclusion

TDL has been designed to address existing challenges and streamline the test development process. By abstracting away from implementation details, TDL enables test engineers to focus on the task of describing the test scenarios that cover the given test objectives, rather than work their way through a specific test execution framework. It can also make test specifications easier to review by non-testing experts. This is beneficial for the overall productivity and quality of test development both in industry and in the standardisation process.

In this article, we discussed the evolution of TDL from its conception into a multipart standard including a meta-model, standardised graphical syntax, exchange format, and a UML profile. To accelerate the adoption of TDL a reference implementation is provided both for users to get started with using TDL and for tool vendors to build their own solutions on top of it or integrate it with their existing products. To bring test purpose specifications into the modeling world and streamline the test specification process even further, an extension to TDL was developed to enable the specification of structured test objectives within TDL. The extension is based on TPLan and is targeted particularly towards supporting the standardised test development processes at ETSI.

The road ahead for TDL includes two main directions for the near future—mapping TDL to TTCN-3 and investigating the requirements for the adaptation of TDL to specific testing needs, such as security and performance testing. Mapping of TDL test descriptions to TTCN-3 test cases will enable generating of executable tests from TDL test descriptions in a semi-automatic way and allow re-using of existing TTCN-3 test tools and frameworks for test execution. A standardised mapping will leverage the impact of TDL and ensure that there is a consistent and common way of implementing test cases based on TDL test descriptions. This will significantly increase the efficiency of the test creation process and thus decrease cost and time-to-market of software products.

During the launch event at UCAAT 2015, multiple stakeholders expressed interest in adopting TDL for security and performance testing. However, they also requested certain features that they rely on. In addition, there are ongoing activities on security testing within TC-MTS. A next step is to identify and catalogue the requirements for the adaptation of TDL to different domains and types of testing in order to determine new language features and extensions.

The TDL working group within TC-MTS is dedicated to maintaining and updating TDL according to evolving user needs. With contributions from numerous partners from industry, academia, and standardisation, TDL is aiming to address testing needs from a wide spectrum of users across different domains.

Acknowledgement. The work on TDL has been funded by ETSI in the context of the STF projects 454, 476, and 492.

References

1. Docx4j. http://www.docx4java.org. Accessed 25 June 2016
2. Papyrus. https://www.eclipse.org/papyrus/. Accessed 20 June 2016
3. Robot framework. https://robotframework.org. Accessed 20 June 2016
4. Sirius. https://www.eclipse.org/sirius/. Accessed 20 June 2016
5. Tdl. http://tdl.etsi.org. Accessed 20 June 2016
6. Xtext. https://eclipse.org/Xtext/. Accessed 20 June 2016
7. Association for Standardisation of Automation, Measuring Systems (ASAM): Release Presentation: ASAM AE ATX V1.0.0, Automotive Test Exchange Format, July 2012. http://www.asam.net/nc/home/asam-standards.html
8. Bouquet, F., Grandpierre, C., Legeard, B., Peureux, F., Vacelet, N., Utting, M.: A subset of precise uml for model-based testing. In: Proceedings of the 3rd International Workshop on Advances in Model-based Testing, A-MOST 2007, pp. 95–104. ACM, New York (2007)
9. ETSI EG 203 130: Methods for Testing and Specification (MTS); Model-Based Testing (MBT); Methodology for Standardised Test Specification Development, v1.1.1. European Telecommunications Standards Institute (ETSI), Sophia-Antipolis, France, April 2013
10. ETSI ES 201 873–1: Methods for Testing and Specification (MTS); The Testing and Test Control Notation version 3; - Part 1: Core Language, v4.8.1. European Telecommunications Standards Institute (ETSI), Sophia-Antipolis, France, July 2016
11. ETSI ES 202 553: Methods for Testing and Specification (MTS); TPLan: A notation for expressing Test Purposes, v1.2.1. European Telecommunications Standards Institute (ETSI), Sophia-Antipolis, France, June 2009
12. ETSI ES 202 951: Methods for Testing and Specification (MTS); Model-Based Testing (MBT); Requirements for Modelling Notations, v1.1.1. European Telecommunications Standards Institute (ETSI), Sophia-Antipolis, France, July 2011
13. ETSI ES 203 119–1: Methods for Testing and Specification (MTS); The Test Description Language (TDL); Part 1: Abstract Syntax and Associated Semantics, v1.3.0. European Telecommunications Standards Institute (ETSI), Sophia-Antipolis, France, July 2016
14. ETSI ES 203 119–2: Methods for Testing and Specification (MTS); The Test Description Language (TDL); Part 2: Graphical Syntax, v1.2.0. European Telecommunications Standards Institute (ETSI), Sophia-Antipolis, France, July 2016
15. ETSI ES 203 119–3: Methods for Testing and Specification (MTS); The Test Description Language (TDL); Part 3: Exchange Format, v1.2.0. European Telecommunications Standards Institute (ETSI), Sophia-Antipolis, France, July 2016
16. ETSI ES 203 119–4: Methods for Testing and Specification (MTS); The Test Description Language (TDL); Part 4: Structured Test Objective Specification (Extension), v1.2.0. European Telecommunications Standards Institute (ETSI), Sophia-Antipolis, France, July 2016
17. ETSI ES 102 840: Methods for Testing and Specification (MTS); Model-Based Testing (MBT); Model-Based Testing in Standardisation, v1.2.1. European Telecommunications Standards Institute (ETSI), Sophia-Antipolis, France, February 2011
18. Grossmann, J., Müller, W.: A formal behavioral semantics for TestML. In: Second International Symposium on Leveraging Applications of Formal Methods, Verification and Validation, ISoLA 2006, pp. 441–448, November 2006
19. Guduvan, A., Waeselynck, H., Wiels, V., Durrieu, G., Fusero, Y., Schieber, M.: A meta-model for tests of avionics embedded systems. In: MODELSWARD 2013, Proceedings of the 1st International Conference on Model-Driven Engineering and Software Development, Barcelona, Spain, 19–21 February 2013, pp. 5–13 (2013)

20. International Telecommunication Union (ITU): Recommendation Z.120 Annex B: Formal Semantics of Message Sequence Chart (MSC), 04/98. Online: Z.120 Annex B (04/98), Standard document. URL: http://www.itu.int/rec/T-REC-Z. 120-199804-I!AnnB/en

21. International Telecommunication Union (ITU): Recommendation Z.120: Message Sequence Chart (MSC), 02/11. Online: Z.120 (02/11), Standard document. URL: http://www.itu.int/rec/T-REC-Z.120-201102-I/en

22. ISO: Road vehicles - Open Test sequence eXchange format - Part 1: General information and use cases. International ISO multipart standard No. 13209–1 (2011)

23. ISO: Road vehicles - Open Test sequence eXchange format - Part 2: Core data model specification and requirements. International ISO multipart standard No. 13209–2 (2012)

24. ISO: Road vehicles - Open Test sequence eXchange format - Part 3: Standard extensions and requirements. International ISO multipart standard No. 13209–3 (2012)

25. ISO/IEC: Information Technology - Open Systems Interconnection - Conformance testing methodology and framework - Part 1: General Concepts. International ISO/IEC multipart standard No. 9646–1 (1994–1998)

26. Kanstrén, T., Puolitaival, O.P., Rytky, V.M., Saarela, A., Keränen, J.S.: Experiences in setting up domain-specific model-based testing. In: 2012 IEEE International Conference on Industrial Technology (ICIT), pp. 319–324, March 2012

27. Kolovos, D.S., Paige, R.F., Polack, F.A.C.: On the evolution of OCL for capturing structural constraints in modelling languages. In: Abrial, J.-R., Glässer, U. (eds.) Rigorous Methods for Software Construction and Analysis. LNCS, vol. 5115, pp. 204–218. Springer, Heidelberg (2009). doi:10.1007/978-3-642-11447-2_13

28. Micskei, Z., Waeselynck, H.: The many meanings of UML 2 Sequence diagrams: a survey. Softw. Syst. Model. **10**(4), 489–514 (2010)

29. Object Management Group OMG: UML Profile For MARTE: Modeling and Analysis of Real-Time Embedded Systems, Version 1.1. OMG Document Number: formal/2011-06-02, Standard document, June 2011. URL: http://www.omg.org/spec/MARTE/1.1/

30. Object Management Group OMG: Object Constraint Language, Version 2.3.1. OMG Document Number: formal/2012-05-09, Standard document, May 2012. URL: http://www.omg.org/spec/OCL/2.3.1/

31. Object Management Group OMG: UML Testing Profile (UTP), Version 1.2. OMG Document Number: formal/2013-04-03, Standard document, April 2013. URL: http://www.omg.org/spec/UTP/1.2/

32. Object Management Group OMG: CCDL Whitepaper. Razorcat Technical Report, 23 January 2014, January 2014. http://www.razorcat.eu/PDF/Razorcat_Technical_Report_CCDL_Whitepaper_02.pdf

33. Object Management Group OMG: Meta Object Facility Core, Version 2.4.2. OMG Document Number: formal/2014-04-05, Standard document, April 2014. URL: http://www.omg.org/spec/MOF/2.4.2/

34. Object Management Group OMG: XML Metadata Interchange (XMI), Version 2.4.2. OMG Document Number: formal/2014-04-06, Standard document. URL: http://www.omg.org/spec/XMI/2.5.1/

35. Pajunen, T., Takala, T., Katara, M.: Model-based testing with a general purpose keyword-driven test automation framework. In: ICSTW, pp. 242–251. IEEE, March 2011

Object-Oriented Operational Semantics

Andreas Prinz[1][(✉)], Birger Møller-Pedersen[2], and Joachim Fischer[3]

[1] Department of ICT, University of Agder, Grimstad, Norway
andreas.prinz@uia.no
[2] Department of Informatics, University of Oslo, Oslo, Norway
birger@ifi.uio.no
[3] Department of Computer Science, Humboldt University, Berlin, Germany
fischer@informatik.hu-berlin.de

Abstract. Operational semantics is one way of providing meaning to an executable language. On a high level of abstraction, operational semantics means to define an interpreter or an abstract machine for the language. In this article, we review the concept of operational semantics in the scope of meta-model-based language definitions and identify challenges and issues. We provide a clean conceptual approach using an object-oriented runtime environment and state change operations, which relies on an underlying abstract virtual machine. We present the approach using a sample language.

1 Introduction

Modelling and meta-modelling are important approaches in the scope of OMG's MDA framework [8]. The table below shows the OMG four level architecture and the corresponding concepts for grammar-based definition of languages.

OMG level	Examples	Grammar example	OCL example
M3: meta-languages	MOF	EBNF	MOF
M2: languages	UML metamodel	Java grammar	OCL language
M1: models	UML model	a program	a formula
M0: instances	runtime objects	a run	a truth value

MDA is mostly concerned with models and programs, which are placed on OMG level M1. Extending MDA to domain-specific languages lifts the focus from M1 to M2, where languages are described.

We start with the understanding that a language on M2 is the collection of instances of the metaclasses that define the language together with their semantics. An instance of a programming language is called a program, and an instance of a modelling language is called a model. In this paper, we use the term language instance for both of them.

When (formally) describing languages on M2, one would typically consider the three aspects structure, presentation, and semantics. A language *structure* defines the set of all possible language instances and restrictions on this set.

© Springer International Publishing AG 2016
J. Grabowski and S. Herbold (Eds.): SAM 2016, LNCS 9959, pp. 132–147, 2016.
DOI: 10.1007/978-3-319-46613-2_9

It consists of metaclasses for its concepts. The *presentation* aspect can include descriptions of textual, graphical, and tabular presentations and a mixture of these. The *semantics* aspect describes the meaning of language instances. It can be given using different methods, e.g. describing language instance execution (execution or operational semantics), mapping into another language (transformation semantics), or defining a mathematical relation between input domain and output domain (denotational semantics).

This paper focuses on structural operational semantics (SOS), which is a way of directly defining how language constructs are executed by providing execution sequences (traces of configurations) as the semantics of a program. The traces are given by a set of inference rules, describing how state changes happen.

Let us consider configurations with three parts $< i, v, s >$, with a language instance i, a current value v, and a storage s. To describe the semantics of a statement **skip**, we use the following rule, which states that **skip** can be replaced by the empty language instance ($\bot$). The arrow denotes the state change relation.

$$\overline{< \mathbf{skip}, v, s > \to < \bot, v, s >}$$

SOS also allows introducing steps on different levels as shown with a sample inference rule handling an assignment of a location L with an expression E. The precondition of the rule is that the expression E is reduced with several steps ($\to^*$) to empty ($\bot$), thereby producing the value v' and the state s' (i.e. E evaluates to v'). The rule itself turns the assignment statement into a state update, where the value for the location L is changed to v'. So the assignment has one step of updating L, but underneath there are several intermediate steps of evaluating E. In this case we use the transitive closure of the steps ($\to^*$) instead of a single step ($\to$).

$$\frac{< E, v, s > \to^* < \bot, v', s' >}{< L := E, v, s > \to < \bot, v', s' \uplus \{L \mapsto v'\} >}$$

Defining SOS for **while** statements is a bit more involved, as the following example shows. The first rule tells us that the while statement does nothing in case the condition B evaluates to **false** in the current state. The second rule handles the case where B evaluates to **true**. In this case, we have to execute the body S followed by the complete loop.

$$\frac{< B, v, s > \to^* < \bot, false, s' >}{< \mathbf{while} \ B \ \mathbf{do} \ S, v, s > \to < \bot, v, s' >}$$

$$\frac{< B, v, s > \to * < \bot, true, s' >}{< \mathbf{while} \ B \ \mathbf{do} \ S, v, s > \to < S; \ \mathbf{while} \ B \ \mathbf{do} \ S, v, s' >}$$

This last example shows the roots of SOS in functional programming, where it is a normal idea that programs can change at runtime. For non-functional programming languages this style might not be as appealing. For object-oriented languages in particular, there are some inconveniences with this style of language definition.

1. In the programming world the program itself is typically considered to be fixed. As the last example shows, the language instances in the configurations are changed in order to indicate the position of execution. For imperative programming, one would rather think of a program counter to indicate the current position.
2. The state of execution is only partly considered. For object-oriented programming, a rich object-structure would be envisioned.
3. Typical runtime structures as program counters and call stack are not directly visible in SOS.

This paper tries to provide a way to describe operational semantics for an object-oriented situation. The paper is conceptual, and uses an example to explain the approach. It does not propose a concrete tool or language.

We continue this paper in Sect. 2 with a discussion of operational semantics and introduce the sample language in Sect. 3. We look into configurations in Sect. 4, and the relation of operational semantics to an execution platform in Sect. 5. After discussing execution semantics in Sect. 6, we summarize in Sect. 7.

2   Operational Semantics Description

There are several forms of operational semantics, in particular structural operational semantics (SOS - also called small-step semantics) [12] and natural semantics (also called big-step semantics) [7]. The first class focuses on the individual computation steps, while the second has more focus on how the computation results come about. For our purpose these differences are marginal and we use SOS as a reference. Operational semantics use the understanding that computations are sequences of runtime states, where the states are called configurations (see e.g. [4,7,10,12]). An SOS transition system is given by a set of configurations, a set of labels and labelled transitions, as well as a set of initial states and a set of final states. The typical idea of an SOS is to change configurations. Control information is often encoded by changes to the current language instance.

Similar elements are defined in other approaches for semantics definition. Rewrite-based approaches as K [13] and Maude [2] relate to configurations with the main aim to reduce the computation to its final value. Rascal [9] provides similar support as SOS, but is more code-oriented as also our approach.

For our definition of operational semantics, we use similar elements. We assume a structure aspect description of the language L. The structure could be defined using MOF (EMF) [3], but any other suitable language would work. Starting from the structure of L, we need to define two parts of semantics. First, we define the *structural part* of the runtime of L, i.e. its set of runtime states (configurations)[1], which we call runtime environment ([15]). Second, we have to handle the *dynamic part* (execution in terms of state changes).

---

[1] Please note the difference between structure of the language (its constructs, e.g. if-construct), and structure of the runtime (its runtime elements, e.g. a stack frame).

Commonly, the *structural part* is called instantiation semantics or structure-only semantics [15]. It defines how the elements of the language relate to runtime elements that can be created and used at runtime. For classes, this would typically be objects, while for methods, we envision stack frames. Depending on the language, also message buffers, or an exception stack could appear. In traditional operational semantics approaches, the main focus is on state changes, while the configurations are defined ad-hoc. However, in our object-oriented approach, configurations are very important.

The *dynamic part* describes the actual state changes that take place at runtime. All execution sequences are based on trivial changes, which are implied by the structural part. These trivial changes are creating new objects, setting values, and adding objects to collections. The dynamic part describes how to combine the trivial changes into bigger changes, in many cases a complete run.

In the operational semantics world, the main focus is on describing languages with a completely defined runtime behaviour, i.e. in any state the possible next states are determined. For example, this would be the case for Java. In practical terms, it means that the program runs to completion.

In interpreted languages and script languages, the combined trivial changes are not complete runs, but runs that can be put together by a user to even bigger runs. An extreme is a language like MOF, which only defines trivial state changes, which can be combined by a user using an editor. We discuss in Sect. 6 how state changes defined by a program are sequences and combinations of these trivial changes.

The main contribution of this paper is the handling of the structural part in Sect. 4, and its relation to the underlying machine and the structural part of this machine as discussed in Sect. 5. Operational semantics normally considers this underlying machine as given, and is not aware of its structure and behaviour. In our approach, the language designer may choose the features of the underlying machine and design the operational semantics combining trivial behaviour and underlying behaviour.

3   SLS - A Sample Language

In order to illustrate and discuss our approach, we consider SLS, a simplified version of SLX [6], an executable language for simulation of dynamic systems. SLS is based on principles of next-event-progressions. Models of existing or hypothetical systems are built in SLS by describing their components as *objects* of classes. For each *class* of objects, attributes and methods are defined describing the structure of the identified system components and their behavior.

SLS distinguishes active and passive classes (and objects). Passive objects are objects that can only be acted upon. Active objects have a *main()* method describing the sequence of executable statements by which they operate on their own. The behaviors of all existing active objects including the system specification determine at runtime the complete behavior of the system.

A *main()* method can only be called indirectly, by activating the corresponding active object from another active object: **activate** obj_reference.

If the *main*() executes a **wait**, the further execution of the active object is frozen. It can be continued by another object: **reactivate** obj_reference.

SLS features global dimensionless model time, i.e. time that is controlled by the execution of the system, and that is not external to the execution. This allows to mimic a real system by having multiple activities carried out at the same time. An active object can experience scheduled delays in model time using the **advance** construct. In SLS, model time is viewed as a succession of instants. At any given instant in model time, the runtime system of SLS processes one by one all events that take place at that time. After that, the runtime system advances the model time to the next imminent event time.

For each active object, the runtime system needs to keep track of at least three things: (1) the location of the next statement to be executed for the activity in the program, (2) the location of data local to that object, and (3) the model time at which the object is to resume (in case of scheduled delays).

In Fig. 1, we show a simple SLS example. Our system consists of two factories (objects of class *Factory*) who produce products (objects of class *Product*) with an individual production time. Both factories run in parallel and deposit their products in a common collection (*ProductList*). As soon as 1000 products are produced, the simulation run should stop with a printout.

The *Factory* is an active class and the *Product* is passive. The *productList* is also a passive object (essentially a set of *Products*). Both the current number of deposited products and the maximum number have been defined as attributes of the global system (active) class *Production*.

The *dynamic semantics* of SLS is a simulation of the system, sometimes called simulation semantics. The *execution* of the SLS sample system starts with an instance of the system specification (here *Production*). The actual run is started by calling the *main*() method of *Production*. At runtime, each active

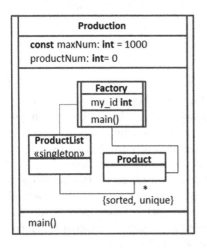

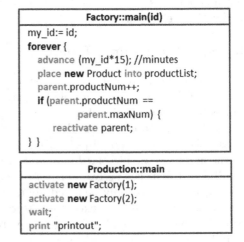

Fig. 1. Sample SLS specification

class (including the system specification) object has its own thread of control as well as a state. The following states are possible.

State	Semantics	Sorting principle
moving	The object is in the *moving* list. It is active or waits for execution. The time of the object is the current model time.	position in *moving* list
scheduled	The object is in the scheduled list. It is delayed by a defined time.	time of next move
waiting	The object is in the waiting list. It is suspended for unknown model time.	FIFO
terminated	*main()* of the object is finished; object cannot be reactivated	none

Now we look at the simulation run of our example, see the table below. The *Production* object is in the *moving* list, its time is 0 and the model time is 0. Its *main()* is called and generates two active *Factory* objects. Both of them get move time 0, and are placed in the *moving* list. Then *Production* executes a **wait** and is transferred into the *waiting* list, keeping its current execution state.

Time	Who	What	Delay until
0	Production	Create Factory(1) and Factory(2)	Infinite
0	Factory (1)	Delay 15	15
0	Factory (2)	Delay 30	30
15	Factory(1)	Create product-1	30
30	Factory(2)	Create product-2	60
30	Factory(1)	Create product-3	45
45	Factory(1)	Create product-4	60
...			
9975	Factory(1)	Create product-997	9990
9990	Factory(2)	Create product-998	10020
9990	Factory(1)	Create product-999	10005
10005	Factory(1)	Create product-1000, resume Production	10020
10005	Production	Finish simulation run	stop

The control now turns to the first entry of the *moving* list, the *Factory*(1) object. Its *main()* just delays for 15 units (we consider this to be minutes). Doing so, the *Factory*(1) will be placed into the *scheduled* list with move time 15. A similar action is done for *Factory*(2) with a move time of 30.

Because the *moving* list has become empty, it will be filled with all objects in the *scheduled* list with minimum move time. This also advances the model time to that time. Here, only *Factory*(1) is at time 15. It generates a new *Product* object, places it in the global *productList*, and delays for 15 more units. The further processing is indicated in the table. We show the runtime situation at system time 45 in Fig. 2.

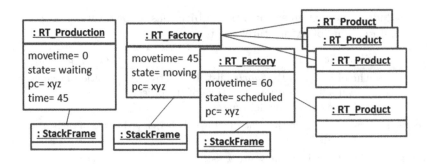

Fig. 2. Runtime situation at system time 45

Finally, the maximum is reached and the waiting *Production* is reactivated. After printing some information, the *main()* of *Production* finishes and this stops the simulation, because *Production* is the system instance.

4   Runtime Environment: Configurations

The runtime environment (RTE) is the set of possible states at runtime, i.e. configurations. Runtime states are purely structural and the state changes (Sect. 6) are based on them, see also [14]. The RTE depends on the language, i.e. the RTE description has to be done on level M2. In addition, the RTE can depend on the specific language instance, which has to be handled on level M1. We want to distinguish several kinds of RTE elements.

– The *read-only program* is included in the RTE, such that the execution can refer to the program.
– *Global elements* are only dependent on the language, e.g. predefined libraries, and program counter. They are independent of the specific program.
– *Local elements* are runtime elements that relate to language concepts and describe how these are instantiated. They are related to their respective concepts, but are independent of the language instance. There are three main cases as follows.
  1. *None-elements*, which means that the language concept does not have a runtime representation. An example would be statements and constant declarations in SLS. The relation from concept to runtime is 1:0.
  2. *One-elements* are extensions of concepts in terms of a 1:1 relationship. An example are locations for global variables in SLS, or the instance of the SLS system specification.
  3. *Many-elements* are also related to concepts, but with the possibility of many instances of the same element. A property of a passive SLS class is an example - it exists for each instance of the class. A stack frame for a method is another example, which exists for each call of the method. They have a 1:n relation from concept to runtime.

– *Dependent elements* are similar to local elements, but they depend on the specific language instance. Active and passive classes in SLS are examples here. They cannot be defined statically on level M2. Instead, on M2 a mapping from the language concepts to the runtime structures can be defined.

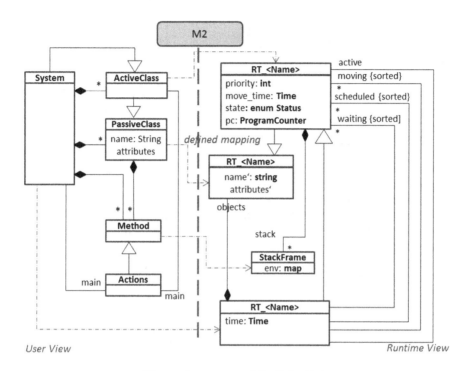

Fig. 3. Structure and RTE for SLS

When defining the RTE of SLS, we start at level M2. As the RTE defines instantiation semantics, it defines the transition from M1 to M0. We assume an underlying mechanism that can instantiate objects from classes, which is called MOF-VM. It is explained in more detail in the next section. For the RTE we describe which MOF-VM classes to use on M1, which implies the possible MOF-VM objects on M0. The crossing of the level boundary between M1 and M0 is done by the MOF-VM semantics. At level M2 it is not possible to define M1 classes. Therefore, at M2 we define a mapping from language concepts to RTE (see Fig. 3). This mapping is applied for the actual language instance, which yields the RTE at level M1 (see Fig. 4). Being a mapping, the RTE is defined on M2, and still depends on the language instance on M1. In Fig. 3, the *dependent elements* are active and passive classes as well as the system. The dependency in all cases are the available attributes. Please note that the mapping for SLS classes is not as trivial as for UML classes, as we need to take care of concurrency by including program counter (pc), call stack and time in the classes. For methods, we define a *local element* mapping to stack frames.

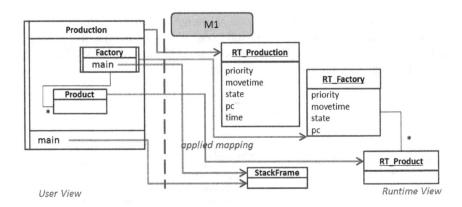

Fig. 4. RTE for the sample language instance

Figure 4 shows how the RTE mapping is applied to our sample language instance at level M1. The RTE mapping defined at M2 is now applied, and yields the MOF-VM classes *RT_Factory*, *RT_Product*, *RT_Production*, and *StackFrame*. Using this RTE, it is straightforward to instantiate the MOF-VM classes, yielding the situation at time 45 at level M0 as shown in Fig. 2.

This way, the RTE is defined at M2 as a mapping from the language instance on M1 to MOF-VM classes on M1, which then get instantiated at M0. Any mapping notation can be used, for example QVT [11]. In this article, we use an ad-hoc notation in order to explain the main idea.

The same approach is used for handling initial states and final states. All these states have to be formed according to the RTE. They are also given by mappings that are defined on level M2, and applied on level M1. Finally, initial states and final states are used on level M0.

5   Execution Platform: MOF-VM

Instantiation semantics is based on an underlying mechanism that provides basic instantiation. This could be very low level as in machine code, where an indication of a memory area leads to the provision of actual memory, thereby providing very simple instantiation. It could be more high level like a Java virtual machine, where a class instantiation mechanism is available. We assume a machine that can instantiate objects from classes, which we call MOF-VM ([5]). MOF-VM instantiation is the only way to do instantiation, such that all instances existing are MOF-VM objects, including the objects on M2, M1, and M0.

In Fig. 5 we show how the language definition and the instantiation semantics work together for the semantics of the M3 language MOF. The concepts of SLS are defined on level M2 as instances of the *Class* concept of MOF (which is defined on level M3), e.g. the class *ActiveClass* on the top left. This class has a MOF-VM RTE as defined for MOF, which is shown on the top right part of Fig. 5. Remember that MOF-VM is independent of the levels and provides the

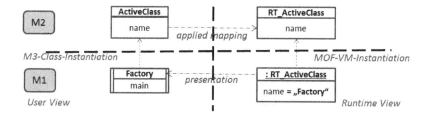

Fig. 5. MOF-VM instantiation versus language instantiation.

general way of crossing from one level to the one below. Using *RT_ActiveClass*, it is possible to create instances using MOF-VM semantics, and provide an object with name *Factory* (bottom right). This object can be presented using the custom presentation for *ActiveClass* (within SLS). This leads to the presentation on the bottom left of Fig. 5.

On the left side, *Factory* is a MOF instance of *ActiveClass*. This language-defined instantiation is based on the MOF-VM instantiation (right side) via the applied mapping and the presentation.

Going one level up, the applied mapping is based on the defined mapping on M3 (Fig. 6). There will be all of the three *presentation*, *defined* and *applied* mappings on the levels M2 and M3; for better understandability, we have only shown the relevant ones.

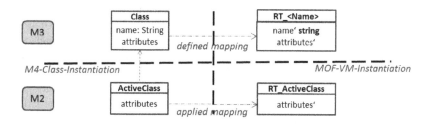

Fig. 6. Defined mapping versus applied mapping.

It is important to be aware that the underlying machine itself has already some built-in runtime structure that may or may not be used by the definition of the operational semantics. When we look at SOS as a language itself, the SOS-VM is functional[2], which means we expect it to be able to keep local values, and to handle (recursive) functions (see also Sect. 6). Look at the following SOS rule for a sequence construct to understand what that could imply.

---

[2] SOS as a language (on M3) is functional, not the language described using SOS (on M2). Of course, SOS can be used to describe all kinds of languages.

$$< S_1, v_0, s_0 > \rightarrow * < \bot, v_1, s_1 >$$
$$< S_2, v_1, s_1 > \rightarrow * < \bot, v_2, s_2 >$$
$$\overline{< S_1; S_2, v_0, s_0 > \rightarrow < \bot, v_2, s_2 >}$$

The precondition of the rule is that a statement S_1 is evaluated to v_1, and S_2 to v_2. Then the sequence of S_1 and S_2 is evaluated to v_2 in one step. The steps inside S_1 and S_2 are intermediate steps in this case. In this rule, it is not clear where the value v_2 is stored – it is implicit in the underlying machine. This is possible, because the SOS-VM allows to transfer the value from the precondition (intermediate steps: above the line) to the top-level step (below the line) by just giving its name. This way the local intermediate value is kept in the RTE of the SOS-VM, and not in the RTE of the language. Similarly, the evaluation of a statement can imply stack frames to be created. This is not explicit here, because the SOS-VM facilities are used. Again, this means this part of the RTE is hidden by using the SOS-VM.

The language developer has to decide where to place the RTE elements like stack frames and local intermediate values. Either they are visible in the defined RTE, or they are hidden and implicit by using the SOS-VM or MOF-VM.

6   Run Versus Step: Dynamic Semantics

As discussed in Sect. 2, an operational semantics has to describe configurations, initial and final states, as well as state changes. In this section, we discuss state changes based on the configurations defined in Sect. 4.

The RTE object structure has an implied navigation along its links, including the navigation from objects to the language instance itself, and back. We assume that the navigation is rich enough to also include basic elementary functions of the underlying basic data types (MOF-VM data types), like boolean, integer, and collection operations. This way, the navigation is a query facility allowing to extract values in a very general sense (r-values). Furthermore, the navigation allows to extract locations, where it is possible to change the state (l-values). Simple updates are also implied by the RTE, and form the trivial state changes.

Defining executions is the combination of these trivial state changes into larger changes. It is the language that defines the granularity of the state changes.

For the object-oriented version, we use an adaptation of abstract state machines (ASM) [1] as the meta-language to define state changes. ASM normally come with an own underlying sub-language for the description of locations and values, but here this is implied by the RTE as follows.

– The RTE provides expressions (navigation/queries) and locations including the notation **new**(C) to create a new element of a MOF-VM class C.
– An RTE update has the following syntax. <location> := <expression>

On top of these trivial updates, we use the following ASM constructs for grouping of updates. As the semantics of the constructs is obvious, we do not describe it here and refer the reader to [1] in case of doubt. In ASM, an instruction is called *rule*.

- Decision instruction: if <expression> then <rule> [else <rule>]
- Parallel execution: <rule> <rule>
- Sequential execution: <rule> seq <rule>
- Named rule: <name>(<name-list>) { <rule> }
- Calls of named rules: <name>(<expression-list>)
- Local names: let <name> = <value> in <rule>
- The ASM constructs **forall**, **extend**, and **choose** are not used here.

ASM normally have a global view on state changes, and would define the semantics as a collection of global rules. As we are interested in an object-oriented approach, we attach the rules to the appropriate classes. These classes can be RTE classes or metamodel classes. As an example for RTE classes, we show methods of the *RT_Factory* runtime class. Essentially, the system (*RT_Factory*) delegates the handling of program counter and stack to the currently active object. Please compare with the runtime structure in Fig. 3.

```
RT_Factory::setPC(newPC) { active.pc:= newPC }
RT_Factory::setValue(idx,v) { active.stack.top.env.add(idx,v) }
RT_Factory::getValue(i) { return active.stack.top.env.value(i) }
RT_Factory::push(stackframe) { active.stack.push(stackframe) }
RT_Factory::pop() { active.stack.pop() }
```

We explain our approach with the three SLS statements shown in Fig. 7.

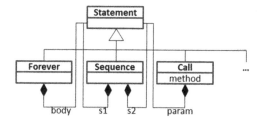

Fig. 7. Some SLS statements shown as part of the SLS metamodel

In SOS, this abstract syntax would be formalized as follows, where S are instances of statements, and M is a method name.

```
statement ::= forever S | S1;S2 | call M(S)
```

There are two possible ways of defining state changes in our approach, which we call STEP and RUN. Doing the STEP variant means to specify the steps of the language soleily based on changes in the RTE without using MOF-VM RTE. The RUN approach is to specify the whole execution including all the steps, possibly making use of the MOF-VM RTE. It is often easier to define the RUN approach, but it will hide part of the RTE as it is kept in the underlying MOF-VM RTE. We explain the operational semantics using the STEP and the

RUN approach by defining methods $step()$ and $run()$, and contrast it with the SOS version. Please note, that STEP and RUN are alternatives, and in a real case the language developer would select one of the two (and not both).

The semantics of the **forever** statement has to handle two situations. (1) When entering a forever loop, the first step is to enter the body. (2) After finishing the body, the forever has to be re-entered again.

The SOS semantics of it is given with a rule that just calls the *body* and then calls the **forever** again. Thus, in SOS both situations are handled by a change to the program code.

$$< \textbf{forever } body, v, s > \rightarrow < body;\ \textbf{forever } body, v, s >$$

The definition using RUN is very similar to SOS, the main difference being the attachment of the rule to the syntax class. Both situations are handled by calls to the $run()$ method. A sequencing of the underlying machine (**seq**) is used to separate these two (big) steps.

```
Forever::run() { body.run() seq self.run() }
```

In STEP, the current position in the execution has to be handled explicitly. Situation (1) is covered by the $step()$ routine of class *Forever*, setting the program counter. Situation (2) is covered when the inner statement is finished. In this case, a continuation has to be provided by its parent, which is done with the $nextPC()$ method of class *Forever*. The definition of the semantics of the sequence construct shows the use of the $nextPC()$. We use $RTroot$ in order to refer to the root of the runtime environment of type $RT\_Factory$. This example shown nicely how the code of the syntax class *Forever* interacts with the code of the RTE class $RT\_Factory$.

```
Forever::step() { RTroot.setPC(body) }
Forever::nextPC(node) { return self; }
```

The semantics of the *SLS sequence statement* includes three situations to handle. (1) When entering the sequence, we start with the first statement. (2) When the first statements is finished, we continue with the second statement. (3) When the second statement is finished, the result of the sequence is the result of the second statement.

In SOS, it is given by the following two tules. The first rule handles the case where the first statement can be reduced to an empty statement starting from a state s. In this case, it is sufficient to start the second statement from this new state, implementing the second situation. If this is not possible, the second rule describes that the first step in the execution of the sequence is the first step of the first statement, which implements the first situation. The second statement is unchanged in this case. The third situation does not need an extra handling in this specification, as the value of the second statement is automatically the final value. A different formulation is discussed in Sect. 5.

$$\frac{< s1, v, s > \rightarrow < \perp, v', s' >}{< s1; s2, v, s > \rightarrow < s2, v', s' >} \qquad \frac{< s1, v, s > \rightarrow < s1', v', s' >}{< s1; s2, v, s > \rightarrow < s1'; s2, v', s' >}$$

In RUN, the first two situations are handled with a call to the $run()$ methods of $s1$ and $s2$. This is achieved with the sequence operator of ASM, thereby introducing an intermediate step. The third situation is implied as with SOS.

```
Sequence::run() { s1.run() seq s2.run() }
```

In STEP, the situation is more tricky. The first situation is handled in the $step()$ method, where the pc is set to the first statement. The second situation is handled in the first branch of the $nextPC()$ method, where the continuation after $s1$ is $s2$. The third situation is handled in the second branch of $nextPC()$. The value of $s2$ is retrieved, and set as value of the sequence itself. Then the next step is given by the continuation of the parent.

```
Sequence::step() { RTroot.setPC(s1) }
Sequence::nextPC(node) {
    if (node==s1) then return s2
    else
        let value = RTroot.getValue(s2) in
            RTroot.setValue(self, value)
            return nextPC(parent)
}
```

Finally, we look at the handling of a *method call*, for simplicity with just one parameter. The following situations have to be handled for the semantics. (1) The value of the parameter is evaluated. (2) The value of the parameter is attached to the name of the parameter. (3) The body of the method is executed. (4) The return value of the body is the value of the call.

SOS uses a precondition to handle the first situation, introducing intermediate steps. The second situation is done by extending the name mapping with the appropriate name and value for the call of the body. The third situation is given by replacing the active code. Finally, the fourth situation is implied by the handling of return values in SOS-VM.

$$\frac{< e, v, s >\rightarrow * <\bot, v', s' >}{< \textbf{call } m(e), v, s >\rightarrow< m.body, v', s' \uplus \{m.parName \mapsto v'\} >}$$

In RUN, the first situation is covered by a call to the $run()$ of the parameter, introducing intermediate steps with the underlying sequence operator (**seq**). The value is attached to the name using the underlying parameter handling of the $run()$ method of *body*, which also handles the third situation. Finally, the result value handling is implied by the return result handling of MOF-VM.

```
Call::run() { value := param.run() seq method.body.run(value) }
```

In STEP, the first situation is given by the $step()$ method. The second and third situations are handled in the first alternative of $nextPC()$. Here, a new stack frame is created in order to keep the parameter value. Then the program counter is set to the *body*. Finally, the fourth situation is handled in the second alternative of $nextPC()$. The stack frame is removed and the value is attached to the call. The next step is given by the continuation of the parent.

```
Call::step() { RTroot.setPC(param) }
Call::nextPC(node) {
    if (node==param) then
        let sf = new(StackFrame) in
        let value = RTroot.getValue(param) in
            sf.env.add(method.parameter.definition, value)
            RTroot.push(sf)
            return method.body
    else //return from call
        let value = RTroot.getValue(method.body) in
            RTroot.pop() seq RTroot.setValue(self,value)
            return nextPC(parent)
```

The formulation of *run*() and *step*() can also be done using other formalisms with sufficient formality, e.g. UML activities or Java code.

7 Summary

In this paper, we have discussed what operational semantics entails and how it can be defined in an object-oriented setting. We have distinguished between structure semantics and dynamic semantics, where structure semantics describes the instantiation of the language constructs and dynamic semantics involves collections of trivial state changes. For both kinds of semantics, it is essential to rely on an underlying abstract machine providing some kind of semantics. We have used the combination of MOF-VM and ASM as such a machine.

The proposed operational semantics is object-oriented because it gives a clear indication of the runtime structure used with all the objects and their connection to each other. In contrast to standard SOS, it allows to have a clear distinction between the RTE of the language and the RTE of MOF-VM.

The paper has detailed the relation between operational semantics with its two parts and the underlying machine. The semantics is described using methods attached to runtime objects and to syntax objects. It is the task of the language designer to decide where to place the semantic methods.

The RTE provides explicit elements for runtime configurations, thereby solving all the problems as indicated in the introduction. The next step is to turn this approach into a meta-language for defining operational semantics and implementing it in an appropriate tool.

Acknowledgements. We thank the anonymous reviewers for their helpful questions and remarks.

References

1. Börger, E., Stärk, R.F.: Abstract State Machines: A Method for High-Level System Design and Analysis. Springer, Secaucus (2003)
2. Clavel, M., Duran, F., Eker, S., Lincoln, P., Marti-Oliet, N., Meseguer, J., Quesada, J.F.: Rewriting logic and its applications maude: specification and programming in rewriting logic. Theor. Comput. Sci. **285**(2), 187–243 (2002)
3. OMG Editor. OMG Meta Object Facility (MOF) Core Specification Version 2.4.2. Technical report, Object Management Group (2014)
4. Felleisen, M., Findler, R.B., Flatt, M.: Semantics Engineering with PLT Redex, 1st edn. The MIT Press, Cambridge (2009)
5. Gjøsæter, T., Prinz, A., Nytun, J.P.: MOF-VM: instantiation revisited. In: Proceedings of the 4th International Conference on Model-Driven Engineering and Software Development, pp. 137–144 (2016)
6. Henriksen, J.O.: SLX: the X is for extensibility [simulation software]. In: Proceedings of Simulation Conference, Winter, vol. 1, pp. 183–190 (2000)
7. Kahn, G.: Natural semantics. In: Brandenburg, F.J., Vidal-Naquet, G., Wirsing, M. (eds.) STACS 1987. LNCS, vol. 247, pp. 22–39. Springer, Heidelberg (1987). doi:10.1007/BFb0039592
8. Kleppe, A., Warmer, J.: MDA Explained. Addison-Wesley, Boston (2003)
9. Klint, P., Storm, T., Vinju, J.: EASY meta-programming with rascal. In: Fernandes, J.M., Lämmel, R., Visser, J., Saraiva, J. (eds.) GTTSE 2009. LNCS, vol. 6491, pp. 222–289. Springer, Heidelberg (2011). doi:10.1007/978-3-642-18023-1_6
10. Mosses, P.D.: Structural operational semantics modular structural operational semantics. J. Logic Algebr. Program. **60**, 195–228 (2004)
11. OMG. Meta Object Facility (MOF) 2.0 Query/View/Transformation Specification, Version 1.1, January 2011
12. Plotkin, G.D.: A structural approach to operational semantics. Technical report DAIMI FN-19, AARHUS UNIVERSITY (DK) (1981)
13. Roşu, G., Şerbănuţă, T.F.: An overview of the K semantic framework. J. Logic Algebr. Program. **79**(6), 397–434 (2010)
14. Scheidgen, M., Fischer, J.: Human comprehensible and machine processable specifications of operational semantics. In: Akehurst, D.H., Vogel, R., Paige, R.F. (eds.) ECMDA-FA 2007. LNCS, vol. 4530, pp. 157–171. Springer, Heidelberg (2007). doi:10.1007/978-3-540-72901-3_12
15. Wider, A.: Model transformation languages for domain-specific workbenches. Ph.D. thesis, Humboldt-Universität zu Berlin (2015)

Model Driven Upgrade Campaign Generation for Highly Available Systems

Oussama Jebbar[1], Margarete Sackmann[1], Ferhat Khendek[1(✉)], and Maria Toeroe[2]

[1] Concordia University, Montreal, Canada
{ojebbar,m_sackma,khendek}@encs.concordia.ca
[2] Ericsson Inc., Montreal, Canada
maria.toeroe@ericsson.com

Abstract. Highly available applications undergo upgrades like any software system. Because of the high availability requirement, such applications cannot be taken offline for performing the upgrade and then put back into service. The upgrade has to be performed while the application is providing services, and it has to avoid service outage as much as possible. The Service Availability Forum (SAF) has defined and standardized a set of middleware services to support high availability and enable application portability. Among these services, the Software Management Framework (SMF) is in charge of the upgrade, mainly through the execution of the upgrade campaign specification, which is seen as an orchestration of the upgrade. The structure and concepts of an upgrade campaign, like procedures, steps and upgrade methods, are defined in the standard. The way these concepts are applied to the elements of an application in a given campaign defines the orchestration of their upgrade and needs to be thought through. For this one has to take into account the dependencies between the elements of the application. Indeed, breaking these dependencies is the main source of outage during upgrade. In this paper we propose a model driven approach for the generation of upgrade campaign specifications taking into account these dependencies, the initial system configuration and the target one.

Keywords: High availability · Upgrade campaign · Service Availability Forum (SAF) · Availability Management Framework (AMF) · Software Management Framework (SMF) · Dependencies · Model driven engineering

1 Introduction

Software systems may undergo upgrades for various reasons, including the upgrade of software versions and fine-tuning of the configuration to improve performance. For systems with the constraint of providing highly-available services, i.e. services available 99.999 % of the time, the upgrade has to be performed while the system is providing its services. The Service Availability Forum (SAF) [1], a consortium of several computing and telecommunication companies, defined and standardized a set of middleware services for enabling the building and the management of highly available application services using Commercial-Off-The-Shelf (COTS) components. Among the SAF middleware services, the Availability Management Framework (AMF) [2] manages the availability of

© Springer International Publishing AG 2016
J. Grabowski and S. Herbold (Eds.): SAM 2016, LNCS 9959, pp. 148–163, 2016.
DOI: 10.1007/978-3-319-46613-2_10

the redundant components composing the application while the Software Management Framework (SMF) [3] is responsible for the live upgrade of this application.

The upgrade of a system from a source configuration to a target one, by upgrading software versions, adding and/or removing application elements, is performed by SMF according to a roadmap, which is known as the upgrade campaign specification [3]. An upgrade campaign specification is composed of a set of procedures, which are composed of a set of steps. Each procedure has an upgrade method, rolling or single step, and a scope. The rolling upgrade method is very useful for highly available systems built with redundant entities as one can roll the upgrade over the redundant entities. Coming up with such a roadmap, its procedures with their upgrade methods and execution order that avoid/minimize service outage during execution is not an easy task. One has to take carefully into account the dependencies among the entities involved in the upgrade as breaking these dependencies is the main source of service outage during upgrades.

In this paper, we propose a model driven approach for the generation of upgrade campaign specifications. The approach takes as input a source configuration, a target configuration, and a set of Entity Types Files (ETFs) [3], and through a set of transformations generates an optimized upgrade campaign specification. The first transformation determines the difference between the configurations and accordingly the upgrade actions needed to migrate the system from the source to the target configuration. However, these actions cannot be performed in any order or grouping, and this has to take carefully into account the dependencies between the involved entities as well as the well-formedness of an upgrade campaign specification as described in the standard. This is achieved through a set of transformations that take into account all these aspects.

Our approach consists of a set of transformations to automate the process of the generation as well as a set of metamodels that describe the different models involved. With a model driven approach, the focus is mainly on including the domain knowledge in the transformations rather than investigating how this knowledge should be applied to achieve a good performance in the generation process. Thus, we are only enabling an implementation, which would be both performant and cost-effective, we do not strive for it. The model driven approach also provides a good basis for further abstractions to widen the scope of applicability in the future.

The rest of the paper is organized as follows, Sect. 2 provides the necessary background on the SAF standards, AMF and SMF. In Sect. 3 we introduce the different metamodels used in our approach. In Sect. 4, we present our approach for upgrade campaign specification generation and discuss the different transformations as well as the prototype implementation. Before concluding in Sect. 6, we briefly review the related work in Sect. 5.

2 Background

Out of the SAF middleware services, AMF [2] and SMF [3] are most relevant to system upgrades. AMF is responsible for managing the components composing an application to maintain service availability. Components are the smallest building blocks of an AMF application and can provide basic services, called component service instances (CSI). Components are logically grouped into service units (SU) that provide service instances (SI) composed of the CSIs of their components. SUs are in turn grouped into service groups to provide redundancy and protect services. To provide a highly available service, an SG must have at least two SUs, so that in case of failure the SIs it provides/protects can be shifted from the faulty SU to the redundant healthy one. An SU may be active – provide the service – or standby, which does not provide service but might receive state information from the active SU so that service continuity can be ensured in case of failure. An application consists of a number of SGs that are deployed on the nodes of a cluster. An SG may have SUs on each node in the cluster, or on a subset of nodes referred to as a Node Group (NG). AMF does not provide APIs for querying and modifying the AMF configuration, this has to be done via another service called Information Model Management (IMM) service [4].

On the other hand, SMF [3] orchestrates the upgrade following a roadmap called an upgrade campaign specification, which contains the changes to be done in IMM and how these changes should be done. An upgrade campaign specification describes one and only one upgrade campaign by providing its initialization actions, campaign body, and wrap-up actions. Initialization actions are taken at the beginning of the campaign to prepare the system for the upgrade and for the changes that will take place during the execution of the body of the campaign. Wrap-up actions are the post campaign and verification actions that should take place at the end of the campaign. The campaign body is specified as a set of upgrade procedures. In addition to proper initialization and wrap-up actions, each procedure has a set of attributes, a scope, an upgrade method, actions to be performed, and attributes common for its steps. The upgrade scope identifies the entities that will be impacted by the upgrade procedure and it can be either a set of Nodes, a set of SUs, or a set of Components. SMF supports only two upgrade methods: 1) the single step upgrade method in which all the entities targeted in the scope are upgraded at once; and 2) the rolling upgrade method which is commonly used for upgrading highly available systems as it rolls over the redundant entities to be upgraded, thus enabling some entities to provide the service while other redundant entities are being upgraded. At runtime, based on the specified scope and upgrade method, SMF decomposes every procedure into the appropriate number of steps and executes these procedures step by step taking out of service some entities referred to as the deactivation unit (DU) at the beginning of the step and at the end of the upgrade step putting back into service the appropriate ones, which are referred to as activation unit (AU). The order of procedures is specified using the execution level attribute, the procedures with lower execution levels are executed before the procedures with higher execution levels, while procedures of the same execution level can be executed in any order or simultaneously depending on the SMF implementation.

From software delivery perspective, every software bundle is accompanied by an ETF file [3] which describes the components and other entity types the bundle delivers and the service types they can provide. ETF files are provided by the software vendor, and contain data about the deployment constraints of a given delivered type.

3 Modeling Framework

We designed several metamodels used in the generation of upgrade campaign specifications. We briefly describe them in this section.

3.1 Dependencies Metamodel

The dependencies metamodel (shown in Fig. 1) captures the different dependencies that may exist between entities in an AMF configuration and their relations. As discussed in [5] it is important to characterize these different dependencies as they impose certain ordering during the upgrade of the involved entities. We have three categories: directed, symmetrical and collocation dependencies. The metamodel of Fig. 1 allows capturing not only the dependencies existing in a given configuration but also the different entities involved. In the following we describe briefly the dependencies:

- SI dependency: this dependency exists between two SGs, where one of them (called Sponsor SG) is protecting a sponsor SI and the other (called Dependent SG) is protecting a dependent SI.
- Proxy-Proxied dependency: the proxy-proxied is a deployment pattern which is part of the AMF standard. This pattern consists of a component (Proxy) that implements AMF management operations to extend the control over components (Proxied) that do not implement the AMF APIs. Thus, the proxy-proxied dependency exists between two SGs, one of them (Sponsor SG) is composed of SUs that contain the proxy components, and the other one (Dependent SG) is composed of SUs that contain the proxied components.
- Instantiation dependency: This is a dependency between components belonging to the same SU, and which have to be instantiated in a given order. The component that has to be instantiated first is the sponsor while the one that must be instantiated later is the dependent.
- CSI dependency: between CSIs of the same SI. The sponsor CSI shall be assigned before the dependent CSI.
- Container-Contained dependency: the container-contained is yet another deployment pattern defined in the AMF standard. It implies a lifecycle dependency between two components, meaning that one component (the contained) cannot exist or offer the service without the existence and service of another component (the container) in the same physical node. This dependency captures the container as being the sponsor and it is identified by its SG and its type. The contained is identified similarly and plays the role of the dependent in this dependency.
- Component-CSI dependency: for some components, imposing an order of instantiation is impossible given the nature of these components. The AMF solution for this case is to order the assignment of CSIs instead of the instantiation of the components. So, this dependency is used for components of this kind, and in this case a component (dependent) is said to depend on another component (sponsor) if: 1) all the CSIs that can be handled by the dependent depend on at least one CSI handled by the sponsor;

and 2) none of the CSIs that can be handled by the sponsor depend on any of the CSIs that can be handled by the dependent.

- SU collocation dependency: exists between components in the same SU.
- Node collocation dependency: exists between SUs configured for the same Node, or SGs that have a Node in common.
- Node Group collocation dependency: exists between SGs sharing the same Node Group.
- Container collocation dependency: this dependency is derived from container-contained dependency, and identifies the pairs of (dependent type, dependent SG) that share the same pair of (sponsor type, sponsor SG).
- Peer dependency: exists between components of SUs of the same SG.
- Service protection dependency: this dependency exists between SUs of the same SG as they all together protect services assigned to the SG.

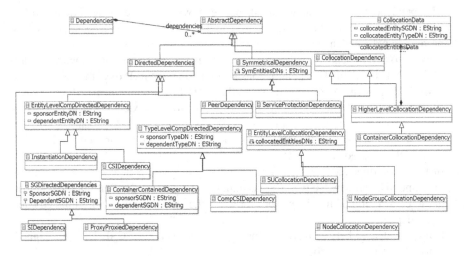

Fig. 1. The dependencies metamodel.

3.2 Change Metamodel

The change metamodel (shown in Fig. 2) is used to describe the changes to be performed to take the system from the source configuration to the target configuration. These changes, can be either IMM configuration related changes (ModifyImm, AddToImm, RemoveFromImm) or software related changes (SoftwareChange).

Software related changes (SoftwareChange) can be for the installation (SwInstallation) or removal (SwRemoval) of software bundles in/from a set of nodes (UCGNode).

The proposed metamodel captures two key aspects of the configuration related changes:

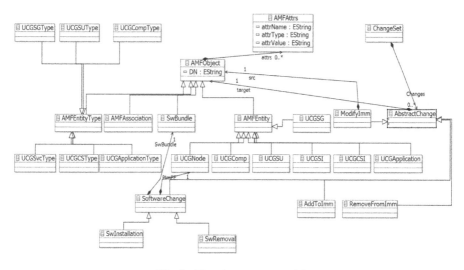

Fig. 2. The change metamodel.

- The nature of a change: Since the input data for a change depends on its nature (addition, removal, or modification), the change metamodel captures all the possible cases from the addition (which requires all the attributes), to the removal (which only requires the target's name).
- The nature of the target of a change: the target of a change can be an AMF entity, an AMF entity type, or an AMF association. The placement of this change in the right section of the upgrade campaign specification is done based on this information. This will be elaborated further in Sect. 4 where we discuss the generation of upgrade campaign specifications.

3.3 Upgrade Campaign Specification Metamodel

The upgrade campaign specification metamodel (shown in Fig. 3) captures the concepts needed to describe a SAF compliant upgrade campaign specification as specified in [3]. It is described using upgrade objects (UCG_UpgradeObject). Every upgrade object is defined through its initialization, body, and wrap up sections. The main upgrade objects (UCG_UpgradeObject) used to specify an upgrade campaign are:

- The upgrade campaign (UCG_UpgradeCampaign): It is the root element of the upgrade campaign specification.
- The upgrade procedure (UCG_UpgradeProcedure): The upgrade objects composing the upgrade campaign's body specifying the changes that the SMF engine should perform and how it should perform them.

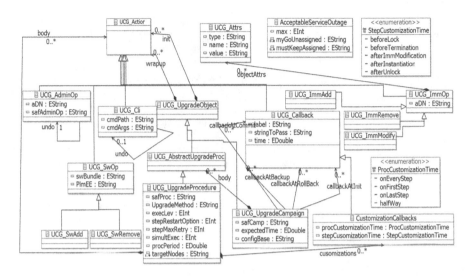

Fig. 3. The upgrade campaign specification metamodel.

The upgrade campaign body as mentioned earlier is composed of upgrade procedures, while the upgrade procedure body is composed of the upgrade step description, which is an ordered list of upgrade actions (UCG_Action) and their respective target entities. The initialization and the wrap up sections are also composed of ordered upgrade actions. An upgrade action can be:

- An IMM configuration related operation (UCG_ImmOp): like addition, removal or modification of an object in IMM representing an AMF entity.
- A software related action (UCG_SwOp): like installations and removals of software bundles; usually called based on the software bundle DN and the node on which the installation should be done (PlmEE).
- An administrative operation (UCG_AdminOp): administrative operations (Lock, Unlock, Lock-Instantiation, and Unlock-Instantiation), defined in the AMF standard, are called on AMF entities based on their DNs. For every administrative operation we should specify how it should be done in the upgrade and at its rollback (doing and undoing of the administrative operation).
- A Callback (UCG_Callback): called on entities deployed in the system, based on their DNs.
- A CLI Command (UCG_Cli): called using the Command Line Interface (CLI). A CLI command is specified using the path of the command, its arguments, and the nodes on which it should be called. For each command, we specify how it is called at upgrade and at its rollback (doing and undoing the command).

4   Upgrade Campaign Specification Generation

We first give an overall view of the generation process before describing each transformation.

4.1   Overall View of the Generation Process

The overall view of our approach is shown in Fig. 4. The starting point is the input which consists of:

- A source configuration: The configuration describing the system as it is currently.
- A target configuration: Describing the new desired configuration of the system.
- ETFs: Describing the software available in the software repository, the software bundles deployed and to be deployed in the system, as well as the AMF types they can provide.

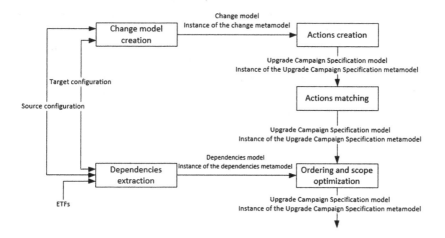

Fig. 4.   Overall view of the approach.

As shown in Fig. 4 the approach consists of several transformations, each one realizing a specific function required in the generation process. The first transformation consists of extracting the dependencies between the AMF entities into a dependencies model (instance of the dependencies metamodel) from each of the configurations and the provided ETFs. Using a second transformation, we create a change model (instance of the change metamodel). This is based on the work done in [6] for the comparison of two configuration models. It has been adapted to provide the difference as a change model that describes the changes to be performed on the source configuration to obtain the target configuration. From this change model, and using a third transformation, we generate an elementary upgrade campaign specification model (instance of the upgrade campaign specification metamodel) containing an upgrade campaign element for each change in the change model. This upgrade campaign specification model goes then through yet another transformation which groups upgrade campaign elements to be performed in the same upgrade procedure. For each group, all the upgrade campaign elements are merged into an upgrade procedure and the elements not required anymore are deleted from the upgrade campaign specification model. Finally, the resulting upgrade campaign model is refined using a fifth transformation that takes into consideration the dependencies between the system's entities to create a partial order and to determine the optimal scope for each procedure.

4.2   The Transformations

4.2.1   Dependencies Extraction

In this transformation we extract from the ETFs, the source and the target configurations the different dependencies between the system's entities. Some dependencies, such as SI dependency, Proxy-Proxied dependency, Container-Contained dependency and CSI dependency are easier to extract than others since they are explicitly mentioned in the AMF configuration. The rest of the dependencies on the other hand, are harder to discover as they either have to be deduced from the way entities relate to each other and their extraction might involve some deep querying of the configuration or they depend on some vendor provided values (such as compatibility information) and might require a lookup into more than one ETF. In order to perform this task, we took advantage of the fact that all transformation languages use OCL as a mean for model querying and navigation as illustrated by the example in Fig. 5. Thus, providing us with a suitable environment to implement easily and execute efficiently these queries.

```
rule CSIDep
    transform csi: CONF!t_object
    to csid: Dep!CSIDependency
    {guard: csi.a_class.matches("SaAmfCSI")
                and csi.c_attr.select(
                    a|a.c_name.text.first().asString().matches("saAmfCSIDependencies")
                    ).first().c_value.text.size()>0
            var spons = csi.c_attr.select(a|a.c_name.text.first().asString().matches("saAmfCSIDependencies")).first().c_value.text;
            if(spons.size()>0){
                for (s in spons){
                    var depp : new Dep!CSIDependency;
                    depp.sponsorEntityDN = s;
                    depp.dependentEntityDN = csi.c_dn.text.first();
                    deps.dependencies.add(depp);}}
        delete csid;}
```

Fig. 5. ETL rule to create CSI dependencies.

4.2.2   Change Model Creation

The change model describes the actions that have to be performed to take the system from the current configuration to the target one. This transformation is based on the work done in [6] for comparing two AMF configuration models. The comparison of two AMF configuration models is done along the following lines: Since the source and the target configurations may not use the same naming for the configuration entities (e.g. if the target configuration is generated automatically from scratch) the assumption is that at least the SIs, which are provided before, after and throughout the upgrade have the same name in the two configurations. Starting with this assumption we identify the provider SG of each SI in each of the configurations and map them to each other. Subsequently we map the SUs of the SGs and their components based on other unchangeable properties of the configuration. Thus, this way we create a consistent mapping between the entities of the two configurations that we can compare as follows:

- If an entity in the source configuration matches an entity in the target configuration and they both have the same values for all attributes, we conclude that the entity in the source configuration has not been changed and therefore no action will be included in the change model for this entity.
- If an entity in the source configuration matches an entity in the target configuration but they do not have the same values for all attributes, we create a ModifyImm element in our change model with the entity in the source configuration as the source of this element (entity being changed), and the entity in the target configuration as the target of this element.
- For every entity in the source configuration that does not match any entity in the target configuration we create a RemoveFromImm element with this entity as a target of the removal.
- For every entity in the target configuration that does not match any entity in the source configuration we create an AddToImm element with this entity as a target.

Software bundle installations and removals are detected based on the changes in their association classes with the AMF Node entity. Additions of an instance of this AMF association class will imply the addition of a SwInstallation element in the change model. Similarly a removal of any one of these entities will imply the instantiation of a SwRemoval element in the change model.

4.2.3   Actions Creation

This transformation takes the change model as input and creates an elementary upgrade campaign specification model which contains an upgrade campaign element for each change in the change model. These upgrade campaign elements are created according to the standard upgrade campaign schema [3] and they respect the logic described in the SAF specifications. This implies putting the right upgrade actions in the right sections of the upgrade campaign specification, some parts of which require explicit specification of actions and their targets (e.g. initialization, wrap-up), while other parts have standard actions and require only their parametrization (e.g. upgrade step). The elementary upgrade campaign specification model requires further refinements as at this stage some schema elements are only partially defined, e.g. an upgrade procedure may only have an initialization and/or a wrap-up section, but not a body. In this translation from a change model to an upgrade campaign specification we aimed at respecting some rules for compliance with SAF standards such as:

- Only IMM operations targeting software bundles or AMF types are put in campaign initialization or wrap-up, for the rest of the actions we create proper upgrade procedures.

- Only IMM operations targeting Nodes, SUs, or Components are part of the body of a given procedure, otherwise the corresponding upgrade action is put either in the initialization or wrap-up of the procedure.
- Actions that prepare for the body of the procedure (for instance locking an SI before removing it), are put in the initialization of the procedure. Actions that follow from the actions of the body of the procedure are put in the wrap-up of the procedure (unlocking a SI after its addition).

4.2.4   Actions Matching

The actions matching, also called grouping, transformation refines the elementary upgrade campaign specification model generated by the previous transformation by matching and grouping the upgrade campaign elements that should be done within the same procedure. After this matching transformation the upgrade campaign specification model becomes fully compliant to the standard upgrade campaign specification schema. This transformation was implemented using EPSILON Pattern Language (EPL) [21]. In EPL the matching goes through several rounds by detecting the matching patterns in the input model that gets refined after every round until no more matching patterns are found. The matching patterns were formulated based on the following reasoning:

- Elements that are redundant of each other should either all be added or none of them is added. Meaning that failure of addition of one, should imply the undoing of all the additions already done.
- There is no need to have a "useless" logical entity, such as a SG without SUs, or SI without the SG protecting it.
- A software bundle is installed only when at least one of its provided components is configured for a node.
- A software bundle with no configured components should be uninstalled.
- We should not have an AMF association in the configuration without the minimum required participating logical entities.

4.2.5   Ordering and Scope Optimization

The last transformation takes into consideration the dependencies extracted from the source, the target configurations and ETFs to determine the appropriate ordering of the execution of the upgrade procedures. Two categories of dependencies have to be considered for the ordering of the upgrade procedures: Symmetrical and directed dependencies.

- The changes to entities related by a symmetrical dependency are to be ordered as follow:
  - Addition can happen whenever possible with respect to any directed dependencies the entities are involved.
  - Upgrade of an entity cannot happen before the addition of all the entities which need to be added, and which are related to this entity through a symmetrical dependency.

- The removal of an entity cannot happen before the upgrade of all entities which need to be upgraded, and which are related to this entity through a symmetrical dependency.
- The directed dependencies are mainly driven by the compatibility between the sponsor and the dependent entities, and the rationale that the dependent entity cannot exist without the sponsor. The ordering in this case is summarized in Table 1.

Table 1. Ordering rules for directed dependencies

Change on sponsor	Change on dependent	Order
Addition	Addition	Sponsor first
Removal	Removal	Dependent first
Addition	Upgrade	Sponsor first
Upgrade	Addition	Sponsor first
Upgrade	Upgrade	Depends on compatibility
Removal	Upgrade	Dependent first
Upgrade	Removal	Dependent first

The rules described in Table 1 impose an order that allows for performing the changes without violating the different dependencies. However, these rules might not be enough for the design of an optimal upgrade campaign specification. The following factors have determining role in keeping to the minimum any service disruption:

- The choice of AU/DU.
- The choice of the upgrade method.
- If there is a chance for the upgrade campaign triggering a rollback it is preferred if this happens as early as possible in the execution. Rollback is triggered by a failure and implies that all the procedures executed successfully before the failure are rolled back. Hence earlier this happens less impact it has on the system.

We propose some heuristics to optimize an upgrade campaign specification from these aspects. Our assumption is that the Node has the biggest scope of impact, followed by the Container then the SU, while the Component has the smallest scope of impact:

- Heuristic #1: keep the AU/DU to the minimal scope of impact (Node, Container, SU, Component), meaning that the AU/DU will be at most of the scope of impact of the software bundle installation/removal. If the upgrade consists only of IMM modifications then the AU/DU will be modification scope bounded. For instance, if an SU is to be modified, there is no need to lock the Node.
- Heuristic #2: put as many changes as possible into the procedures having a bigger scope of impact. For instance, if the upgrade of a contained entity has the scope of impact of the Container we can upgrade with it all collocated contained entities.
- Heuristic #3: procedures with bigger scope of impact should be executed as early as possible. The rationale is that more actions a step may take more likely it will fail.

Since a step with a Node as its AU/DU, for instance, can take actions on any and all of the hosted entities it is more likely to fail than a step that has an SU as its AU/DU.

- Heuristic #4: an execution level should contain procedures of the same scope of impact.

4.3   Prototype

There exist many environments and tools for model management. The tool we used in this work is EPSILON [20], a family of languages that provide a self-contained model management environment that enables model transformation, verification, merging, comparison and migration among other capabilities. The rationale behind this choice is as follows:

- EPSILON family of languages are concrete syntax agnostic [24], meaning that the model transformations are written only based on the abstract syntax, and using the EPSILON Model Connectivity we can apply them successfully on models expressed as XML, EMF (XMI 2.x), or even Z models [25].
- EPSILON enables and eases the integration with existing tools written in other languages such as JAVA or ATL [26].
- EPSILON defines EPL [21], which enables patterns detection in models on one hand, and the re-execution of the transformation until no more specified patterns are detected in the input models on the other hand. As far as we know, no other model management tool offers such capability that we needed especially in the implementation of the actions' matching, ordering and scope optimization activities.

In our prototype, the dependency extraction is realized as a transformation in EPSILON Transformation Language (ETL) [20, 21], and so was the action creation. For the refinements (actions matching and optimization activities), they have been implemented using EPL. The change creation function extends the work in [6] implemented in JAVA, hence the use of the general purpose language Epsilon Object Language (EOL) [20, 23] in order to integrate this tool in the overall approach. The generation of the xml file from the upgrade campaign specification model, not shown in Fig. 4, is done using the Epsilon Generation Language (EGL) [20, 22].

5   Related Work

The paper touches upon several topics including live upgrade, component dependencies, dynamic reconfiguration and model comparison.

Component dependencies and dynamic reconfiguration of component based systems have been thoroughly investigated in the literature. Chen [7] proposes an approach for dynamic dependency management for dynamic reconfiguration of component based systems. He considers the "static" (design time) known functional dependencies among components, but defines the concept of dynamic dependency that holds temporarily when a client component calls a method in a server component. The idea is that the dependencies defined at design time do not hold all the time during execution but only when a component is using another component. The proposal is to monitor the interactions of each component using a virtual stub that registers ongoing interactions, block interactions when needed for the reconfiguration, and resume blocked interactions after reconfiguration. The proposed approach is not applicable in the context of service high-availability as blocking interactions between components while they are still providing service will certainly lead to service outage.

Matevska et al. [8] tackle the problem for the same kind of dependencies as in [7], with the goal of minimizing service outage. They define the concept of dynamic dependency graph to keep track of which component is currently using which other component. Components can be in different states, free, passive and active. Components are only changed when they are in free and passive states; before the changes are performed they are blocked and incoming invocations are queued. To avoid service outage, the idea is to find the optimal point in time during the evolution of this dependency graph, and change a component when there is no runtime dependency to it. The authors are concerned with high-availability and service outage, but there is no guarantee there will be an optimal point in time and there is no guarantee about the duration of the changes while incoming invocations/requests are blocked. A similar approach, where software modules are only upgraded in safe states and future incoming requests are buffered is described in [9].

Dependencies relevant for upgrades in the context of AMF have been studied in [10]. Two kinds of dependencies are considered: functional dependencies (directed dependencies in this paper) and upgrade dependencies. Upgrade dependencies are dependencies between two upgraded components that did not exist between the original components. A directed graph is created from these dependencies and taken into account for the design of the upgrade campaign. However, not all relevant dependencies are considered (e.g. collocation dependencies) and the type of applications that are considered is limited. Our approach provides an automated method to identify dependencies and design an upgrade campaign whereas the work described in [10] is mainly concerned with the individual upgrades of applications and databases at a lower granularity.

Other works [11, 12] consider component dependencies during dynamic reconfiguration of component based applications from the perspective of application consistency, not removing a component while it is being used by another one, avoiding dangling references, etc., but with no consideration to the service outage and high-availability. Dependencies are determined at runtime and taken into account before removing or updating a component. Other approaches rely on specific operating systems [13], container environments [14] or component models [15] or use low-level approaches with wrapper-like functions [16] or modify source code [17]. An overview of techniques used for dynamic reconfiguration can be found in [18].

Comparing models and determining their differences has been a very active research topic as shown in the review of the different approaches provided in [19]. Our approach for comparing two configuration models is similar to many of these approaches but specialized to the context of AMF configurations where the services instances used in both models are used as starting point for the matching and the differentiation.

6   Conclusion

We devised and implemented a model driven approach for upgrade campaign specification generation. This is part of a larger project for model based software management including model driven configuration generation and model based service level agreement management. A model driven approach leverages the modeling framework designed for the project and increases the level of abstraction. The declarative aspects of the transformations allow to focus on the concepts and their relations. The particular feature of pattern detection of EPL was found particularly useful for the functions of action matching, ordering and scope optimization.

As part of the larger project we have also been working on the simulation and evaluation of upgrade campaign for highly available systems. As future work we plan to use the simulation and evaluation tool to validate the heuristics presented in Sect. 4.2.5, define new heuristics if necessary and validate the whole upgrade campaign specification generation approach.

Acknowledgement. This work has been partially supported by Natural Sciences and Engineering Research Council of Canada (NSERC) and Ericsson.

References

1. SAForum. http://www.saforum.org
2. SAForum: Application Interface Specification, Availability Management Framework specification: SAI-AIS-AMF-B.04.01.AL
3. SAForum: Application Interface Specification, Software Management Framework specification: SAI-AIS-SMF-A.01.02.AL
4. SAForum: Application Interface Specification, Information Model Management specification: SAI-AIS-IMM-A.03.01.AL
5. Davoudian, A., Khendek, F., Toeroe, M.: Ordering upgrade changes for highly available component based systems. In: The Proceedings of IEEE HASE 2014, Florida, January 2014
6. Mishra, A.: Automated AMF configuration difference generation. M.A.Sc. thesis, Electrical and Computer Engineering, Concordia University (2011)
7. Xuejun, C.: Dependence management for dynamic reconfiguration of component-based distributed systems. In: The Proceedings of 17th IEEE International Conference on Automated Software Engineering, pp. 279–284. IEEE Computer Society (2002)
8. Matevska, J., Hasselbring, W.: A scenario-based approach to increasing service availability at runtime reconfiguration of component-based systems. In: The Proceedings of 33rd EUROMICRO Conference on Software Engineering and Advanced Applications (EUROMICRO 2007), pp. 137–148. IEEE, August 2007
9. Yu, L., Shoja, G., Muller, H., Srinivasan, A.: A framework for live software upgrade. In: The Proceedings of the 13th ISSRE, pp. 149–158. IEEE Computer Society (2002)
10. Wolski, A., Laiho, K.: Rolling upgrades for continuous services. In: Malek, M., Reitenspiess, M., Kaiser, J. (eds.) ISAS 2004. LNCS, vol. 3335, pp. 175–189. Springer, Heidelberg (2005)
11. Kon, F., Campbell, R.: Dependence management in component-based distributed systems. IEEE Concurrency **8**(1), 26–36 (2000)

12. Morin, B., Nain, G., Barais, O., Jézéquel, J.-M.: Leveraging models from design-time to runtime. A live demo. In: The Proceedings of the 4th Workshop of Models@runtime, MODELS (2009)
13. Giuffrida, C., Kuijsten, A., Tanenbaum, A.S.: Safe and automatic live update for operating systems. ACM SIGARCH Comput. Architect. News **41**(1), 279–292 (2013)
14. Milazzo, M., Pappalardo, G., Tramontana, E., Ursino, G.: Handling run-time updates in distributed applications. In: The Proceedings of the ACM SAC 2005, New York, USA (2005)
15. Almeida, J., Wegdam, M., van Sinderen, M., Nieuwenhuis, L.: Transparent dynamic reconfiguration for CORBA. In: The Proceedings of the 3rd International Symposium on Distributed Objects and Applications. IEEE Computer Society (2001)
16. Ajmani, S., Liskov, B., Shrira, L.: Scheduling and simulation: how to upgrade distributed systems. In: The Proceedings of the 9th Conference on Hot Topics in Operating Systems. USENIX, May 2003
17. Chen, H., Yu, J., Chen, R., Zang, B., Yew, P.-C.: POLUS: A POwerful Live Updating System. In: Proceedings of ICSE 2007, pp. 271–281. IEEE, May 2007
18. Miedes, E., Munoz-Escoi, F.D.: A survey about dynamic software updating. Instituto Universitario Mixto Tecnologico de Informatica, Universitat Politecnica de Valencia, Technical report (2012)
19. Kolovos, D.S., Di Ruscio, D., Pierantonio, A., Paige, R.F.: Different models for model matching: an analysis of approaches to support model differencing. In: The Proceedings of the ICSE Workshop on Comparison and Versioning of Software Models (CVSM 2009). IEEE Computer Society, Washington, DC (2009)
20. EPSILON. http://www.eclipse.org/epsilon
21. Kolovos, D.S., Paige, R.F., Polack, F.A.: The Epsilon Transformation Language. In: Vallecillo, A., Gray, J., Pierantonio, A. (eds.) ICMT 2008. LNCS, vol. 5063, pp. 46–60. Springer, Heidelberg (2008)
22. Rose, L.M., Paige, R.F., Kolovos, D.S., Polack, F.A.: The Epsilon Generation Language. In: Schieferdecker, I., Hartman, A. (eds.) ECMDA-FA 2008. LNCS, vol. 5095, pp. 1–16. Springer, Heidelberg (2008)
23. Kolovos, D.S., Paige, R.F., Polack, F.A.: The Epsilon Object Language (EOL). In: Rensink, A., Warmer, J. (eds.) ECMDA-FA 2006. LNCS, vol. 4066, pp. 128–142. Springer, Heidelberg (2006)
24. Francis, M., Kolovos, D.S., Matragkas, N., Paige, R.F.: Adding spreadsheets to the MDE toolkit. In: Moreira, A., Schätz, B., Gray, J., Vallecillo, A., Clarke, P. (eds.) MODELS 2013. LNCS, vol. 8107, pp. 35–51. Springer, Heidelberg (2013)
25. Woodcock, J., Davies, J.: Using Z: Specification, Refinement, and Proof. Prentice Hall, Upper Saddle River (1996)
26. Atlas Transformation Language. https://www.eclipse.org/atl/

Model-Driven Approach to the Optimal Configuration of Time-Triggered Flows in a TTEthernet Network

Sofiene Beji[1], Abdelouahed Gherbi[2(✉)], John Mullins[1], and Pierre-Emmanuel Hladik[3]

[1] Department of Computer and Software Engineering,
École Polytechnique de Montréal, Montréal, Canada
{sofiene.beji,john.mullins}@polymtl.ca
[2] Department of Software and IT Engineering,
École de Technologie Supérieure, Montréal, QC, Canada
abdelouahed.gherbi@etsmtl.ca
[3] LAAS-CNRS, Université de Toulouse, CNRS, INSA, Toulouse, France
pehladik@laas.fr

Abstract. The SAE standard Time-triggered Ethernet defines a strong networking infrastructure, which supports the engineering of avionic systems. Avionic functions are often designed independently and integrated to form the avionic system. The iterative integration approach helps in controlling the design complexity of evolving avionic systems and aims at minimizing the cost associate with the reconfiguration of scheduling parameters of already integrated parts. On the other hand, the iterative approach requires to specify and manage a huge set of constraints, which are then solved to compute the optimal scheduling parameters. In this paper, we focus on this issue of manual specification of these constraints by the system engineer. We propose a model-driven approach, which provides the required abstractions and automation to support the system engineer in using effectively the iterative integration approach. The abstractions consist in a metamodel, which describes the system at a given integration step and a metamodel for the constraints. The automation consists in a model transformation which enables generating automatically the relevant constraints at integration step.

Keywords: Time-Triggered Ethernet · IMA · Model-driven approach · Meta-model · Model transformation

1 Introduction

Avionic embedded systems are now engineered following the principles of Integrated Modular Avionics (IMA) architecture [1]. The IMA architecture is characterized essentially by the sharing of distributed computing resources called modules. Since avionic systems are inherently safety-critical systems, sharing these resources requires to guarantee some safety properties such as the collision-free.

© Springer International Publishing AG 2016
J. Grabowski and S. Herbold (Eds.): SAM 2016, LNCS 9959, pp. 164–179, 2016.
DOI: 10.1007/978-3-319-46613-2_11

Moreover, IMA-based avionic systems are distributed systems which depend on a robust and deterministic networking infrastructure. The Avionic Full Duplex Switched Ethernet (AFDX) [2] has long been adopted as a networking standard for the avionic systems. Therefore, the IMA and AFDX became the main components of a typical architecture model for the recent civil aircrafts such as $B787$ and $A380$. More recently, the SAE standard Time-Triggered Ethernet (TTEthernet) is emerging as a new standard of the avionic network [3]. With respect to AFDX, the TTEthernet standard enables to achieve a best usage of the network resources and is more deterministic. In particular, the TTEthernet network schedule is established off-line.

The avionic functions designed independently need to be integrated within an existing system deployed on a TTEthernet-networked IMA architecture. The integration of avionic system is a complex engineering task. We have presented in [4] an iterative integration approach, which enables the integration of multiple IMA partitions as well as TTEhernet frames. This approach addresses the issue of finding an appropriate scheduling for the partitions and frames. The synthesized schedule may require the reconfiguration of the already integrated frames or partitions which lead to a supplementary re-certification cost that we aim to minimize. We consider this issue as Constraints Optimization Problem (COP) [13] where we satisfy not only a set of constraints but also we optimize the reconfiguration cost function.

In order for avionic engineers to use the iterative integration approach, they have to specify both the existing system and the new avionic functionality using a set of formal constraints. These constraints can then solved effectively using Constraints Programming (CP) techniques. The number and complexity of these constraints grow up very sharply even for small system examples. Therefore, using effectively the iterative integration approach faces a challenging constraints management complexity. In order to overcome this issue, we propose in this paper a model-driven engineering approach, which provides the required abstractions (i.e. metamodels) and defines the transformation process to enable the automatic generation of these constraints.

The paper is organized as follows. Section 2 presents the background knowledge and the model for the iterative integration problem. In Sect. 3, we introduce our model-driven engineering approach. We dedicate Sects. 4 and 5 to present the meta-models of our approach. We define in Sect. 6 the transformation process that generates the constraint program for a given integration problem. Our case study is presented in Sect. 7. We present the related works in Sect. 8 and we conclude the paper in Sect. 9.

2   Iterative Integration on TTEthernet Networks: Backgrounds and Model

The TTEthernet is a layer 2 protocol standardized under *SAE AS6802* [3]. It defines a strategy of clock synchronization in a distributed system. The TTEthernet supports two classes of traffic: time-triggered traffic and event-triggered traffic.

The time-triggered traffic is relevant mainly for the critical applications. In this work, we are only interested in time-triggered (TT) traffic. In contrast to the event-triggered traffic, the time-triggered one is static and fixed time windows are reserved for the transmission of each frame on a given dataflow link.

A TTEthernet network can be represented by a graph $\mathcal{G} = (\mathcal{V}, \mathcal{E})$ where $\mathcal{V}$ represents the nodes of the network and $\mathcal{E}$ the set of physical links. The nodes are of two types: the set of End-Systems (ES) and the set of Network-Systems (NS) Each physical link connecting two nodes defines a bidirectional communications, each of which is a dataflow link.

A TTEthernet frame f_i is communicated from its source to its destinations throughout fixed paths called virtual links. A virtual link vl_i is therefore associated with each frame f_i and defines a tree structure where its nodes are a set of dataflow links. The root element of this tree is the first link on which a frame f_i is transmitted, denoted $first(f_i)$. The leaves are the last dataflow links on which the frame f_i is transmitted, designated $last(f_i)$. We denote by $next(f_i, l)$ the next dataflow links on which the frame f_i is transmitted taking as reference the dataflow link l. We denote by f_i^l the transmission of the frame f_i on the dataflow link l, $f_{i,k}^l$ the kth instance of the frame f_i on the dataflow link l and by $\mathcal{L}_i$ the set of dataflow links on which f_i is defined.

The transmission of each frame f_i is characterized by the parameters: the period of f_i, $f_i.Period$, and its transmission delay on a dataflow link $f_i.Length$. The periodic pattern describing the communication of all the frames is called hyper-period (HP) and defined as the least common multiple of all frame periods. We denote by $Instances(f_i)$ the number of instances considered for the frame f_i and formally defined as $\frac{HP}{f_i.Period}$. The schedule of the kth instance of the frame f_i on the dataflow link l is determined by the variable $f_i^l.Offset$ which designate the offset time with the respect to the beginning of HP. The offsets are the only variables of the integration problem.

In the iterative integration problem as defined in [4,9], we have some configured applications which communicate through a TTEthernet network and we want to integrate new ones. To ensure the real-time requirements, we may reconfigure the scheduling of the previous ones. We focus in the scope of this paper on the reconfiguration of the network. This reconfiguration induces an additional cost of the re-certification of the system. We designate by $Cost(f_i)$ the cost of reconfiguring a frame f_i on a given dataflow link. We denote by $\mathcal{F}$ the set of considered frames, $\mathcal{F}_{old}$ the set of configured frames and $\mathcal{F}_{new}$ the set of frames to configure.

For a configured frame f_i, we denote by $f_{i/b}^l.Offset(k)$ the offset of the kth instance of the frame f_i on the dataflow link l before the integration and by $f_{i/a}^l.Offset(k)$ this offset after the integration. When it is clear from the context, we simply designate the offset after the integration by $f_i^l.Offset(k)$. We define by $R_i^l(k)$ the reconfiguration function that returns 1 if the kth instance of frame f_i on the dataflow link l is reconfigured and 0 otherwise. The goal of the iterative integration problem is then to minimize the total reconfiguration cost of the network. The reconfiguration cost of a frame instance $f_{i,k}^l$ is equal to $Cost(f_i) \times R_i^l(k)$.

3   Overall Approach

We present in this section our model-driven engineering approach to automatically generate the constraints program that solves the problem of a given integration step. As shown by Fig. 1, our approach relies on the definition of two meta-models. The first one, called the Integration Specification Meta-Model, characterizes an iterative integration problem on TTEthernet networks. The second one called CP Integration Meta-Model defines the CP formalization to solve this problem. An instance of the first meta-model describes a real case of the iterative integration problem. We specify in this instance the configured frames and the frames to be configured and how they are deployed on the network architecture. An instance of the second meta-model models the CP program that solves a specific iterative integration problem. A transformation tool, which relies on the meta-models, enables transforming a given instance of the Integration Specification meta-model to the corresponding CP model. The latter is then transformed to a CP code structured following the targeted CP language specification and solved by a CP solver to find a new optimal configuration. By defining an intermediate CP model before generating the CP integration code, our approach can target different CP solvers. To test our approach, we have used *MiniZinc* [6] as target CP language. We specify in the following section the Integration Specification meta-model.

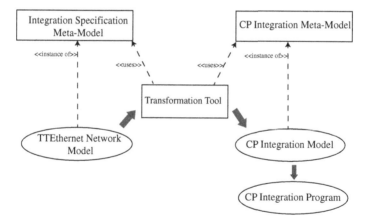

Fig. 1. Approach overview

4   Integration Specification Meta-Model

This meta-model is depicted in Fig. 2. An integration problem is based on the definition of integration steps, which are represented by the metaclass *IntegrationStep*. This metaclass has an attribute *step* which indicates the step order of the integration. It has also the attributes *switchTreatmentDelay* and *HP* which designate respectively the required delay for a switch to handle a frame and the

Hyper-Period for all the frame periods. An *IntegrationStep* is composed of a set of frames to configure and the set of already configured frames if any. A *Configured-Frame* differs from a *FrameToConfigure* by the indication of the *actualOffsets* attribute which indicates the schedule before the integration of each instance of the considered frame on each dataflow link. A *Frame* is characterized by several attributes including *period, length, reconfigurationCost, nbInstances*, etc. A *VirtualLink* is associated with each frame. Each *VirtualLink* is characterized by a source and destinations *DataflowLink*. A *VirtualLink* can be hence composed of a number of DataPaths. Each *DataPath* defines a path from the source to one destination. It is constituted by the adjacent sequence of a dataflow links. A *Schedule* characterizes the allocation of time windows of each frame on each dataflow link. Obviously, many frames can be scheduled on a dataflow link and a frame is transmitted on the different dataflow links that defines its associated virtual link. The *Schedule* of a frame on a dataflow link may be synchronized with another of the same one on another dataflow link. This case occurs when a frame must be relayed simultaneously on different dataflow links.

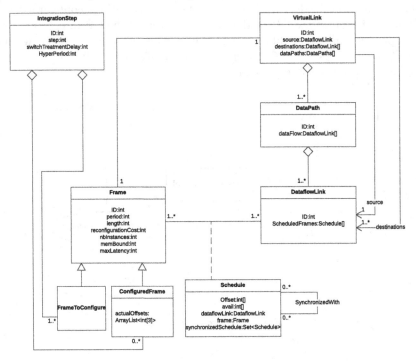

Fig. 2. The integration specification meta-model

5   CP Integration Meta-Model

Our CP Integration Meta-Model is depicted by Fig. 3. It is composed of a set of *VariableDeclaration* metaclasses, a set of *Constraint* metaclasses and a *SolveItem* metaclass. For readability purpose, we do not include in Fig. 3 the comprehensive set of the relationships between these metaclasses. A *SolveItem* models a directive to the solver, which consists in the definition of two attributes, *type*, which is the type of the problem either a satisfaction or minimization problem; and *objective*, which is the optimized objective in the case of an optimization problem. In our case, the optimized objective is the reconfiguration cost.

5.1   Variables Declaration

As shown by Fig. 3, three types of variables are considered to solve the integration problem. The metaclass *FrameInstanceOffsets* specifies the offsets of the different frame instances of a frame on a dataflow link. *FrameInstanceOffsets* has the two attributes *name* and *type*. The attribute *name* is of type *FrameInstanceName* and defines the name of the frame instances on one dataflow link. The *name* is therefore uniquely identified by the *IDFrame* and the *IDLink*. The attribute *type* is of type *int[]*. The metaclass *FrameInstanceReconfig* captures the information whether the offsets of the already configured frame instances are changed after the integration. It has two attributes *name* which is also the name of the considered frame instances on a dataflow link and the attribute *type* of type *bool[]*. The metaclass *ReconfigurationCost* specifies the cost of the schedule after the integration.

5.2   Constraints

To solve the integration problem, we consider nine types of constraints illustrated in Fig. 3. We introduce for the definition of these constraints a new type *Quantifier* which quantifies the instance order of a frame and has four attributes: (1) *ident* which gives an identification name for the quantifier, (2) *type* which specifies the type of the quantifier (e.g. *exists* or *forall*), (3) *min* the minimum value of the quantifier and (4) *max* the max value of the quantifier.

Contention-Free Constraints: A Contention-Free Constraint expresses the mutual exclusion of a transmission on a dataflow link. Given two frames f_i and f_j transmitted on a dataflow link l, the end of transmission of an instance of f_i on l occurs before the beginning of transmission of a given frame instance of f_j or vice versa. The contention free constraints can be formalized as follows:

$$\forall f_i, f_j \in \mathcal{F}, \forall l \in \mathcal{L}_i \cap \mathcal{L}_j, \forall k \in [1..Instances(f_i)], \forall k' \in [1..Instances(f_j)],$$
$$\left(f_i^l.Offset(k) + f_i.Length \le f_j^l.Offset(k')\right) \vee$$
$$\left(f_j^l.Offset(k') + f_j.Length \le f_i^l.Offset(k)\right)$$

In the CP Integration Meta-Model, a Contention-Free Constraint is modeled by the class *ContentionFreeConstraint* which has the attributes (1) *q1* and *q2* as two *Quantifier*s on respectively the instance order k and k', (2) *fio1* and *fio2* the offsets of respectively f_i^l and f_j^l and (3) *length1* and *length2* to designate the transmission delays of f_i and f_j on a dataflow link.

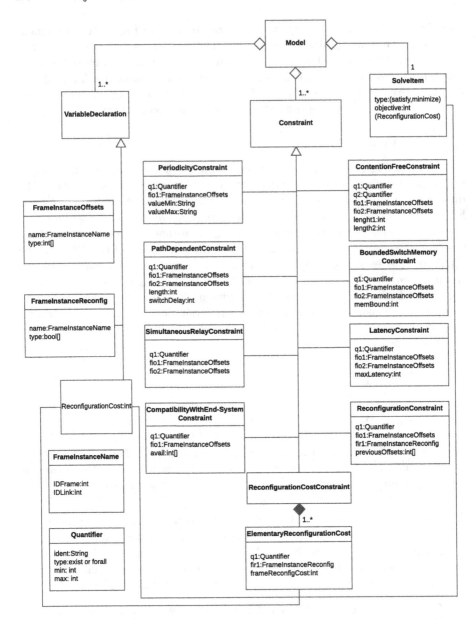

Fig. 3. The CP integration meta-model

Path-Dependent Constraints: We introduce this constraint to express the sequential transmission of a frame f_i along a data path of the virtual link vl_i. Formally this constraint is defined as follows:

$$\forall f_i \in \mathcal{F}, \forall l' \in next(f_i, l), \forall k \in [1..Instances(f_i)],$$

$$\left(f_i^l.Offset(k) + f_i.Length + switch\_delay\right) \leq \left(f_i^{l'}.Offset(k)\right)$$

where, *switch_delay* denotes the processing delay of a frame by a switch. A Path-Dependent constraint is specified in our meta-model by the metaclass *PathDependentConstraint*, which has the following attributes: (1) *q1* as a *Quantifier* on the instance order k of f_i, (2) *fio1* and *fio2* the offsets of respectively f_i^l and $f_i^{l'}$, (3) *length* the parameter $f_i.Length$ and (4) *switchDelay* the processing delay of a frame by a switch.

Latency Constraints: In order to ensure that frames meet their deadline requirements, we define latency constraints. These constraints bound the transmission delay of a frame along their datapaths and are formalized as follows

$$\forall f_i \in \mathcal{F}, \forall l \in last(f_i), \forall k \in [1..Instances(f_i)],$$

$$f_i^l.Offset(k) - f_i^{first(f_i)}.Offset(k) \leq max\_latency_i$$

We represent a latency constraint in our CP meta-model by the metaclass *LatencyConstraint* which has the attributes (1) *q1* to represent the instance order k, (2) *fio1* to designate the offsets of $f_i^{first(f_i)}$, (3) *fio2* to designate the offsets of f_i^l and (4) *maxLatency* the maximal tolerated bound of latency.

Reconfiguration Constraint: The reconfiguration constraints detect if the already configured frames are reconfigured after the integration of new frames. The reconfiguration constraints are formalized as follows

$$\forall f_i \in \mathcal{F}_{old}, \forall l \in \mathcal{L}_i, \forall k \in [1..Instances(f_i)],$$

$$(f_{i/b}^l.Offset(k) = f_{i/a}^l.Offset(k)) \Leftrightarrow (R_i^l(k) = 0)$$

In the CP Meta-Model, a reconfiguration constraint is modeled by the metaclass *ReconfigurationConstraint* which has the attributes (1) *q1* to represent the instance order k, (2) *fio1* to designate the offsets after the integration (3) *fir1* to designate the reconfiguration variables $R_i^l(k)$ and (4) *previousOffsets* which contains the previous offsets of f_i on the dataflow link l.

6   Model Transformation Process

We detail in this section the transformation rules implemented in our *Transformation Tool* to generate automatically the CP Integration Model. We note by *ModelIn* the integration specification model and by *ModelOut* the CP integration model. In the remainder, we detail the transformation rule corresponding to each component of a CP Integration model.

6.1   Variables

For the variables of the CP Model, we define the transformation rule given by Algorithm 1 that generates the *FrameInstanceOffset* instances. In *Line* 1, we select from the input model an instance of the metaclass *Schedule*, denoted by *A*. We create in *Line* 2 an instance of the *FrameInstanceOffsets* metaclass corresponding to *A* that we denote by *B*. In *Line* 3 − 5, we assign the relevant attributes.

Algorithm 1. Generation of *FrameInstanceOffset* Instances

1: **for each** $A = InstanceOf(ModelIn.Schedule)$ **do**
2:      ***create*** B=***new*** $InstanceOf(ModelOut.FrameInstanceOffsets)$
3:      $B.type \leftarrow int[A.Frame.nbInstances]$
4:      $B.name.IDFrame \leftarrow A.frame.ID$
5:      $B.name.IDLink \leftarrow A.dataFlowLink.ID$
6: **end for**

6.2   Constraints

For the constraints, we present only the transformation rule that define the *ContentionFreeConstraint* instances. This rule is specified by Algorithm 2. In *Line* 1 − 2, we select from the input model two instances *A* and *B* of the metaclass *Schedule*. In order to define correctly a Contention-Free Constraint, we must check in *Line* 3 − 4 that *A* and *B* are two instances that define a schedule of two different frames in the same dataflow link. To ensure constraint unicity, we impose that the *ID* of the frame associated with *A* is inferior that of *B*. We create then in *Line* 4 a new instance *C* of the *ContentionFreeConstraint* metaclass. In *Line* 5 − 6, we define the two quantifiers of the created instance *C*. *q1* is reserved for the schedule of the frame associated with the instance *A* and *q2* for that of *B*. In *Line* 7 − 11, we define the attributes *fio1* and *length1* that correspond respectively the schedule and the transmission delay of the frame associated with *A*. Similarly, in *Line* 12 − 16, we define the schedule and the transmission delay of the frame associated with *B*.

6.3   SolveItem

For the *SolveItem*, we have one instance by a CP Model (i.e. a singleton). We generate this instance by following the Algorithm 3. In *Line* 1, we check the existence of any already configured frame. This allows the definition of the nature of the problem. If no frame is already configured which is the case in *Line* 2 − 3, we assign the value *satisfy* to the *type* of the problem. In the contrary case, shown in *Line* 5 − 6, the problem is rather of *type minimize* and the *objective* to minimize is the *ReconfigurationCost*.

Algorithm 2. Generation of *ContentionFreeConstraint* Instances

1: **for each** $A = InstanceOf(ModelIn.Schedule)$ **do**
2: **for each** $B = InstanceOf(ModelIn.Schedule)$ **do**
3:   **if** $(A.frame.ID < B.frame.ID)and(A.dataflowLink = B.dataflowLink)$ **then**
4:    **create** C=**new** $InstanceOf(ModelOut.ContentionFreeConstraint)$
5:    $C.q1 \leftarrow$ **new** $Quantifier("i", forall, 1, A.Frame.nbInstances)$
6:    $C.q2 \leftarrow$ **new** $Quantifier("j", forall, 1, B.Frame.nbInstances)$
7:    **for each** $D = InstanceOf(ModelOut.FrameInstanceOffsets)$ **do**
8:     **if** $(D.name.IDFrame = A.frame.ID)and(D.name.IDLink = A.dataflowLink.ID)$ **then**
9:      $C.fio1 \leftarrow D$
10:      $C.length1 \leftarrow A.frame.length$
11:     **end if**
12:    **end for**
13:    **for each** $D = InstanceOf(ModelOut.FrameInstanceOffsets)$ **do**
14:     **if** $(D.name.IDFrame = B.frame.ID)and(D.name.IDLink = B.dataflowLink.ID)$ **then**
15:      $C.fio2 \leftarrow D$
16:      $C.length2 \leftarrow B.frame.length$
17:     **end if**
18:    **end for**
19:   **end if**
20: **end for**
21: **end for**

Algorithm 3 Generation of *SolveItem*

1: **if** $(nbInstancesOf(ModelIn.IntegrationStep.ConfiguredFrame) = 0)$ **then**
2: $ModelOut.SolveItem.type = satisfy$
3: $ModelOut.SolveItem.objective = null$
4: **else**
5: $ModelOut.SolveItem.type = minimize$
6: $ModelOut.SolveItem.objective = ReconfigurationCost$
7: **end if**

7 Case Study

In this section, we illustrate our model-driven engineering approach through the integration of the communication part of the distributed system whose physical architecture is illustrated by Fig. 4. We identify in this figure the different dataflow links by numbers and we illustrate the direction of each flow by a dashed arrow.

The temporal characterization of the frames is given by Table 1. We propose as shown by the first column to integrate the set of frames in three integration steps. The *IDs* of the frames are indicated in the second column. The frame periods are given by the third column. We reserve the fourth column to the indication of the information availability dates at the ES level. The fifth column indicates the transmission delays of the frames on a dataflow link. We indicate in the last column the structure of the virtual link. We adopt in this field the notation $l_s - \{l_{d_1}, ..., l_{d_n}\}$ to indicate that the associated frame is transmitted first in l_s and the simultaneously in l_{d_1} to l_{d_n}. The reconfiguration cost of each frame in this example is equal to 1.

In the following, we use this case study to illustrate through two examples: (1) the integration specification in input as instance of the *Integration Specification Meta-Model*, (2) an instance of the CP Integration Meta-Model corresponding to the spec input, and (3) the associated *MiniZinc* code relative the to the CP model.

Although this example illustrates the integration of only 26 virtual links, we note that the resolution of each integration step requires about one thousand of code lines. We only illustrate some relevant aspects of our approach using two small examples. We set in the first example as goal to show the generation of some CP variables and frame constraints through the example of a Contention-Free Constraint. In the second example, we explain a constraint that exploits the structure of the virtual link.

7.1   Example 1

Focusing in the first integration step and more precisely the integration of frames f_3 and f_4, we notice that f_3 is scheduled on the dataflow links with the *IDs* 3 and 2. f_4 is scheduled on the dataflow links 3 and 8. The integration specification model corresponding to this part is given by Fig. 5. We illustrate only the schedules $s1$ and $s2$ of frames $f3$ and $f4$ on the dataflow link $l3$. As shown by Fig. 6, two instances $fio1$ and $fio2$ of the class *FrameInstanceOffsets* are defined in our output CP model to represent the schedules $s1$ and $s2$. As the number of instances of f_3 considered in the integration specification model is equal to 4, the *type* attribute of the variable $fio1$ has a value of *int[4]*. The corresponding *MiniZinc* Code is given by Fig. 7. We note that we limit our offsets to the interval [1..120] to have an enough large finite domain that represents the different possible values. Now that we have illustrated the different variables of the CP Integration Model, we present the contention-free constraint of Example 1. This constraint is defined by the instance $c1$ of the metaclass *Contention FreeConstraint* as illustrated by Fig. 8. The instance $c1$ contains the information required to generate the corresponding *MiniZinc* code as illustrated by Fig. 9

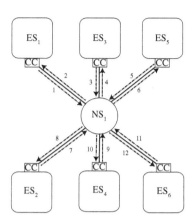

Fig. 4. Physical Architecture of the system

Table 1. Temporal characteristics of integrated frames

Integration step	Frame Id	Frame period	Availabilities	Frame length	Virtual link
1	3	30	$[7, 35, 65, 95]$	1	3-2
	4	30	$[5, 33, 63, 93]$	1	3-8
	40	60	$[21, 21]$	2	3-2
	41	60	$[15, 15]$	4	3-8
	42	60	$[17, 17]$	1	1-4
	43	60	$[17, 17]$	3	7-4
	1030	60	$[9, 9]$	2	1-4
	1031	60	$[9, 9]$	1	7-4
2	2	30	$[9, 41, 67, 97]$	2	3-8
	10	60	$[51, 51]$	3	3-2
	11	60	$[31, 31]$	7	3-8
	12	60	$[27, 27]$	3	3-8
	13	30	$[25, 61, 75, 107]$	4	7-2
	14	60	$[71, 71]$	1	1-8
	15	60	$[89, 89]$	2	7-4
	1000	30	$[17, 53, 89, 105]$	1	1-4
	1001	30	$[19, 55, 69, 101]$	2	7-4
	1002	60	$[63, 63]$	1	1-4
	1003	60	$[7, 7]$	1	7-4
3	0	60	$[35, 95]$	1	9-4
	1	30	$[0, 30, 60, 90]$	1	3-10
	109	60	$[22, 82]$	11	11-{2,4,6,8,10}
	110	60	$[14, 74]$	5	11-{2,4,6,8,10}
	111	60	$[7, 67]$	2	11-{2,4,6,8,10}
	140	60	$[61, 81]$	4	3-6
	141	60	$[44, 104]$	1	5-4

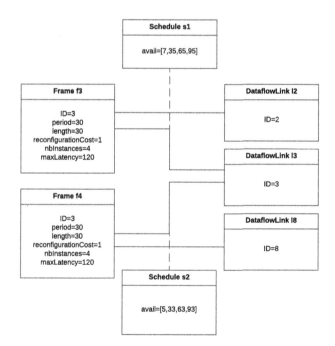

Fig. 5. Integration specification model of Example 1

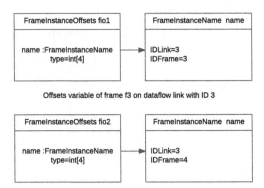

Fig. 6. CP variables considered in Example 1

```
array[1..4]  of var  0..120:Link3Offset3;
array[1..4]  of var  0..120:Link3Offset4;
```

Fig. 7. Declaration of the variables of Example 1 in *MiniZinc*

7.2   Example 2

The frame f_3 is transmitted on the virtual link vl_3 which is composed by the datapath $3 - 8$. The transmission of f_3 on its associated datapath induces the definition of a *Path-Dependent Constraint* that has the structure presented by Fig. 10. In addition to the attributes *switchDelay* and *length*, to define this constraint, we consider from Example 1 the instance $fio1$ to characterize the offsets of f_3 on the dataflow link 2. We consider also the instance $fio3$ that defines the offsets associated to the transmission of f_3 on the dataflow link 2. The corresponding *MiniZinc* code corresponding to this constraint is given by Fig. 11.

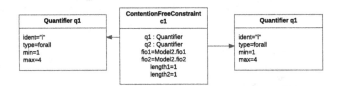

Fig. 8. Contention-Free constraint considered in Example 1

```
constraint forall(i in 1..4,j in 1..4)
((Link3Offset3[i]+1<=Link3Offset4[j])\/
(Link3Offset4[j]+1<=Link3Offset3[i]));
```

Fig. 9. Example 1: Contention-Free constraint code in *MiniZinc*

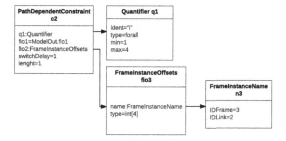

Fig. 10. CP integration model of Example 2

```
constraint forall (i in 1..4)
(Link3Offset3[i] + 1 + 1 <= Link2Offset3[i]);
```

Fig. 11. Example 2: Path-Dependent constraint code in *MiniZinc*

8   Related Works

The constraint programming approach to the scheduling problems in avionic systems is now a very active and popular research field. Several formal definitions and frameworks have been proposed for reasoning about the problem of scheduling in IMA architecture (e.g. [10,11]), the problem of scheduling in Time-Triggered Networks (e.g. [7,12,14,15]) and the cost optimization problems for evolving avionic systems (e.g. [9]). The most related work to ours is the recent paper of Lauer et al. [9] and the one of Steiner [14]. In [9], the authors address the problem of an iterative integration in an *IMA* Architecture. Its objective is to find an optimal scheduling configuration that minimizes the cost of the integration. However, it does only consider the integration of IMA partitions and the proposed iterative approach handles only the scheduling of system model that evolves by adding a single partition at each iteration. The work in [4] extends the work in [9] to consider a SMT-based approach that handles not only the integration of IMA partitions but also TTEthernet flows.

The combination of model-driven software engineering approach and constraints programming approach has been the focus of some other research works including [5,8]. In [8], the authors propose a formalization of constraint programming solving tasks in a model-driven process chain. In [5], the authors discuss the need for a visual high level modeling language and the quality of metamodeling techniques to implement the transformations. In particular, they present a platform called s-COMMA, which efficiently implements the chain from modeling to solving constraint problems.

9   Conclusion

In this paper, we have proposed a model-driven engineering approach to support the automatic synthesis of programs that resolve the integration of TT flows of

TTEthernet. The proposed approach relies on the definition of two meta-models. The first one specifies an integration problem on TTEthernet networks. The second one describes the structure of the corresponding CP program. Further to the two meta-models, this approach is based also on the definition of transformation processes that automatizes the generation of the CP model to a given integration problem. The resulted CP model is transformed to a CP code which is resolved by a CP solver to find the new optimal configuration of the network. As Future Work, we plan to extend our approach by considering the schedule of IMA partitions. We expect no difficulties to extend the two meta-models to consider the integration of IMA partitions and their associated constraints. We will define also the necessary transformation process to automatize the synthesis of IMA constraints.

Acknowledgment. This work was supported by the Natural Sciences and Engineering Research Council of Canada (NSERC).

References

1. Integrated modular avionics (ima). AERONAUTICAL RADIO, INC., ARINC 653 (2006)
2. ARINC 664, part 7: Avionics full duplex switched ethernet (afdx). AERONAUTICAL RADIO, INC. (2009)
3. AS6802: Time-triggered ethernet (ttethernet). SAE Aerospace (2011)
4. Beji, S., Hamadou, S., Gherbi, A., Mullins, J.: Smt-based cost optimization approach for the integration of avionic functions in ima and ttethernet architectures. In: Proceedings of the 2014 IEEE/ACM 18th International Symposium on Distributed Simulation and Real Time Applications, pp. 165–174. IEEE Computer Society (2014)
5. Chenouard, R., Granvilliers, L., Soto, R.: Model-driven constraint programming. In: Proceedings of the 10th International ACM SIGPLAN Conference on Principles and Practice of Declarative Programming, pp. 236–246. ACM (2008)
6. Optimisation Research Group. Minizinc 2.0, February 2016. http://www.minizinc.org/ide/index.html
7. Huang, J., Blech, J.O., Raabe, A., Buckl, C., Knoll, A.: Static scheduling of a time-triggered network-on-chip based on SMT solving. In: Proceedings of the Conference on Design, Automation and Test in Europe, pp. 509–514. EDA Consortium (2012)
8. Kleiner, M., Del Fabro, M.D., Albert, P.: Model search: formalizing and automating constraint solving in MDE platforms. In: Kühne, T., Selic, B., Gervais, M.-P., Terrier, F. (eds.) ECMFA 2010. LNCS, vol. 6138, pp. 173–188. Springer, Heidelberg (2010). doi:10.1007/978-3-642-13595-8_15
9. Lauer, M., Mullins, J., Yeddes, M.: Cost optimization strategy for iterative integration of multi-critical functions in IMA and ttethernet architecture. In: 2013 IEEE 37th Annual Computer Software and Applications Conference Workshops (COMPSACW), pp. 139–144. IEEE (2013)
10. Lee, Y.-H., Kim, D., Younis, M., Zhou, J., McElroy, J.: Resource scheduling in dependable integrated modular avionics. In: Proceedings International Conference on Dependable Systems and Networks, DSN 2000, pp. 14–23. IEEE (2000)

11. Lee, Y.-H., Kim, D., Younis, M., Zhou, J.: Scheduling tool and algorithm for integrated modular avionics systems. In: Proceedings of the 19th Conference on Digital Avionics Systems Conference, DASC 2000, vol. 1. IEEE (2000). p. 1C2-1
12. Majumdar, R., Saha, I., Zamani, M.: Performance-aware scheduler synthesis for control systems. In: Proceedings of the Ninth ACM International Conference on Embedded Software, pp. 299–308. ACM (2011)
13. Rossi, F., Van Beek, P., Walsh, T.: Handbook of Constraint Programming. Elsevier, New York (2006)
14. Steiner, W.: An evaluation of smt-based schedule synthesis for time-triggered multi-hop networks. In: 2010 IEEE 31st Real-Time Systems Symposium (RTSS), pp. 375–384. IEEE (2010)
15. Tamas-Selicean, D., Pop, P., Steiner, W.: Synthesis of communication schedules for ttethernet-based mixed-criticality systems. In: Proceedings of the Eighth IEEE/ACM/IFIP International Conference on Hardware/software Codesign and System Synthesis, pp. 473–482. ACM (2012)

Feature Location Through the Combination of Run-Time Architecture Models and Information Retrieval

Lorena Arcega[1,2]([⊠]), Jaime Font[1,2], Øystein Haugen[3], and Carlos Cetina[1]

[1] SVIT Research Group, Universidad San Jorge, Zaragoza, Spain
{larcega,jfont,ccetina}@usj.es
[2] Department of Informatics, University of Oslo, Oslo, Norway
[3] Department of Information Technology, Østfold University College,
Halden, Norway
oystein.haugen@hiof.no

Abstract. Eighty percent of the lifetime of a system is spent on maintenance activities. Feature location is one of the most important and common activities performed by developers during software maintenance. This work presents our approach for performing feature location by leveraging the use of architecture models at run-time. Specifically, the execution information is collected in the architecture model at run-time. Then, our approach performs an Information Retrieval technique at the model level. We have evaluated our approach in a Smart Hotel with its architecture model at run-time. We compared our architecture-model-based approach with a source-code-based approach. The rankings produced by the approaches indicate that since models are on a higher abstraction level than source code, they provide more accurate results. Our architecture-model-based approach ranks the relevant elements in the top ten positions of the ranking in 84 % of the cases; in the top positions in the ranking of the source-code-based approach, there are false positives associated with some programming patterns and true positives are spread between positions 12 and 100.

Keywords: Arquitecture model · Models@Run-time · Feature location · Information retrieval · Reverse engineering

1 Introduction

In software development, all systems evolve over time as new requirements emerge or when bug-fixing becomes necessary. Lehman et al. [13] pointed out that up to 80 % of the lifetime of a system is spent on maintenance and evolution activities. Feature location is one of the most important and common activities performed by developers during software maintenance and evolution [8]. Currently, research efforts in feature location are concerned with identifying software artifacts that are associated with a program functionality (a feature).

© Springer International Publishing AG 2016
J. Grabowski and S. Herbold (Eds.): SAM 2016, LNCS 9959, pp. 180–195, 2016.
DOI: 10.1007/978-3-319-46613-2_12

Models at run-time provide a kind of formal basis for reasoning about the current system state, for reasoning about necessary adaptations, and for analyzing the consequences of possible system adaptations. Models at run-time development approaches have the proven capability to deliver complex, dependable software effectively and efficiently. In this paper, we show that the information extracted from architecture models at run-time can be useful in the field of feature location. In models at run-time [5], there is a causal connection between the system and the run-time model (i.e., there is a bidirectional relation between the source code and the run-time model).

This work proposes an approach that combines architecture models at run-time and Information Retrieval (IR) for feature location. In the first step of our approach, the software engineer executes a scenario, which uses the desired feature to be located. The execution information is collected in the architecture model at run-time. Then, our approach filters the trace in order to extract the relevant elements of the models. We adapt an information retrieval technique, Latent Semantic Indexing (LSI). This technique allows the software engineers to write queries that are relevant to the feature to be located. Finally, the software engineers obtain a ranked list of model elements that are related to the feature based on the similarity to the query.

We have evaluated our approach in a Smart Hotel that is defined with an architecture model at run-time. The Smart Hotel presents sixty-eight model elements in the architecture model that are implemented in 268 Java classes (about 67,207 methods of source code). We have compared our approach based on models with a feature location approach that is based on source code, which is presented in [14]. We chose this approach because it outperforms all other source-code-based approaches that use a single scenario and information retrieval [8].

The results indicate that the information gathered at a high level of abstraction of architecture models is closer to natural language queries of software engineers; hence, the rankings are more accurate. Our architecture-model-based approach ranks the relevant elements in the top ten positions of the ranking in 84 % of the cases; in the top positions in the ranking of the source-code-based approach, there are false positives associated with some programming patterns and true positives are spread between positions 12 and 100.

The remainder of the paper is structured as follows. In Sect. 2, we present the Smart Hotel. In Sect. 3, we introduce our approach for feature location with architecture models at run-time. In Sect. 4, we evaluate our approach with the Smart Hotel and we discuss the results. In Sect. 5, we examine the related work of the area, and we present our conclusions in Sect. 6.

2   The Smart Hotel

The running example and the evaluation of this paper are performed through a Smart Hotel [6]. The Smart Hotel is reconfigured in response to changes in the context, for example if there is a client in the room or not, and what activities they may be performing (sleeping, watching TV, ...). This section shows the language used for specifying the architecture model of the Smart Hotel. This section also shows how the architecture model is reconfigured at run-time in response to context changes.

2.1   The Architecture Model

We use Pervasive Modeling Language (PervML) [16] to describe the Smart Hotel architecture. PervML[1] is a DSL that describes pervasive systems using high-level abstraction concepts based on Meta-Object Facility (MOF)[2]. This language is focused on specifying heterogeneous services in specific physical environments such as the services of a Smart Hotel. This DSL has been applied to develop solutions in the Smart Hotel domain. The PervML language provides different models to specify the services and devices of a pervasive system.

Due to space constraints, in this paper, we only focus on the subset of PervML that specifies the relationships among devices and services. This subset specifies the components that define a particular configuration system (services and devices) and how these components are connected with each other (channels). Services are depicted by circles, devices are depicted by squares, and the channels connecting services and devices are depicted by lines (see Fig. 1).

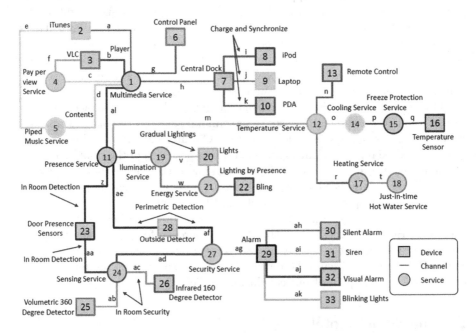

Fig. 1. Smart hotel architecture model

---

[1] https://tatami.dsic.upv.es/pervml/index.php.
[2] Meta object facility (MOF) 2.0 core specification, 2003.

2.2   The Architecture Model Reconfiguration

The Smart Hotel reconfiguration engine determines how the system should be reconfigured in response to a context change, and then it modifies the PervML architecture model accordingly. The Monitor uses the run-time state as input to check context conditions. If any of these conditions are fulfilled, the Analyzer queries the run-time models about the necessary modifications. The response of the models is used by the Planner to elaborate a reconfiguration plan. This plan also contains reconfiguration actions, which modify the architecture model and maintain the consistency between the PervML architecture model and the system. The Execution of this plan modifies the system by executing reconfiguration actions that deal with the activation and deactivation of software components and the creation and destruction of channels among components. For more details about the reconfiguration engine see [6].

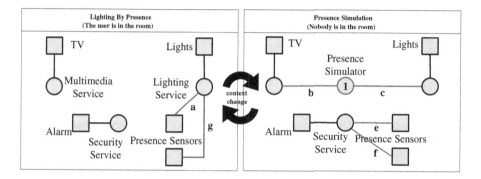

Fig. 2. Smart hotel architecture model reconfigurations

Figure 2 shows two Smart Home configurations according to the concrete syntax of the PervML. Figure 2 (left) shows a *User in the room* configuration, while Fig. 2 (right) shows a *Nobody in the room* configuration. As it can be observed, movement sensors are not used for lighting (left); instead, they are used to provide information to the security service (right). In addition, the Occupancy simulation service is activated in the *Nobody in the room* configuration, and the connections that are required for this service to communicate with multimedia, lighting, and security services are established.

3   Feature Location with Architecture Models at Run-Time

Figure 3 shows an overview of our feature location approach. In the Dynamic Analysis phase, the software engineer executes a scenario, which uses the target feature to be located. The run-time architecture model obtained from the running scenario contains the elements of the model that are related to the target feature.

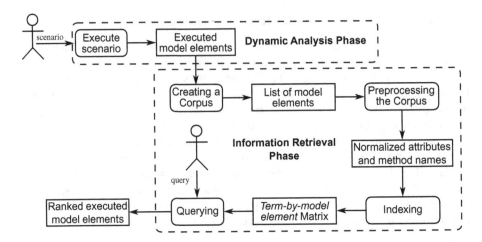

Fig. 3. Feature location approach based on architecture models at Run-Time

In the Information Retrieval phase, the approach filters the run-time architecture model to extract the relevant elements of the target feature to be located. To achieve the filtering, we adapt an Information retrieval (IR) technique named Latent Semantic Indexing (LSI) [12], which allows the software engineers to write queries that describe the feature to be located. The result is a ranked list of model elements that are related to the feature based on the similarity to the provided query.

The following subsections present the details of each one of the steps of our approach that must be carried out in order to perform the feature location at the model level. We use the Smart Hotel presented in Sect. 2 throughout the different subsections to illustrate the details with a running example.

3.1   The Dynamic Analysis Phase

Execution information is gathered via dynamic analysis (see Fig. 3), which is commonly used in program comprehension and involves executing a software system under specific conditions. Invoking the desired feature during run-time generates a feature-specific execution trace. In other words, the input for the execution is a scenario that runs the specific feature.

For example, we depict a scenario where we want to fix a bug in the gradual lights in the Smart Hotel. Therefore, the feature that we must locate is the Gradual Lighting service. We follow the information from the bug report to define the scenario that executes the targeted feature. In this case, the scenario is as follows:

'The software engineer simulates an empty Smart Hotel room. The lights are off. The software engineer simulates that a client enters the room. The lights gradually turn on. The software engineer simulates that the client leaves the room, and then the lights gradually turn off.'

3.2   The Information Retrieval Phase

Textual information in source code (represented by identifier names and internal comments) embeds domain knowledge about a software system. In our case, textual information corresponds to the names, attributes and methods of the model elements. This information can be leveraged to locate the implementation of a feature through the use of IR. IR works by comparing a set of artifacts to a query and ranking these artifacts by their relevance to the query.

There are many IR techniques that have been applied for feature location tasks. However most feature location research efforts have shown better results when LSI is applied [14,17,18]. To perform LSI, our approach follows five main steps: creating a corpus, preprocessing, indexing, querying, and generating results (see Fig. 3 Information Retrieval phase).

We adapted each step of the LSI technique to work with architecture models. Instead of using the source code files, we used the architecture model that contains the executed model elements from the dynamic analysis. The adaptation is performed as follows:

Creating a corpus. In the first step of LSI, a document granularity needs to be chosen to form a corpus. A document lists all the text found in a contiguous section of source code (methods, classes, or packages). A corpus consists of a set of documents. In this work, each document corresponds to a model element of the architecture model. Each document (model element) includes text from the names of the attributes and methods.

Preprocessing. Once the corpus is created, it is preprocessed. Preprocessing involves normalizing the text of the documents. For source code, operators and programming language keywords are removed. In addition, identifiers and compound words are split. In this work, the type of the attributes and the type of the parameters in the methods are removed. Then, all the identifiers are split; for example "IlluminationService" becomes "illumination" and "service".

Indexing. The corpus is used to create a *term-by-document matrix*. Each row of the matrix corresponds to each term in the corpus, and each column represents each document. Each cell of the matrix holds a measure of the weight or relevance of the term in the document. The weight is expressed as a simple count of the number of times that the term appears in the document. In other words, each term-document pair has a number that indicates the number of times this term appears as part of the names of attributes or methods of this model element. In this work, in the term-by-document co-occurrence matrix, the terms (rows) correspond to the names of the attributes or methods (i.e., intensity) of the run-time architecture model and the documents (columns) correspond to the model elements (i.e., IlluminationService) that have appeared in the run-time architecture model.

Figure 4 shows this term-by-document co-occurrence matrix with the values associated to our running example. Each row in the matrix stands for each one of the unique words (terms) extracted from our run-time architecture model. Figure 4 shows a set of representative keywords in the domain such as 'room',

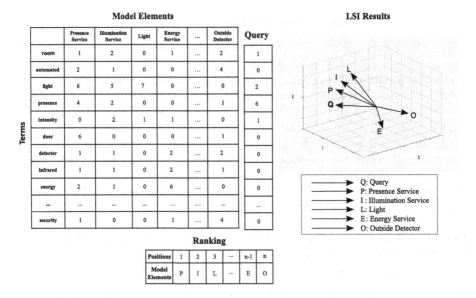

Fig. 4. Information retrieval via Latent Semantic Indexing (LSI)

'light', or 'presence' as the terms of each row. Each column in the matrix stands for the model elements of the run-time architecture model. Figure 4 also shows the names of the model elements in the columns such as 'PresenceService' or 'IlluminationService', which represent the model elements of the run-time architecture model. Each cell in the matrix contains the frequency with which the keyword of its row appears in the document denoted by its column. For instance, in Fig. 4, the term 'light' appears 6 times in the 'PresenceService' model element.

Querying. A user formulates a query in natural language consisting of words or phrases that describe the feature to be located. Since LSI does not use a predefined grammar or vocabulary, users can originate queries in natural language. In this work, we use the bug reports to formulate the queries. Only the relevant terms are taken into account, and words such as determinants and connectors from the language are avoided.

In Fig. 4, the query column represents the words that appear in the bug report. Each cell contains the frequency with which the keyword of its row appears in the query. For instance, the term 'light' appears 2 times in the query.

Generating results. In LSI, the query and each document correspond to a vector. The cosine of the angle between the query vector and a document vector is used as the measure of the similarity of the document to the query. The closer the cosine is to 1, the more similar the document is to the query. A cosine similarity value is calculated between the query and each document, and then the documents are sorted by their similarity values. The user inspects the ranked list to determine which of the documents are relevant to the feature.

We obtain vector representations of the documents and the query by normalizing and decomposing the term-by-document co-occurrence matrix using a matrix factorization technique called singular value decomposition (SVD) [14]. SVD is a form of factor analysis, or more precisely, the mathematical generalization of which factor analysis is a special case. In SVD, a rectangular matrix is decomposed into the product of three other matrices. One component matrix describes the original row entities as vectors of derived orthogonal factor values, another describes the original column entities in the same way, and the third is a diagonal matrix that contains scaling values such that when the three components are matrix-multiplied, the original matrix is reconstructed.

A three-dimensional graph of the LSI results is provided in Fig. 4. The graph shows the representation of each one of the vectors, labeled with letters that represent the names of the model elements, which are referenced in the box below the graph. The graph reflects the 'PresenceService' model element vector as being the closest to the query vector, followed by the 'IlluminationService' model element vector.

The goal of our approach is to rank model elements relevant to the feature to locate within the top positions. The ranking of model elements is ordered by the values of the cosines. In the running example (see Fig. 4, Ranking), the 'PresenceService' element is in the first position and therefore is the most relevant, while the 'OutsideDetector' element is in the last position and is the less relevant.

4   Evaluation: Feature Location in the Smart Hotel

We evaluated whether our feature location approach with architecture models at run-time achieves better results than current approaches [14] that use source code to perform feature location. We choose the approach presented in [14] because is the one that shows the best results for feature location in source code [8,20].

We defined the experimental design of our study using the Goal-Question-Metric method (GQM) [2]. We used the template presented in [3]. The GQM method was defined as a mechanism for defining and interpreting a set of operation goals using measurements. In this evaluation, according to GQM template our goal was the following:

– Object: Our Smart Hotel
– Purpose: Evaluation
– Issue: The accuracy of the results in our architecture-model-based feature location approach
– Context: Feature location in the run-time architecture model

To fulfill this goal, we focused on answering the following research question: Does our architecture-model-based approach for feature location provide better results than a source-code-based approach?

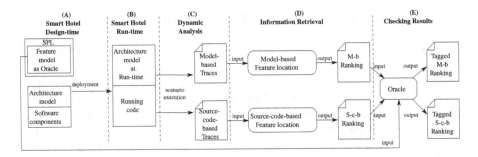

Fig. 5. The evaluation process followed in the Smart Hotel

Figure 5 shows the entire process that we followed for this evaluation.

(A) Smart Hotel Design-time. The Smart Hotel was developed using a Dynamic Software Product Line (DSPL) [4]. The architecture model and the source code of the Smart Hotel were configured with a feature model [7]. The feature model specifies the 39 different features that the Smart Hotel has implemented. We used the feature model of the software product line as an oracle to evaluate our approach. In other words, we made use of a set of PervML models and implementation codes whose feature realizations are known beforehand and will be considered as the ground truth. This enables us to compare the oracle with the results provided by our approach and the source-code approach.

The Smart Hotel presents sixty-eight model elements (thirteen services, twenty devices, and thirty-five channels) in the architecture model. The software components of the Smart Hotel consist of 268 classes that are implemented in about 67,207 methods of Java source code.

(B) Smart Hotel Run-time. In the evaluation set-up, a scale environment with real KNX[3] devices was used to represent the Smart Hotel. In our case, we chose to carry out in-virtuo experiments [2,21], where the real world is described as computer models. This experiment involves the interaction among participants and a computerized model of reality. The simulated environment offers major advantages regarding the cost and the feasibility of replicating a real-world configuration. In addition, some scenarios, such as fires or floods, cannot be replicated in the real world.

(C) Dynamic Analysis. We then ran the scenario that executes the feature to be located. For this case study, we executed 30 independent runs (as suggested by [1]) for each of the 39 features. The execution of the scenario generated the Smart Hotel run-time architecture model and source code traces.

(D) Information Retrieval. Our architecture-model-based feature location approach and the source-code-based feature location approach used the Smart Hotel run-time architecture model and source code traces, respectively. Our architecture-model-based feature location approach produced a ranking of

---

[3] KNX technology is a standard for applications in home and building control (http://www.knx.org/).

model elements (see Fig. 5, M-b Ranking) and the source-code-based feature location approach produced a ranking of methods (see Fig. 5, S-C-b Ranking) for the targeted feature.

(E) Checking Results. The feature model oracle enabled us to know how many of the model elements or methods in the rankings were the ones that realized the target feature. We tagged the model elements (see Fig. 5, Tagged M-b Ranking) and methods (see Fig. 5, Tagged S-C-b Ranking) that belonged to the targeted feature. This allowed us to know their positions in the rankings.

4.1   Results

We performed this evaluation with the thirty-nine features that compose the Smart Hotel. We defined the scenarios based on bug reports of each one of the features. On average, the traces generated were the following: 46 model elements in the architecture-model-based feature location approach and 3,817 methods in the source-code-based feature location approach.

Figure 6 shows the position of the first model element and the first method that belong to the target feature in the ranking for each one of the thirty-nine features. The x-axis represents the features, and the y-axis represents the position in the ranking. The blue dots represent the first model element for each feature and the red Xs represent the first source code method for each feature. The position of the first model element that belongs to each one of the features has values between 1 and 28, where the 84 % of the results are in the top ten positions. However, the position of the first source code method that belongs to each one of the features has values between 12 and 100.

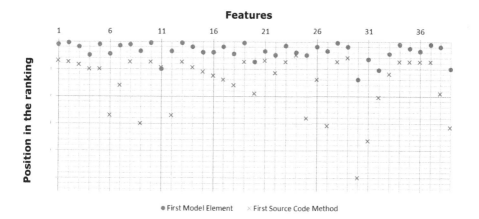

Fig. 6. Position of the first model element and the first method that belong to the target feature in the ranking for each one of the features

Does Our Architecture-model-based Approach for Feature Location Provide Better Results Than the Source-code-based Approach? Our architecture-model-based approach ranks the relevant elements in the top ten positions of the ranking in 84 % of the cases; in the top positions in the ranking of the source-code-based approach, there are false positives associated with some programming patterns and true positives are spread between positions 15 and 100 (see Fig. 6).

It is accepted by the feature location community [14,18] that, a feature location approach is considered better than another feature location when it produces a ranking where the elements that belong to the feature are in higher positions than in the ranking of the other approach. In our evaluation with the Smart Hotel, our architecture-model-based feature location approach obtained better positions in the rankings than the source-code-based approach.

4.2   Analysis of the Results

The results of our evaluation confirms that introducing architecture models at run-time outperforms the equivalent technique at source code level.

Figure 7 shows the graphical representation of the ranking for the 'Gradual Lighting' feature (feature number five in Fig. 6). Due to space constraints, we only show the graphical representation for one feature, however, all the rankings follow a similar distribution in the results.

The query is the vector that is on the x-axis. The remainder of the vectors are model elements in the architecture-model-based feature location approach or methods in the source-code-based feature location approach. Those that have been tagged by the oracle have a r_i label at the end of the arrow, while those

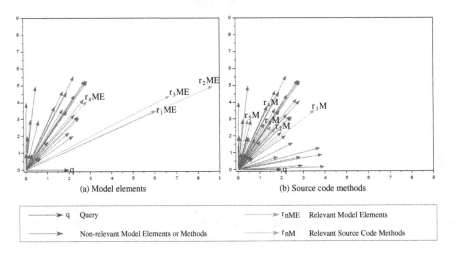

(a) Model elements   (b) Source code methods

→ q	Query		→ r_nME	Relevant Model Elements
→	Non-relevant Model Elements or Methods		→ r_nM	Relevant Source Code Methods

Fig. 7. Vectorial representation of the model elements and source code methods in the Ranking of the 'Gradual Lighting' feature

that have not been tagged have nothing at the end of the arrow. The angle corresponds to the cosine with which we calculated the position in the ranking (see Sect. 3.2); the closer the model element or method is to the query, the higher the position in the ranking. The length of each vector indicates the number of times that the terms appear in each model element or method. The longer the vector is, the more terms appear in the model element or method.

The graph of the left corresponds to the architecture-model-based feature location approach, of the total of vectors (model elements), forty-six, the graph only shows the thirty-three which have positive cosines, the rest, thirteen, are in the left of the y-axis and have few relevance for the query. The graph on the right corresponds to the source-code-based feature location approach, of the total of vectors (methods), 3,817, the graph only shows the 1,302, which have positive cosines, the rest, 2,515, are in the left of the y-axis.

The first difference between the architecture-model-based approach and the source-code-based approach lies in the size of the search space in which the feature must be located. The goal of a feature location technique is to reduce the effort required by software engineers to find the desired feature. Our architecture-model-based approach on average requires searching in less than fifty model elements while a source-code-based approach on average requires searching in more than three thousand eight hundred methods.

The graphical representation of Fig. 7 allows us to see that the architecture-model-based approach discriminates better than the source-code-based approach. The majority of the model elements that belong to the feature achieve better results than the ones that do not belong. However, in the source-code-based approach, the source code methods that belong to the feature and the source code methods that do not belong to the feature are not differentiated.

In addition, the vectors of the model elements that belong to the feature are closer to the query vector than the vectors of the source code methods that belong to the feature (see Fig. 7). Therefore, the model-based approach provides searches that are more accurate.

Since architecture models at run-time allow working on a high level of abstraction, the words used at the model level (i.e., *room, presence*) are closer to the query than the ones used at source code level (i.e., *save or run*). The result is that queries using a natural language show better results with the architecture-model-based approach. In the source-code-based approach some auxiliary terms are taken into account. Some terms, like *controller or run*, can proceed from some programming patterns. By raising the level of abstraction with the architecture model, we can prevent auxiliary methods and variables from interfering with the feature location.

Finally, in our Smart Hotel, we realized that the model elements that contained few attributes and methods got worse positions in the ranking than the ones that contained more attributes and methods. For example, one of the elements related to the feature 'Gradual Lighting' in Fig. 7 obtained position 27 in the ranking. This is because this element corresponds to a channel element that connects two services. This particular channel only has three attributes that describe the information that goes through the channel. The information required by this element was not as detailed as the other model elements when specifying the model. For this reason, the model element corresponding to this channel got a lower position in the ranking. In contrast, other kinds of channels got better positions since, on average, they have about twenty attributes and methods.

4.3   Threats to Validity

In this section, we discuss some of the issues that might have affected the results of the evaluation and may limit the generalizations of the results.

One issue is whether or not the software system used in the evaluation is representative of those used in practice. Given the scale and complexity of our Smart Hotel (sixty-eight model elements and 67.207 methods), we consider our evaluation to be a good starting point for representing a realistic case. However, this threat can be reduced if we experiment with other software systems of different sizes and domains.

Furthermore, the DSL model used in this study is a language in a specific domain. PervML is a DSL that describes pervasive systems using high-level abstraction concepts. However, other experiments with other DSLs should be performed to validate our findings.

Another issue is the selection of the scenarios based on the bug reports to obtain the execution trace. Since we are experts in the Smart Hotel system, we can claim that our scenarios are good representatives of features that have been necessary to locate in order to solve the most common bugs of the Smart Hotel. Thus, depending on the chosen scenarios, the results may differ. The more knowledge the software engineer has about the system, the better the scenarios and the queries will be, leading to better results.

5   Related Work

Some approaches that are related to feature location use design-time models to extract variability. Although they do not use architecture models at run-time, their works are based on extracting features using models.

Font et al. [9] suggest that model fragments that are extracted mechanically may not be recognizable units by the application engineers. They propose identifying model patterns by human-in-the-loop and conceptualizing them as reusable model fragments. Their approach provides the means to identify and extract those model patterns and further apply them to existing product models. In [10], the work from [9] is extended to handle situations where the domain expert fails to provide accurate information. The authors propose a genetic algorithm for feature location in model-based software product lines. When this method was compared with another approach that did not use a genetic algorithm, the results showed that their approach was able to provide solutions for situations where the information of the domain expert was inaccurate, while the other approach failed.

Martinez et al. [15] propose an extensible framework that allows features to be identified, located, and extracted from a family of models. They introduce the principles of this framework and provide insights on how it can be extended for use it in different scenarios. As a result, the initial investment required by the task of adopting a software product line from a family of models is reduced.

Xue et al. [22] present an approach to support effective feature location in products variants. They exploit commonalities and differences of product variants by software differencing and formal concept analysis (FCA) techniques so that IR techniques can achieve satisfactory results.

All of these works are based on extracting model fragments from a given set of models taking into account their commonalities and variabilities. However, these approaches do not take into account the run-time behaviour of the systems and are not focused on feature location. Nevertheless, all of them can be used as a basis for the extraction of the model fragments that correspond to the feature to be located.

There are many more research efforts in dynamic feature location techniques that are based on source code analysis. Some of these works combine other kinds of analysis (i.e., information retrieval) to obtain more accurate results.

Liu et al. [14] combine information from an execution trace and from the comments and identifiers from the source code. They executed a single scenario (which runs the desired feature), and all executed methods are identified based on the collected trace using LSI. The result is a ranked list of executed methods based on their textual similarity to a query. Similarly, Koschke et al. [11] develop a semi-automated technique using a combination of static and dynamic program analysis. However, they use FCA to explore the results of the dynamic analysis.

Revelle et al. [18] apply data fusion for feature location. Their technique combines information from textual, dynamic, and web mining analysis applied to a software system. Their input is a single scenario that executes the feature; after running the scenario, they construct a call graph that contains only the methods that were executed. Then, they apply a web-mining algorithm, and the system filters out low-ranked methods. The remaining set of methods is scored using LSI based on their relevance to the input query that describes the feature.

Similarly to our approach, all these feature location techniques use information from different sources. Additionally, Revelle and Poshyvanyk [19] present an exploratory study of feature location techniques that use various combinations of textual, dynamic, and static analysis. Also, they introduces a new way of applying textual analysis by which queries are automatically composed by identifiers of a method known to be relevant to a feature. Although they are based on locating feature in source code, some of the ideas could be applied to our architecture-model-based feature location approach to obtain more accurate results.

6   Conclusions

This work proposes an approach that combines architecture models at run-time and information retrieval for feature location. Specifically, our approach uses a scenario that executes the desired feature to be located. In addition, our approach ranks all of the model elements that are executed to extract the model elements that are related to the feature. We adapt an information retrieval technique called LSI to work with architecture models at run-time. The ranked list of model elements is obtained based on the similarity of these model elements to a query in a natural language.

Both models and feature descriptions are on a higher abstraction level than source code. This means that models are closer to natural language queries, and the results are more accurate. The comparison of our architecture-model-based feature location approach with a source-code-based feature location approach for the Smart Hotel case study demonstrate this outcome.

Our architecture-model-based approach ranks the relevant elements in the top ten positions of the ranking in 84 % of the cases. In the top positions of the source-code-based approach ranking, there are false positives associated with some programming patterns and true positives are spread between positions 12 and 100.

Acknowledgments. This work has been partially supported by the Ministry of Economy and Competitiveness (MINECO) through the Spanish National R+D+i Plan and ERDF funds under the project Model-Driven Variability Extraction for Software Product Line Adoption (TIN2015-64397-R).

References

1. Arcuri, A., Briand, L.: A hitchhiker's guide to statistical tests for assessing randomized algorithms in software engineering. Softw. Test. Verif. Reliab. **24**(3), 219–250 (2014). doi:10.1002/stvr.1486

2. Basili, V.R.: The role of experimentation in software engineering: past, current, and future. In: Proceedings of the 18th International Conference on Software Engineering, ICSE 1996, pp. 442–449 (1996). http://dl.acm.org/citation.cfm?id=227726. 227818

3. Basili, V.R., Caldiera, G., Rombach, H.D.: The goal question metric approach. In: Calvo, J. (ed.) Encyclopedia of Software Engineering. Wiley, Hoboken (1994)

4. Bencomo, N., Hallsteinsen, S., Santana de Almeida, E.: A view of the dynamic software product line landscape. Computer **45**(10), 36–41 (2012)

5. Bencomo, N., France, R., Cheng, B.H.C., Aßmann, U. (eds.): Models@run.time. Foundations, Applications, and Roadmaps. LNCS, vol. 8378. Springer, Heidelberg (2014)

6. Cetina, C.: Achieving autonomic computing through the use of variability models at run-time. Ph.D. thesis, Universidad Politécnica de Valencia (2010)

7. Czarnecki, K., Helsen, S., Eisenecker, U.: Staged configuration using feature models. In: Nord, R.L. (ed.) SPLC 2004. LNCS, vol. 3154, pp. 266–283. Springer, Heidelberg (2004). doi:10.1007/978-3-540-28630-1_17

8. Dit, B., Revelle, M., Gethers, M., Poshyvanyk, D.: Feature location in source code: a taxonomy and survey. J. Softw. Maintenance Evol. Res. Pract. **25**(1), 53–95 (2011)

9. Font, J., Arcega, L., Haugen, Ø., Cetina, C.: Building software product lines from conceptualized model patterns. In: Proceedings of the 2015 19th International Software Product Line Conference, SPLC 2015, Nashville, TN, USA (2015)

10. Font, J., Arcega, L., Haugen, Ø., Cetina, C.: Feature location in model-based software product lines through a genetic algorithm. In: Kapitsaki, G.M., Santana de Almeida, E. (eds.) ICSR 2016. LNCS, vol. 9679, pp. 39–54. Springer, Heidelberg (2016). doi:10.1007/978-3-319-35122-3_3

11. Koschke, R., Quante, J.: On dynamic feature location. In: Proceedings of the 20th IEEE/ACM International Conference on Automated Software Engineering, ASE 2005, NY, USA, pp. 86–95 (2005). http://doi.acm.org/10.1145/1101908.1101923

12. Landauer, T.K., Foltz, P.W., Laham, D.: An introduction to latent semantic analysis. Discourse Process. 25(2–3), 259–284 (1998)

13. Lehman, M.M., Ramil, J., Kahen, G.: A paradigm for the behavioural modelling of software processes using system dynamics. Technical report, Imperial College of Science, Technology and Medicine, Department of Computing, September 2001

14. Liu, D., Marcus, A., Poshyvanyk, D., Rajlich, V.: Feature location via information retrieval based filtering of a single scenario execution trace. In: Proceedings of the Twenty-Second IEEE/ACM International Conference on Automated Software Engineering, ASE 2007, NY, USA, pp. 234–243 (2007). http://doi.acm.org/10.1145/1321631.1321667

15. Martinez, J., Ziadi, T., Bissyandé, T.F., Le Traon, Y.: Bottom-up adoption of software product lines: a generic and extensible approach. In: Proceedings of the 2015 19th International Software Product Line Conference, SPLC 2015, Nashville, TN, USA (2015)

16. Muñoz, J.: Model driven development of pervasive systems. building a software factory. Ph.D. thesis, Universidad Politécnica de Valencia (2008)

17. Poshyvanyk, D., Gueheneuc, Y.G., Marcus, A., Antoniol, G., Rajlich, V.: Feature location using probabilistic ranking of methods based on execution scenarios and information retrieval. IEEE Trans. Softw. Eng. 33(6), 420–432 (2007). doi:10.1109/TSE.2007.1016

18. Revelle, M., Dit, B., Poshyvanyk, D.: Using data fusion and web mining to support feature location in software. In: 2010 IEEE 18th International Conference on Program Comprehension (ICPC), pp. 14–23, June 2010

19. Revelle, M., Poshyvanyk, D.: An exploratory study on assessing feature location techniques. In: IEEE 17th International Conference on Program Comprehension, ICPC 2009, pp. 218–222, May 2009

20. Rubin, J., Chechik, M.: A survey of feature location techniques. In: Reinhartz-Berger, I., Sturm, A., Clark, T., Cohen, S., Bettin, J. (eds.) Domain Engineering, pp. 29–58. Springer, Berlin (2013)

21. Travassos, M.O., Barros, M.O.: Contributions of in virtuo and in silico experiments for the future of empirical studies in software engineering. In: Proceedings of the ESEIW 2003 Workshop on Empirical Studies in Software Engineering. IEEE Computer Society (2003)

22. Xue, Y., Xing, Z., Jarzabek, S.: Feature location in a collection of product variants. In: 2012 19th Working Conference on Reverse Engineering, pp. 145–154, October 2012

Exchanging the Target-Language in Existing, Non-Metamodel-Based Compilers

Dorian Weber[✉], Markus Scheidgen, and Joachim Fischer

Humboldt-Universität zu Berlin, Berlin, Germany
{weber,scheidge,fischer}@informatik.hu-berlin.de

Abstract. When looking for solutions to automatically translate from high-level source to target code in heterogeneous programming environments and under budgetary restrictions, one often encounters the problem that affordable compilers with front-end support for a particular source language don't map to the desired target-language. The goal of this paper is to present an approach for adapting existing compilers in a non-intrusive way that keeps the front-end intact and replaces the back-end with a component that supports the translation into any language with a context-free text-based syntax. This is achieved by introducing a domain-specific language for code generation to the compiler pipeline that offers a programmable interface to access internal representations of parsed source code in its programs. We formulate a set of requirements for this language and show how compiler developers can use the supplied interface in combination with the domain-specific language to adapt the textual output to their needs.

Keywords: Legacy compiler · Code generation · Meta-model · ASN.1 · Meta-language · Domain-specific language

1 Introduction

Work on a sophisticated project often requires the cooperative use of multiple programming languages that describe different aspects of the software. It is in this context that one often finds the need to generate high-level code, e.g. from formal specifications, to be used in conjunction with high-level code written in some other language. In these situations, one would be looking for a compiler that translates the source into its target-language representation. In this paper, *language* refers to the concrete syntax of a language, *compiler* refers to any program that translates a *source* into a *target-language* and the implementation language of the compiler is called the *host-language*. Compilers for established formal languages usually exist, but may lack support for the desired target or are prohibitively expensive. In consequence, one has to spend resources to either employ a team of programmers that render the specification manually, abandon the use of source or target-language in favor of a combination with better tool support, or develop a new compiler. These choices imply a potentially costly binding of resources: rendering the specification manually could be expensive and introduces redundancies, abandoning the use of source or target-language might not be feasible and is certainly not desirable, and developing a new compiler is

© Springer International Publishing AG 2016
J. Grabowski and S. Herbold (Eds.): SAM 2016, LNCS 9959, pp. 196–210, 2016.
DOI: 10.1007/978-3-319-46613-2_13

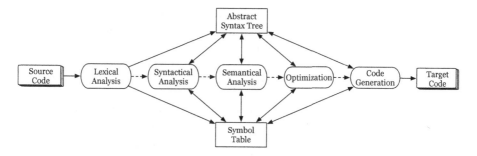

Fig. 1. Canonical compiler architecture according to [4]. Passive structures and external files are represented by rectangles and stacks respectively and rounded boxes indicate active phases. Dotted arrows point in the direction of the control flow, solid arrows show data flow. Arrows pointed towards structures indicate permission to write, while arrows pointing away from them indicate read access.

uncertain to pay off in the long term, especially if decisions like these are made on a by-project basis.

Given access and permission to modify the code of an existing compiler for the source language, we propose a method to add support for an additional target-language while keeping the front-end intact, thereby removing it from the cost-equation. By providing optimized means of expressing the generation of high-level code through the use of a domain-specific language that is deployed as part of the adapted compiler we can facilitate the construction of additional compiler extensions by parties that are otherwise unaffiliated with compiler development. We call domain-specific languages for code generation *meta-languages*. Figure 1 on page 2 shows the traditional compiler architecture according to Garlan and Shaw [4]. Our fundamental assumption is that front- and back-end can be separated in the original compiler. We propose to replace the code generating component with a generic module that provides an interface for importing the abstract syntax in combination with a meta-language that can access these structures. Although this approach could be used for compilers with low-level language targets, we focus on high-level text-based output in this paper, since we regard applications involving the translation of specification-type source languages into implementation-type target-languages as more common.

The paper is organized as follows. First we take a look at related work in Sect. 2 and discuss the relationship to the problem presented here. We continue by comparing different approaches in Sect. 3 and follow up with a description of our generic module for code generation in Sect. 4. Section 5 contains a case study for an ASN.1-to-C compiler using our approach. We finish with our conclusions and outlook in Sect. 6.

2   Related Work

The LLVM-project as described by Lattner and Adve [5] solves a very similar problem: the abstract syntax of a source language is to be translated for multiple target architectures. By decoupling source and target via mapping into an intermediate language for a low-level virtual machine, they modularize both front-and back-ends, allowing them to be exchanged independently to support arbitrary combinations of source and target-language. This technique isn't unique to LLVM and the intermediate language is commonly known as IR (intermediate representation). The LLVM-approach is to use a canonical IR for arbitrary source languages. The key difference between the problem solved with LLVM compared to the one solved in this paper is our need to generate high-level as opposed to low-level target code. Since LLVM ultimately generates machine code, the canonical IR is executable by design. This restriction would not be appropriate for our source and target-languages because our models might not be executable.

Parr uses his *StringTemplate* library [6] to generate high-level documents using string templates. *String templates* are sequences of static text and dynamically evaluated expressions with access to the model and other string templates. The problem is similar because many different document formats can be generated from the same source. He specifically prevents the library to be turing-complete in order to separate model and view [7] and points out that string templates can be used to generate any context-free text-based language due to the structural similarity between string templates and context-free grammars. This makes string templates a suitable tool for generating context-free text-based languages. The key difference is that we don't assume our target-language to be context-free, e.g. C isn't context-free because it requires prior declaration of identifiers.

In the context of model-transformation, the combination of Xtext and Xtend can be used to implement code generators for different language targets [2]. The fundamental idea is to use information inherently present in the concrete syntax specification of the source language in order to derive the abstract syntax in Xtext [3] as a form of text-to-model transformation and import it into Xtend for code generation as a model-to-text transformation. This technique requires a shared metamodel of the abstract syntax and a compatible execution platform. Our problem differs because we cannot assume a standardized metamodel for representing the abstract syntax in legacy compilers. We discuss benefits and drawbacks of metamodel-based rewrites for legacy compilers in Sect. 3.

3   Comparing Different Methods for Exchanging the Target-Language

In this section we analyze different methods that can be used to exchange the language emitted by a compiler. Ideally, we would like to support both the existing as well as any additional target-language in the same program. We have divided this task into two steps:

1. Prepare the compiler to be extended through additional code generators by introducing a generic module for code generation.
2. Specialize or extend the generic module with one or more code generators for the desired target-languages.

This separation helps us to weigh the amount of work needed to implement the first additional target-language versus any following ones. The workload differs because later extensions benefit from mechanisms that are in place after the first target-language has been introduced. We observe a sliding scale in flexibility with respect to new target-languages: putting a larger (fixed) amount of work into the first step tends to reduce the (dynamic) costs for the second step and vice versa. We continue by analyzing three specific approaches on that spectrum with varying demands regarding the costs of the first and the second steps.

3.1   Metamodel

Characterization. A *model* is an abstraction of an aspect of reality. A *meta-model* is the model of a model. In our paper, the metamodel contains data structure definitions specific to the source language, i.e. the abstract syntax. Metamodel instances are produced as the result of the parsing process and capture all aspects that are relevant to code generation for any given input. The metamodel-based approach of language development aims to reduce the costs of implementing new compilers by employing domain-specific languages throughout the development process and standardizing exchange formats between different phases via compliance to a shared metamodel. This architecture allows for easy replacement of compiler components as well as semi-automated derivation of auxiliary tools like editors and debuggers.

Analysis. Languages developed using this approach benefit from flexible backends and only need to exchange their code generator components to facilitate different target-languages. However, it is not trivial to transform a Non-Metamodel-Based compiler into one using explicit metamodels if the former hasn't specifically been constructed with a shared metamodel in mind. This is because the metamodel-based approach relies on a language-agnostic specification of navigable intermediate structures with a standardized interface that is rendered into concrete data types for the various languages that are used in the development of the compiler. It is not customary in traditional compiler development to specify intermediate structures in a language different from the host-language, meaning that supporting tools, e. g. lexer and parser generators, usually support code injections in the host-language that access and manipulate these structures. Because of the multitude of specifications in different domain-specific languages, automatically refactoring the use and construction of these structures to abide by a new interface is a complex task. Manually exchanging intermediate structures implies a workload about the same order of magnitude as redeveloping the compiler from scratch using a metamodel-based approach.

Conclusion. This approach requires a costly first step while the second step benefits from the use of a meta-language during code generation. With a comparatively small amount of extra work, additional tools like editors and debuggers can be derived. Initial compiler development can gain the most with this approach, but compilers with high demands in terms of supported target-languages that would benefit from custom editors and debuggers could profit as well.

3.2   Meta Language

Characterization. A *meta-language* is a programming language that includes domain-specific facilities aimed at improving the description of code generators. Meta-languages have been developed alongside metamodel-based techniques and can also be used in absence of an explicit metamodel. One example for this is Xtend, a JVM-based language typically used to implement code generation for language specifications written in Xtext. Even though Xtext and Xtend are designed with each other in mind they don't have to be used in combination allowing Xtend to implement the back-end of compilers that are not using explicit metamodels. Due to their domain-specificity, meta-languages can significantly reduce the amount of work needed to support target-languages. One can distinguish between declarative meta-languages that unparse the abstract syntax tree through recursive application of unparse-rules and imperative meta-languages similar to general-purpose languages with built-in facilities for the generation of high-level code. Both variants require access to the abstract syntax.

Analysis. In order to provide access to the abstract syntax in absence of an explicit metamodel, it will usually be necessary to employ a compatibility layer between host- and meta-language. The layer could be formed via compliance to a shared metamodel or using an interface provided by the meta-language that is used to feed data into it. Once the structures are accessible, one uses the meta-language to implement code generators as if the metamodel-based approach had been used to begin with. The approach differs from the metamodel-based one, since the metamodel is not needed for the other translation phases.

Conclusion. This approach offers a good compromise of balancing the fixed amount of work needed for setting up the extension mechanism with the dynamic amount of work for implementing additional code generators. It allows the use of meta-languages for the back-end of the compiler but doesn't support automatic derivation of editors and debuggers, since these applications require access to the grammar of the source language.

3.3   General-Purpose Language

Characterization. Instead of using meta-languages in the compiler back-end, one can simply use an existing general-purpose language augmented with a programming library suitable for generating high-level code. The need to recompile the compiler for each additional code generator can be overcome through the use of a well-defined interface in combination with dynamic linking or by employing an interpreted (general-purpose) language. A library for code generation could include support for common tasks such as access to intermediate structures via iterators, file and exception handling as well as support for string templates. Compared to common strings that don't support dynamic expressions or recursion, string templates conserve the structure of the generated text, improving the readability of generators for high-level code.

Analysis. Using the host-language to generate target code requires the implementation of a library that is useful in processing the generated structures. Since the required functionality of that library, e.g. iterating complex structures, file and exception handling, is very common, it is likely that one can choose an existing library for the task. This reduces the work necessary to prepare the extension mechanism to designing a generic interface for code generators.

The second step, extending the compiler with additional code generators, is more complex. Only some advantages of meta-languages can be emulated through library functions. Using the host-language as the language to implement the code generators has the following drawbacks compared to using a well designed meta-language:

– the general-purpose language lacks support for domain-specific features, such as string templates with access to the surrounding variable scope,
– compiling dynamically linked libraries requires OS dependent code changes that need to be adapted for each platform,
– bugs in the code generator cannot easily be traced back to the offending code since source code will usually not ship alongside the compiler,
– the code generator is not isolated from the main program, bugs may have ramifications further down the execution path.

Some of these disadvantages can be circumvented through the use of an interpreted general-purpose language, but those will typically

– be designed for stand-alone usage, assuming script rather than host-language driven control and manipulating global program states,
– ship with extensive programming libraries unrelated to code generation and increase the memory footprint of any compiler they are deployed with,
– offer minimal support for using host-language structures inside of script files.

Conclusion. This approach requires a minimal amount of work for preparing the compiler and can benefit from existing support through programming libraries. Extending the compiler with additional target-languages can be much more complicated compared to the use of a meta-language because in addition to concentrating on the complex task of code generation one must also deal with the idiosyncrasies of the host-language. This can include memory and file management, platform dependent integer types as well as a lack of standardized iteration mechanisms, exception handling and object oriented features further complicating debugging and maintenance of any additional target-language.

4 A Generic Module for Code Generation

In this section we discuss how a generic module may be constructed that can be used in place of a code generator for existing compilers. The module contains a compiler or interpreter for a meta-language as well as an interface to import structures from the host-language. Given the existence of such a module, the key steps to extend an existing compiler are:

1. provide an interface for compiler users to switch language targets,
2. give access to the abstract syntax of the source language to code generators,
3. supply code generators written in the meta-language.

The first step depends on internal compiler specifics, so we cannot comment on it. The second step can be accomplished through the use of the module's import interface. Using the code generators developed in the third step, the compiler can generate target-language-specific code utilizing the module's support for the meta-language.

We begin by listing our design goals for a generic module for code generation, followed by an overview of our implementation. In order to verify the merits of our proposition we have developed a meta-language called *Glue*. The next section showcases an example for using *Glue* to extend an existing open source ASN.1-compiler.

4.1 Design Goals

We make five basic assumptions about scenarios in which the module is used. These are:

1. Compiler and code generator are developed by independent parties.
2. Compiler developers want to minimize their work when preparing the compiler for target-language extensions.
3. Code generator developers are not familiar with the meta-language but have programming experience.
4. Translation of the source language is a complicated task.
5. Code generators are developed incrementally and may contain bugs.

Under these assumptions, here are five factors that we have identified as important for the design of the domain-specific language and module:

1. The meta-language should have domain-specific features for code generation, e.g. string templates or rule-based unparsing of abstract syntax trees.

   Rationale: *Domain-specificity is the key reason for preferring the meta-language over any general-purpose language.*
2. Importing external data structures should only require dealing with the parts that are actually useful in meta programs. Navigation and member access shouldn't require prior decomposition and reconstruction.

Rationale: *Structures associated with the abstract syntax have to be imported into the meta-language. Keeping the translation interface simple helps to reduce the amount of work that needs to be invested in order to prepare the compiler.*

3. Code not directly contributing to the translation effort should be minimized. Examples include
   - managing dynamic memory,
   - assigning data types to variables,
   - dealing with platform dependencies,
   - handling runtime errors.

   Rationale: *It is helpful to keep the focus on essential elements of the respective code generator during development and for maintenance purposes.*

4. The generic module should be deployed as a platform independent and autonomous programming library for the host-language.

   Rationale: *External dependencies of the component may lead to restrictions in the platform of potential applications.*

5. The syntax should exercise minimality (no redundant concepts), orthogonality (no overlapping concepts), and familiarity (syntactical similarity to popular languages).

   Rationale: *These are qualities that allow external developers and end users to quickly pick up the language and follow code generator implementations.*

In order to fulfill these requirements, we have decided to deploy an interpreter for a meta-language called *Glue* as part of our generic module. Our goal is to provide a platform independent C-based alternative to the Java-based Xtend, so we look to Xtend for domain-specificity, to C for syntactical cues and to Python for simplicity. The resulting language looks like C with Python-like type inference and garbage collection as well as built-in support for Xtend-style string templates.

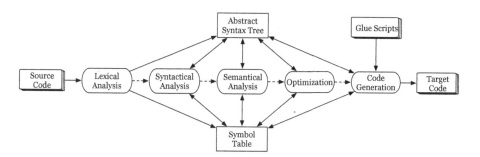

Fig. 2. Modified compiler architecture after integration of our generic module. *Glue* script files describe specialized code generators, conceptionally taking the place of Xtend.

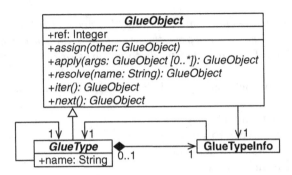

Fig. 3. UML class diagram depicting the relationship between objects and types handled by the *Glue* interpreter. The interface for GlueObject-instances is incomplete and only contains the methods relevant to this paper.

4.2   Implementation

Our module contains a platform independent, autonomous interpreter for a meta-language we refer to as *Glue*. It is used to replace the code generating component of a compiler in a manner consistent with Fig. 2 on page 9. In order to expose host language structures to script files, one can use the interface depicted in Fig. 3 on page 9 to define new types of GlueObject. In practice this means that for every type used in the abstract syntax, the compiler developer needs to provide an instance of GlueType that is used as a gateway to the internal representation. Note that this doesn't require the reconstruction of host structures as *Glue* structures; GlueObjects only need to hold a reference to the specific part they provide access to and atomic attributes like strings or numbers can be converted on-the-fly into equivalent *Glue* types.

The interpreter interacts with GlueObjects through their virtual interface, e.g. by calling assign() in order to assign a new value to a GlueObject. GlueObject's other methods shown in Fig. 3 on page 9 are used to implement function calls (apply()), attribute resolution (resolve()), iterator construction (iter()) as well as advancement (next()). Additional methods have been omitted for brevity. Since the module is C-based, pointers to these methods reside in a virtual function table as part of a GlueTypeInfo-object. Types are represented by instances of GlueType whose role is that of a factory producing instances of their type. Since they are derived from GlueObject, this construction allows *Glue*-scripts to reason about the types and meta-types of objects. A simple single-inheritance scheme is supported.

The *Glue*-syntax borrows heavily from C/C++ syntax but includes automatic, reference based garbage collection, built-in string templates with access to the surrounding variable scope, exception handling, and runtime type inference. It ships with a library that contains support for file and path handling, container types like sets, maps, lists and tuples as well as atomic types like strings and unbounded integers. The inheritance scheme is used to provide reasonable default behavior for unimplemented methods.

5   Case Study: ASN.1 to C

In this section we demonstrate how to exchange the target-language in a concrete compiler using our approach. To this end, we consider a subset of ASN.1 [9] and explain the necessary modifications performed at an open source ASN.1-compiler. We show the *Glue* script files that are used to generate C-code and conclude by analyzing the overall quality of the compiler output for a concrete specification.

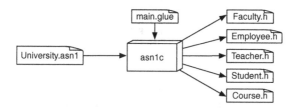

Fig. 4. Illustration of inputs and outputs for the discussed example.

5.1   Scenario

We have integrated our module for code generation into Lev Walkin's open source ASN.1-compiler *asn1c* [8] and use it here to translate an ASN.1-fragment into equivalent C-structures. The source language supports type-definitions using SEQUENCE, CHOICE, SEQUENCE OF, type references, and the terminal type VisibleString. This subset is interesting because it allows types to be complex, recursive, anonymous, aliased, and self-referential. We chose to describe the abstract syntax of our subset of ASN.1 in ASN.1 in order to emphasize that it is powerful enough to express its own abstract syntax, i.e. the abstract syntax shown in Listing 1 is a valid input to a compiler accepting only the subset described therein.

However, in order to avoid confusing different meta-levels, our demonstration uses the specification in Listing 2 as compiler input. The Listing also shows the value of the abstract syntax the way it can be navigated in *Glue* scripts and Fig. 4 on page 10 shows input and output files. The difficulties addressed with this example are:

1. SEQUENCE, CHOICE and SEQUENCE OF are complex types in C.
   Example: *Faculty, Employee and Course are of meta-type SEQUENCE OF, CHOICE and SEQUENCE respectively.*
2. Types may refer to other types and require a prior declaration.
   Example: *Employee refers to Teacher using the attribute teacher.*
3. Directly embedding ASN.1 types requires a distinction between named and unnamed types.

```
1    AbstractSyntax DEFINITIONS AUTOMATIC TAGS ::=
2    BEGIN
3      AST ::= SEQUENCE OF SEQUENCE {
4        module VisibleString,
5        member SEQUENCE OF Named-Type
6      }
7
8      Named-Type ::= SEQUENCE {
9        name VisibleString,
10       type Embedded-Type
11     }
12
13     Embedded-Type ::= CHOICE {
14       typeref VisibleString,
15       sequence SEQUENCE OF Named-Type,
16       choice SEQUENCE OF Named-Type,
17       sequenceOf Embedded-Type
18     }
19   END
```

Listing 1. Abstract syntax of the ASN.1-subset defined as an ASN.1-specification. This representation is made navigable in *Glue* scripts using a global variable of type AST. According to the specification, an abstract syntax tree is a list of modules, each with a name and a list of named types. A named type is a pair consisting of a name and an embedded type definition. Type definitions are either references to other types, tuples/selections of attributes, or lists of embedded types.

```
1    University DEFINITIONS                          asn1 AST ::= {{ module "University", member {
2    AUTOMATIC TAGS ::= BEGIN
3      Faculty ::= SEQUENCE OF SEQUENCE {              { name "Faculty", type sequenceOf: sequence: {
4        name VisibleString,                             { name "name", type typeref: "VisibleString"},
5        member SEQUENCE OF Employee,                    { name "member", type sequenceOf: typeref: "Employee" }
6        courses SEQUENCE OF Course                      { name "courses", type sequenceOf: typeref: "Course" }
7      }                                              }},
8
9      Employee ::= CHOICE {                            { name "Employee", type choice: {
10       teacher Teacher,                                { name "teacher", type typeref: "Teacher" },
11       student Student                                 { name "student", type typeref: "Student" }
12     }                                              }},
13
14     Teacher ::= SEQUENCE {                           { name "Teacher", type sequence: {
15       name VisibleString,                             { name "name", type typeref: "VisibleString" },
16       courses SEQUENCE OF Course                      { name "courses", type sequenceOf: typeref: "Course" }
17     }                                              }},
18
19     Student ::= VisibleString                        { name "Student", type typeref: "VisibleString" },
20
21     Course ::= SEQUENCE {                            { name "Course", type sequence: {
22       title VisibleString,                            { name "title", type typeref: "VisibleString" },
23       instructor Teacher,                             { name "instructor", type typeref: "Teacher" },
24       students SEQUENCE OF Student                    { name "students", type sequenceOf: typeref: "Student" }
25     }                                              }}
26   END                                            }}}
```

Listing 2. ASN.1-specification serving as input next to its abstract syntax. The concrete syntax on the left is exposed to *Glue* as the abstract value on the right, expressed in terms of the abstract type AST of Listing 1. Each line on the left-hand-side directly corresponds to a line on the right-hand-side.

Example: *Faculty is a SEQUENCE OF an anonymous SEQUENCE.*

4. Self-referential types have to be protected from self-inclusion.
   Example: *Teacher and Course depend on one another's definition.*

5.2   Solution

The abstract syntax of the source specification is made accessible to the script through the global variable `asn1` that we define using the interface shown in Fig. 3 on page 9. In accordance with Listing 1 we have implemented `GlueTypes` for `AST`, `Named-Type` and `Embedded-Type`. Since they are responsible for creating their instances, these types have their `apply()`-method implemented. Type instances are views of the underlying abstract syntax, so each of them contains a pointer to the part it wraps. We implemented `resolve()`-methods for `Named-Type`- and `Embedded-Type`-instances for access to the sub-structures as well as an `iter()`-method for `AST`-instances that compiles a `GlueList` of contained modules and returns an iterator to that list. The `resolve()`-methods wrap their attributes on-the-fly either by creating a wrapper instance, by initializing a `GlueList` of wrappers, or by constructing a `GlueString`. The root instance with the name `asn1` is initialized internally and exposed to the script via the interpreter API.

The principal algorithm implemented in the code generator systematically iterates over the abstract syntax tree and recursively translates visited nodes into C-code. Listing 5 shows this loop: each `Named-Type`-node on the module level yields a C-header with an include guard, a list of dependencies (either `#include` or forward declaration) and a type declaration. In order to emit the type, the function `emit()` in Listing 3 is called. Using the attribute `type`, we can distinguish between the different alternatives contained in the `CHOICE Type` and generate the appropriate code.

For `typeref` nodes, we test whether a direct reference to the type would complete a circular inclusion. To that end, the function `contains()` in Listing 4 is used to search the referenced type's closure with regards to its include dependencies for the currently processed top-level `Named-Type`-node. If present, it is necessary to refrain from including the type's header file, instead forward declaring the type and referring to it using a pointer. Since the dependency map is constructed iteratively, this scheme allows the direct inclusion in one direction, referring to the second type via pointer only if a dependency circle were to be completed otherwise. For `sequence` nodes, we generate a `struct` and recursively embed the attributes. The `choice` and `sequenceOf` nodes are implemented through a tagged union and a dynamic list respectively. The terminal type `VisibleString` is mapped to `char*`.

5.3   Observations

The generated header files are shown in Listing 6 with the exception of the header files for *Teacher* and *Student*. We observe that employing string templates to describe the translation has allowed us to automatically derive correctly indented target code. Should we want to improve the generated code, e.g. by adding encode and decode routines or by fixing an error or oversight, it would be obvious which

```
1   new emit(self) {
2     if (self.type == "Typeref") {
3       new type = self.typeref;
4
5       if (contains(self.typeref, expr.name)) {
6         if (self.typeref != expr.name)
7           forwards.insert(self.typeref);
8
9         type = $(struct $type*);
10      }
11      else includes.insert(self.typeref);
12
13      return type;
14    }
15    else if (self.type == "Sequence")
16      return $(
17        $if (self == expr.type)
18        struct ${ expr.name} {
19        $else
20        struct {
21        $$
22          $for (e: self.sequence)
23            ${ emit(e.type)} ${ e.name};
24        $$
25        }
26      );
27    else if (self.type == "Choice")
28      return $(
29        $if (self == expr.type)
30        struct ${ expr.name} {
31        $else
32        struct {
33        $$
34          enum {
35            $for (e: self.choice)
36              ${ self.name.upper}_${ e.name.upper},
37          $$
38          } tag;
39
40          union {
41            $for (e: self.choice)
42              ${ emit(e.type)} ${ e.name};
43          $$
44          } value;
45        }
46      );
47    else if (self.type == "SequenceOf")
48      return $(
49        $if (self == expr.type)
50        struct ${ expr.name} {
51        $else
52        struct {
53        $$
54          int cap, len;
55          ${ emit(self.sequenceOf)}* list;
56        }
57      );
58    else if (self.type == "VisibleString")
59      return "char*";
60  }
```

Listing 3. Code emitting function.

```
62  new containment = Map();
63  new contains(type1, type2) {
64    if (type1 == type2)
65      return true;
66
67    for (it: containment[type1])
68      if (contains(it, type2))
69        return true;
70
71    return false;
72  }
```

Listing 4. Function that recursively searches the convex dependency hull of a type for another type.

```
74  for (module: asn1)
75    for (expr: module.member) {
76      new includes = Set();
77      new forwards = Set();
78      new decl = emit(expr.type);
79
80      Path(expr.name + ".h").open("w").write($(
81        #ifndef ${ expr.name.upper}_H
82        #define ${ expr.name.upper}_H
83
84        $for (include: includes)
85          #include "$include.h"
86        $$
87        $for (forward: forwards)
88          struct $forward;
89        $$
90
91        typedef $decl ${ expr.name};
92
93        #endif
94      ) "\n").commit();
95
96      containment[expr.name] = includes;
97    }
```

Listing 5. The for-loops iterating over the modules and their type definitions, generating a header file for each definition.

```
1    #ifndef FACULTY_H_INCLUDED    #ifndef EMPLOYEE_H_INCLUDED   #ifndef COURSE_H_INCLUDED
2    #define FACULTY_H_INCLUDED    #define EMPLOYEE_H_INCLUDED   #define COURSE_H_INCLUDED
3
4    #include "Course.h"            #include "Student.h"          #include "Student.h"
5    #include "Employee.h"          #include "Teacher.h"          struct Teacher;
6
7    typedef struct Faculty {       typedef struct Employee {     typedef struct Course {
8      int cap, len;                  enum {                        char* title;
9      struct {                         EMPLOYEE_TEACHER,          struct Teacher* instructor;
10        char* name;                    EMPLOYEE_STUDENT,         struct {
11       struct {                      } tag;                        int cap, len;
12         int cap, len;                                             Student* list;
13         Employee* list;            union {                      } students;
14       } member;                      Teacher teacher;          } Course;
15       struct {                       Student student;
16         int cap, len;              } value;                    #endif
17         Course* list;            } Employee;
18       } courses;
19     }* list;                     #endif
20   } Faculty;
21
22   #endif
```

Listing 6. Compiler output for types *Faculty*, *Employee* and *Course* respectively.

part of the code generator to modify. The generating code is easy to read because the structure of the emitted code is eminent and not obstructed by the structure of the emitting code which is another major benefit to using string templates for generating high-level code. Common tasks involving resources and error handling are performed in the background, significantly reducing the complexity of the code generator.

6   Conclusions and Outlook

We have discussed different approaches to exchange the target-language in existing, Non-Metamodel-Based compilers and identified 5 key properties for a generic module for code generation: (1) use of a meta-language, (2) minimal interface for importing host-language structures, (3) focus on essential elements of code generation, (4) deployment as platform independent library, and (5) minimal, orthogonal, and familiar syntax. We presented our module that includes support for the domain-specific language *Glue* and demonstrated its integration and use by modifying an open source ASN.1 compiler to translate a subset of ASN.1 into C-code. Based on the characteristics of the generated code we were able to confirm that the use of a meta-language can be worthwhile when attempting to generate high-level text-based code for multiple targets.

As Arnoldus [1] demonstrated in his PhD thesis, adapting the meta-language to include a syntactical description of the target-language yields a powerful tool for statically detecting syntax errors in the output before attempting to translate any source code. However, this requires modifications to the meta-language during parse-time (of the meta-program) which is technologically challenging. It would be interesting to research whether the syntactical correctness of the target code could be guaranteed without changing the grammar of the meta-language.

References

1. Arnoldus, B.J.: An illumination of the template enigma: software code generation with templates. Ph.D. thesis, Technische Universiteit Eindhoven (2010)
2. Bettini, L.: Implementing Domain-Specific Languages with Xtext and Xtend. Packt Publishing, Birmingham (2013)
3. Efftinge, S., Völter, M.: oAW xText: a framework for textual DSLs. In: Workshop on Modeling Symposium at Eclipse Summit, vol. 32, p. 118 (2006)
4. Garlan, D., Shaw, M.: An introduction to software architecture. Adv. Softw. Eng. Knowl. Eng. **1**(3.4), 24 (1993)
5. Lattner, C., Adve, V.: LLVM: a compilation framework for lifelong program analysis & transformation. In: International Symposium on Code Generation and Optimization, CGO 2004, pp. 75–86. IEEE (2004)
6. Parr, T.J.: String template. http://www.stringtemplate.org/
7. Parr, T.J.: Enforcing strict model-view separation in template engines. In: Proceedings of the 13th International Conference on World Wide Web, pp. 224–233. ACM (2004)
8. Walkins, L.: asn1c. http://lionet.info/asn1c/
9. ASN.1: Specification of basic notation. International Standard X.680, ITU-T (2008)

Towards Rule-Based Detection of Design Patterns in Model Transformations

Chihab eddine Mokaddem, Houari Sahraoui, and Eugene Syriani[(✉)]

University of Montreal, Montreal, Canada
{mokaddec,sahraoui,syriani}@iro.umontreal.ca

Abstract. Model transformations are at the very heart of the Model-Driven Engineering paradigm. As modern programs, they are complex, difficult to write and test, and overall, difficult to understand, maintain, and reuse. In other paradigms, such as object-oriented programming, design patterns play an important role for understanding and reusing code. Many works have been proposed to detect complete design pattern instances for understanding and documentation purposes, but also partial design pattern instances for quality assessment and refactoring purposes. Recently, a catalog of design patterns has been proposed for model transformations. In this paper, we propose to detect these design patterns in declarative model transformation programs. Our approach first detects the rules that may play a role in a design pattern. Then, it ensures that the control flow over these rules corresponds to the scheduling scheme in the design pattern. Our preliminary evaluation shows that our detection mechanism is effective for both complete and partial instances of design patterns.

1 Introduction

Model-driven engineering (MDE) is a recent software development approach that is rapidly growing in popularity [14]. At its core, it makes intensive use of models as a means for automation and reuse. MDE developers use model transformations to perform operations on models, such as: evolving, refactoring, and simulating them [16]. Model transformations, which uses generally a rule-based declarative paradigm [9], are still manually developed. Therefore, like any hand-written software programs, model transformations must be well-designed and implemented in order to be understandable by other developers, be re-used in other projects, and reduce maintenance efforts.

In other paradigms, such as object-oriented programming (OOP), design patterns play an important role in software design [13]. They are proven solutions to recurring design problems that complement practices of developers. Design patterns are described at a higher level of abstraction than the implementation language to ease communication and comprehension. They are considered as micro-architecture building blocks from which more complex designs can be built, thus promoting modularity and reuse. Recently, Lano et al. proposed a thorough catalog of over 20 design patterns for model transformations [17]. They

© Springer International Publishing AG 2016
J. Grabowski and S. Herbold (Eds.): SAM 2016, LNCS 9959, pp. 211–225, 2016.
DOI: 10.1007/978-3-319-46613-2_14

showed that these design patterns reduce complexity and execution time, as well as improve the flexibility and modularity of model transformations. Although the intent and application conditions of each pattern are described rigorously, they chose to define the solution part of the design pattern using a formal notation. To facilitate their understanding for model transformation engineers and to enable the automatic instantiation of design patterns in model transformation implementations, Ergin et al. [10] proposed a dedicated modeling language DelTa with both a graphical and a textual [12] notation.

With the increasing scale and complexity of utilizing models in MDE, the model transformations developed are also increasing in scale and complexity. Furthermore, as with any software product, model transformations are evolving constantly in development projects. This tends to deteriorate their architecture and design, which is a burden of maintenance tasks. Nevertheless, design patterns expressed in DelTa impose structure thanks to the abstraction they use. Therefore, the identification of design patterns implemented in an existing model transformation can tremendously help the developer in understanding the design, as well as document the transformation [22]. Even if a design pattern was not implemented in its integrity in the model transformation, identifying some of its participants provides valuable feedback to the developer: (1) a missed opportunity to implement it in order to improve the quality, (2) a suggestion to correctly implement it through refactoring, or (3) the presence of a modified version of the design pattern, since any design pattern may be implemented with endless variations [20]. Various design pattern detection mechanisms have proven to be very efficient [2,4,7,22]. However, these techniques have been applied to imperative OOP code. Detecting design patterns on model transformations comes with many challenges because they are described (1) declaratively, (2) at the level of meta-models dealing with types and relations rather than instances, and (3) with non-deterministic execution of rules.

In this paper, we present an approach to detect complete or partial instances of design patterns in concrete model transformation implementations. It is a model finding approach based on a rule engine, where we map model transformations to an abstract representation and design patterns to rules that these representations must satisfy. After identifying individual participants of a design pattern, we verify that the scheduling scheme described in the pattern is satisfied in the transformation. We compute an accuracy score at each detection step that is finally aggregated and reported. We implemented a prototype where we encode design patterns defined with the DelTa language as rules and that automatically maps a complete model transformation implemented in a specific model transformation language to the abstract representation. We report preliminary results that show our detection mechanism is effective for both complete and partial instances of design patterns.

In Sect. 2 we provide the necessary background on model transformation and their design patterns. In Sect. 3 we describe our approach on an example. We report the results on the effectiveness of our approach in Sect. 4. Finally, we conclude in Sect. 5.

2   Background

We first review background on model transformations and their design patterns, and then discuss different techniques for detecting design patterns in programs.

2.1   Model Transformation

In MDE, a model transformation is the automatic manipulation of a model following a specification defined at the level of metamodels [16]. A model transformation can be outplace, when it produces a target model from a source model, such as in a translation, or it can be inplace when it modifies a model and the result is an updated version of the source model, such as in a simulation. Typically, a model transformation is defined by a set of declarative rules to be executed. A rule consists of a pre-condition and a post-condition pattern. The pre-condition pattern determines the applicability of a rule: it is the pattern that must be found in the input model to apply the rule. Optionally negative patterns may be specified in the pre-condition to inhibit the application of the rule if present. The post-condition imposes the pattern to be found after the rule is applied. Patterns are made up of structural elements (i.e., model fragments) and of constraints on their attributes. Rules follow a scheduling scheme that defines the order in which they are applied when a transformation is executed. The scheduling can be made explicit by the language with a control flow structure partially ordering rules, such as in Henshin. In some languages, such as ATL, rules are scheduled implicitly, depending on the causal dependence between the post-condition of a rule and the pre-condition of another. Features that model transformation languages support are listed in [9]. A comparison of existing model transformation tools can be found in [18]. Possible scheduling schema of model transformations are described in [21].

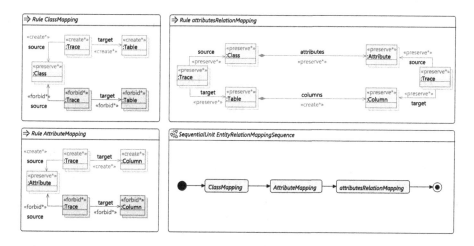

Fig. 1. Model transformation of entity relation in Henshin

For example, consider the model transformation defined in the Henshin language in Fig. 1. It contains three rules that are scheduled to execute in sequence, as depicted on the bottom right. This is an excerpt of transformation that creates database tables and columns from a class diagram. The first rule in the top left states that if a class is present then create a table and link it with a trace element unless such a trace already exists for the class.

2.2   Model Transformation Design Patterns

A design pattern expresses a means of solving a common model transformation design problem: it describes the transformation structure (rules, condition patterns, and scheduling) that constitute the solution idea. A design pattern includes also a description of the problem which motivated the pattern, how such problems can be detected, and the benefits and negative consequences to consider when using the pattern.

In the mid-2000s, several works proposed design patterns for model transformation. Agrawal et al. [8] defined design patterns for graph transformation described in a specific model transformation language. Iacob et al. [15] defined other design patterns for outplace transformations. Levendovszky et al. [19] proposed domain-specific design patterns for model transformation and different domain-specific languages.

More recently, Lano et al. [17] presented the most comprehensive model transformation design pattern study and defined a catalog of 29 patterns classified into five categories. For example, these include a design pattern to map objects before links, to decompose a transformation into phases based on the target model, the criteria to separate rules so they can be executed in parallel, to ensure that elements created by a rule are unique, or to individually process all nodes of a model recursively.

At the same time, Ergin and Syriani [11] presented similar design patterns, as well as new ones, such as modifying a model iteratively until a fixed point is reached, or the execution of a modeling language by translating it into another modeling language that can be simulated.

2.3   DelTa to Describe the Structure of Design Patterns

Lano et al. [17] presented the structure design patterns using a formal language TSPEC in the form of contracts with pre- and post-conditions that a concrete model transformation implementing the pattern should satisfy. However, Ergin and Syriani [12] engineered a domain-specific language, *DelTa*, dedicated to represent the structure of model transformation design patterns. Because an implementation is already available in EMF, we opted to use the DelTa implementations of Lano et al.'s design patterns.

DelTa is a language to define model transformation design patterns with its own syntax and semantics. It is independent from existing model transformation languages. In terms of abstraction, DelTa borrows concepts from various MTLs

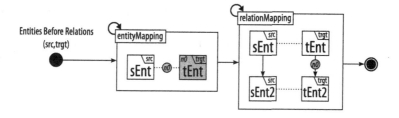

Fig. 2. Entities before relations design pattern

to create a more understandable and common language. Figure 2 represents a model transformation design pattern in its graphical syntax as described in [10].

A DelTa model specifies the minimal rules (the large rectangles) and necessary rule scheduling (the connections between them) that a concrete model transformation implementing it should have. Rules consist of the minimal constraints and actions on elements of the metamodel that concrete transformation rules implementing them should specify. Constraints and actions refer to variables that are typed as entities (rectangles like sEnt) or relations (arrows between entities) of a metamodel, or traces (dotted lines). For example, in rule *entityMapping*, there is a constraint stating that there must be an entity (sEnt). Furthermore, the *n0* symbol on rule elements indicates that trace and the entity tEnt are part of a negative constraint. These two entities come from different metamodels (src and trgt). In DelTa, we only reason about entities and relations, independently from specific metamodel types and relations. Entities are represented using a UML class notation and their metamodel appears on the top right. An "x" symbol on an element inside a rule means that this element should not appear in the concrete transformation rule implementing the DelTa rule.

Color coding of entities and relations inside the rules indicates whether they are part of the constraint or a type of action of the rule. White elements form the minimal application pre-condition that a concrete transformation rule implementing it should have. Gray elements are the minimal elements to be created in the concrete transformation rule. For example, the tEnt and the trace between it and sEnt must be created. Therefore, the rule *entityMapping* dictates that the concrete transformation rule implementing it should look for an entity from one metamodel and create a new entity from another metamodel, as well as a trace between them. Elements in black are the minimal elements to be deleted in the concrete transformation rule.

When a self loop symbol appears on the top left (as it is the case with both rules in Fig. 2), the DelTa rule is exhaustive: the concrete transformation rule implementing it should be applied on all of its matches. This may require to have more than one rule implementing this DelTa rule, for example to match different metamodel types.

In DelTa, the scheduling is depicted using a control flow notation. The start node (filled ball) indicates the initial rule of the design pattern. Arrows between rule blocks indicate a predence order: the concrete transformation rule implementing the *entityMapping* rule should be performed before the one implementing the *relationMapping* rule. A dashed box containing rules specifies that the order of execution of the rules it contains is irrelevant to the design pattern. Entities, rules, and scheduling represent the *participants* of a model transfromation design pattern. In this paper, we use model transformation design patterns expressed in DelTa from [10].

2.4   Design Patterns Detection in Software Engineering

To the best of our knowledge, there is no previous work that tackles the detection of design patterns in model transformation. Most of the detection approaches target the patterns of Gamma et al. in object-oriented programs [13]. These approaches target primarily the structural patterns as these can be detected by matching the structure of code to one of the pattern [3,22]. To improve the detection, some projects combine multiple strategies as in [7]. The detection of behavioral patterns also attracted the interest of the research community. In De Lucia et al. [2], the authors use model checking to improve the detection of behavioral patterns. A work similar to our is one in [5]. In this paper, the authors first identify pattern key participants using a machine learning technique. Then, they check for the other participants of the pattern and the relations between them.

3   Design Pattern Detection for Model Transformation

We propose an approach to detect complete and partial instances of design patterns in concrete model transformations. We consider design pattern detection as a constraint satisfaction problem where a design pattern imposes a specific structure that a concrete model transformation should contain, and we solve it using a declarative strategy based on an inference rule engine.

3.1   Overview

As shown in Fig. 3, the detection of a design pattern is encoded as a set of *rules*. These rules apply to a set of *facts* representing the model transformation. The facts conform to *fact templates*: a generic abstract representation of transformation components relevant to design pattern detection. This abstract representation makes our approach independent from a specific model transformation language. The mapping to of a concrete model transformation is performed by a model-to-text transformation.

The detection process is performed in three automated steps. First, the transformation is mapped to an abstract representation (i.e., facts) using a higher-order transformation. Second, we identify which rules of the model transformation can play the role of the participants of the design pattern. Third, once the participant candidates are identified, we verify that their execution satisfies the scheduling scheme specified in the design pattern.

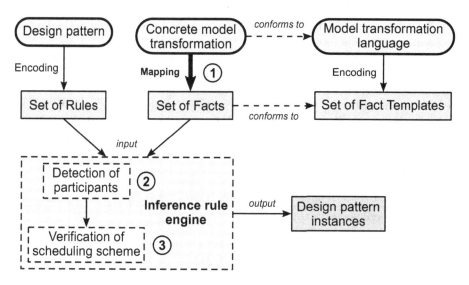

Fig. 3. Architecture overview of design pattern detection

In the remainder of this section, we describe how concrete model transformations are mapped to generic facts and then explain the two steps of the detection process.

3.2 Mapping Model Transformations to Generic Facts

Fact Template. To describe model transformations, we defined a fact-based language inspired by the Henshin transformation language [1]. The motivation behind this decision is that design patterns, as defined in [17], deal mainly with the manipulation (creation/modification/deletion) of model elements by rules as well as with the rule execution scheduling. All these constructs can be described by the Henshin concepts.

The main fact template to describe a transformation is `Rule`. A `Rule` is composed of nodes, each corresponding to an action on a model element present in the pre- or post-condition of a model transformation rule. Nodes are described by the fact template `Node`. Nodes have several attributes to define the element name and type they represent, a reference to the rule in which they appear, and also an action. If the action slot is assigned "create", "update" or "delete", then the node is part of the post-condition of the transformation rule. If it is assigned "preserve" or "forbid", then the node is part of the pre-condition (positive or negative constraint, respectively) of the transformation rule. Nodes may also be related with the `Edge` fact template when the action in one node depends on another node, e.g., an element is created and its attributes are set according to those of another element. For rule execution scheduling, we define the fact template `Sequence` that specifies the precedence between two rules.

The precedence relationship may also involve control events such as the beginning and the end of a loop.

Listing 1.1 shows fact templates for Rule, Node, and Sequence expressed in the Jess language [6]. In Jess, each template has a name and a set of slot definitions. When asserting a fact, the slots must be set with values. Some slots are used to describe the fact properties such as Name in Rule and Action in Node. Others are used to connect facts. For example, the slot RuleId in Node is set with the Id of the Rule which the node belongs to. Similarly, SourceId and TargetId in Sequence refer respectively to the Ids of the preceding and following rules.

Listing 1.1. Fact Templates representing a model transformation language

```
1  (deftemplate Rule (slot Id)(slot Name))
2
3  (deftemplate Node (slot Id)(slot RuleId)(slot Action)
4  (slot Occurrences)(slot Name)(slot Type))
5
6  (deftemplate Sequence(slot SourceId)(slot TargetId))
```

Fact. Listing 1.2 shows the Jess facts of a rule having two nodes.

Listing 1.2. Fact representing a concrete model transformation

```
1  (Rule (Id"R1")(Name"Class2TableMapping"))
2
3  (Node (Id"N1")(RuleId"R1")
4  (Action"preserve")(Occurrences"n")(Name"")(Type"Class"))
5
6  (Node (Id"N2")(RuleId"R1")
7  (Action"create")(Occurrences"n")(Name"")(Type"Table"))
```

To be effective for large transformations, we automate the mapping of a given concrete model transformation to a set of facts. Therefore, we need to write a fact generator for each model transformation language considered. To this end, we use Acceleo[1], a template-based model-to-text transformation tool in EMF. These code generation templates encode the semantic equivalence between the transformation language constructs and our fact templates. Listing 1.3 illustrates an example for generating of a fact Rule from a Henshin rule. Although our implementation currently supports Henshin, adapting to another model transformation language simply requires to create a new Acceleo template for it.

Listing 1.3. Fact representing a concrete model transformation

```
1  [template public generateRule(rule:Rule, position:Integer)]
2     (Rule (Id \"["R" + position]\") (Name \"[rule.name/]\"))
3  [/template]
```

---

[1] https://eclipse.org/acceleo/.

3.3   Encoding Design Patterns as Detection Rules

As mentioned in Sect. 2.2, the participants of a model transformation design
pattern are DelTa rules, the elements they contain in their constraint and actions,
and their scheduling scheme. The pattern *Entities Before Relations* in Fig. 2, for
instance, consists of two DelTa rules: *entityMapping* and *relationMapping*. It also
mandates that the former must be executed before the latter. Consequently, our
detection strategy starts by finding concrete model transformation rules that
match the ones in the DelTa model, and then verify if the scheduling specified
in the patterns holds for the concrete matched rules.

Listing 1.4. Rule encoding the complete entityMapping rule of Entities before Relations design pattern

```
1   (defrule CreateEntityMapping_Rule
2     (Rule (Id ?r_1)(Name ?r_2))
3     (Node (Id ?sEnt_1)(RuleId ?r_1)(Action"preserve")
4       (Occurrence ?sEnt_4)(Name ?sEnt_5)(Type ?sEnt_6))
5     (Node (Id ?tEnt_1)(RuleId ?r_1)(Action"forbid")
6       (Occurrence ?tEnt_4)(Name ?tEnt_5)(Type ?tEnt_6))
7     (Node (Id ?tEnt_2)(RuleId ?r_1)(Action"create")
8       (Occurrence ?tEnt_4)(Name ?tEnt_5)(Type ?tEnt_6))
9     (Edge (Id ?ed_1)(RuleId ?r_1)(SourceId ?sEnt_1)
10       (TargetId ?tEnt_1))
11     (Edge (Id ?ed_2)(RuleId ?r_1)(SourceId ?sEnt_1)
12       (TargetId ?tEnt_2))
13   =>
14     (assert
15      (EbR_entityMapping
16       (Id (str-cat ?r_1 ?sEnt_1 ?tEnt_1 ?tEnt_2 ?Ed_1 ?Ed_2))
17       (RuleId ?r_1)
18       (sEnt_1Id ?sEnt_1)
19       (tEnt_1Id ?tEnt_1)
20       (tEd_1Id ?ed_1)
21       (tEnt_2Id ?tEnt_2)
22       (tEd_2Id ?ed_2)
23       (accuracy 1))
24     )
25   )
```

The detection of instances of a DelTa rule is encoded as a *rule* in Jess.
For example, Listing 1.4 rule detects complete instances of *entityMapping*. The
Jess rule first filters all transformation rule facts that have a "preserve" node
connected to a "forbid" node and to a "create" node. For each rule satisfying
these conditions, it asserts a fact *EbR_entityMapping*. Another Jess rule will filter
the concrete rules that can play the role of *relationMapping* and asserts for each
match a fact *EbR_relationMapping*. The encoding of DelTa rules into Jess rules
can be implemented with Acceleo templates.

Once the potential participants are detected, the next step is to ensure if the
execution schedule of the concrete rules corresponds to the one of the pattern.
In the case of the pattern *Entities Before Relations*, a Jess rule filters facts

EbR_entityMapping and *EbR_relationMapping*, and a `Sequence` fact relating the rules respectively involved in the participant facts.

3.4   Accuracy for Complete and Partial Instances

In the case of complete instance detection, all the conditions (participants and scheduling) should be fully satisfied, i.e., accuracy equals 1.

When detecting partial instances, rules variants are defined for participants and scheduling detection. These rules may omit one of the conditions and adjust the value of fact accuracy accordingly. For example, in the detection of *entityMapping* participants, a variant rule can consider rules with "preserve" and "create" nodes, but without a "forbid" node. This is depicted in Listing 1.5. The accuracy is then adjusted to 0.66 for example. The scheduling verification rule, calculate the global accuracy of the pattern instance from the accuracy values of the participants facts and one of the scheduling itself.

Listing 1.5. Rule encoding a partial entityMapping rule of Entities before Relations design pattern

```
1   (defrule CreateEntityMapping_Rule
2     (Rule (Id ?r_1)(Name ?r_2))
3     (Node (Id ?sEnt_1)(RuleId ?r_1)(Action"preserve")
4       (Occurrence ?sEnt_4)(Name ?sEnt_5)(Type ?sEnt_6))
5     (not (Node (Id ?tEnt_1)(RuleId ?r_1)(Action"forbid")
6       (Occurrence ?tEnt_4)(Name ?tEnt_5)(Type ?tEnt_6))
7     ...
8   =>
9     (assert
10     (EbR_entityMapping
11       (Id (str-cat ?r_1 ?sEnt_1 ?tEnt_1 ?tEnt_2 ?Ed_1 ?Ed_2))
12       (RuleId ?r_1)
13       (sEnt_1Id ?sEnt_1)
14       (tEnt_1Id"")
15       (tEd_1Id"")
16       (tEnt_2Id ?tEnt_2)
17       (tEd_2Id ?ed_2)
18       (accuracy 0.66))
19     )
20   )
```

4   Preliminary Evaluation

4.1   Setup

A preliminary evaluation of this work consists in selecting a subset of design patterns and detect their instances on a sample of model transformations. The goal here is to analyze qualitatively how our detection approach applies to concrete transformations.

We selected 13 Henshin transformations[2] with different characteristics (see Table 1). As we had to analyze manually the results, we opted for small-medium transformations having 1 to 13 rules. We also paid attention to the control complexity as most of the transformation design patterns deal with the rule execution control. Indeed, some of the selected transformations use default implicit control (no control specified), and others have up to 13 rule scheduling units with loops and calls between the units. Additionally, we varied the complexity of the rules with respect to the number of involved model elements, with an average number of nodes per rule between 3 and 11.

Table 1. Selected transformations.

Model transformations	# rules	# sch-unit	# nodes	# relations	# calls	# loop
bank	3	0	12	12	0	0
bankmap	1	0	5	4	0	0
comb	2	1	22	38	1	1
diningphils	4	0	22	34	0	0
ecore2genmodel	8	6	55	59	12	2
gossipingGirls	2	0	7	9	0	0
grid-full	4	5	18	27	8	3
grid-sparse	3	4	11	16	6	2
java2statemachine	13	13	77	59	27	5
petriM	2	0	15	27	0	0
sierpinski	1	0	6	12	0	0
sort	1	1	3	2	1	1
entityRelationMapping	3	1	16	14	3	0

In this preliminary evaluation we experimented with the detection of three patterns, selected from the catalog of [17]. Two of them deal with the rule modularization (*Entities Before Relations* and *Construction and cleanup*), and one with optimization (*Unique Instantiation*).

Entities Before Relations. The goal of this pattern (Fig. 2), also called *Map Objects Before Links*, is to create the entities and then their relations. As mentioned in Sect. 3.3, three rules are defined for the detection of this pattern: (1) detection of entities creation, (2) detection of relations creation, and (3) precedence checking between the two creations. In addition to the detection of complete instances, we implemented the detection of one kind of partial instance, i.e., the situation in which the transformation program have rules for creating the entities before the creation of their relations, but does not check if an entity exists before it creates a new one (see Sect. 3.4).

---

[2] https://www.eclipse.org/henshin/examples.php.

Construction and Cleanup. As shown in Fig. 4, this pattern consists in separating rules which create model elements from those which delete elements [17]. Like for the previous patterns, the detection is done in three phases: (1) finding element creation rules, (2) finding element deletion rules, and (3) precedence checking between the two.

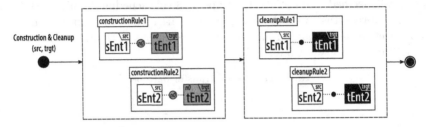

Fig. 4. Construction & cleanup - Structure in DelTa

Unique Instantiation. This pattern, sketched in Fig. 5, aims at avoiding multiple creations of the same model element. This may happen in two situations: (1) two rules creating the same model element or (2) a rule creating a model element, and that appears in a loop inside a rule execution schedule. We defined detection rules for each situation, i.e., identifying element-creation rules, and checking duplications and loops.

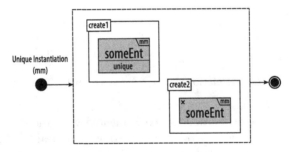

Fig. 5. Unique instantiation - structure in DelTa

4.2   Qualitative Analysis

Entities Before Relations. Surprisingly, our prototype did not find complete instances of the pattern *Entities Before Relations*. To understand this, we manually inspected the automatically detected partial instances. We noticed that, in many cases, the *EntityMapping* participants were identified with an accuracy of 1. However, the *relationMapping* participants did not satisfy the condition of the non-existence of a relation before its creation. All the detected partial instances satisfied the execution schedule conditions with perfect accuracy. Figure 1 illustrates two examples of partial instances found in the *entityRelationMapping* e rules transformation. The rules *ClassMapping* and *AttributeMapping* are both complete instances of *entityMapping*. Conversely, in rule *attributeRela-tionMapping*, the relation between "Class" and "Attribute" is mapped to a relation between "Table" and "Column" without ensuring that such a relation does not already exist (not a "forbid" action). Although the scheduling is perfectly accurate, i.e., both *ClassMapping* and *AttributeMapping* rules precede *attributeRelationMapping*, the aggregated accuracy is lower than 1.

Construction and Cleanup. The prototype found many instances of the design pattern *Construction and cleanup*. An interesting instance is one found in the *Java2StateMachine*. In this transformation, only one rule has a "delete" action (*updateAction* on the right of Fig. 6). All the other rules create elements. This rule appears at the last step of the execution schedule (on the left of Fig. 6). This is a non trivial instance to detect because of the modularization of the execution schedule. In our detection program, we implemented a function that reconstructs a flat schedule by resolving the schedule step references.

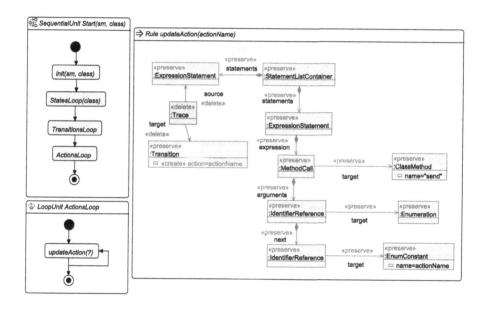

Fig. 6. An example of instance of the pattern *Constr*uction and Cleanup

Unique Instantiation. This is by far the most frequent pattern and many of its instances were found in almost all the considered transformations. Some of them have a high accuracy. An example of a complete instance was found in the *Ecore2GenModel* high-order transformation. The *createCustomizationUnit* rule creates an element, which is not created by other rules (Fig. 7a). Moreover, this rule does not appear in a loop in the execution schedule (Fig. 7b).

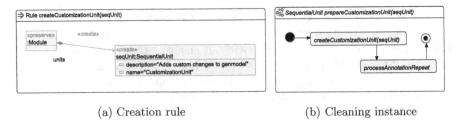

(a) Creation rule   (b) Cleaning instance

Fig. 7. Unique instantiation instance detected in Ecore2Genmode transformation

5   Conclusion

In this paper, we propose an approach and a preliminary implementation for the detection of complete and partial instances of design patterns in model transformations. Our approach follows a declarative strategy which consists in identifying transformation rules that play the roles of design pattern participants and then check if their execution sequence conforms to the schedule specified in the pattern.

We conducted a preliminary evaluation which consisted in applying our detection rules on a set of transformations and in qualitatively analyzing the detection results. Although the obtained results are encouraging, our evaluation revealed some limitations. First, we define explicitly rules for detecting pattern variants [20]. The advantage of this strategy is that we identify acceptable variants of a design pattern. The drawback is that our detection code is very verbose with very similar rules. We plan in the future to have a generic detection of variants by allowing weights to the pattern participants.

Another limitation of our approach resides in the limited number of control structures we handle. In our current implementation, we do not consider alternatives structures. Thus for the pattern *Unique Instantiation*, if two rules respectively in the two branches of the alternative create the same element, we do not detect a valid instance. Handling more control structures is a part of our future work.

References

1. Arendt, T., Biermann, E., Jurack, S., Krause, C., Taentzer, G.: Henshin: advanced concepts and tools for in-place emf model transformations. In: Model Driven Engineering Languages and Systems, pp. 121–135 (2010)
2. De Lucia, A., Deufemia, V., Gravino, C., Risi, M.: Improving behavioral design pattern detection through model checking. In: European Conference on Software Maintenance and Reengineering, pp. 176–185 (2010)
3. Dong, J., Zhao, Y., Peng, T.: A review of design pattern mining techniques. Int. J. Softw. Eng. Knowl. Eng. **19**(06), 823–855 (2009)
4. Guéhéneuc, Y.G., Guyomarc'h, J.Y., Sahraoui, H.: Improving design-pattern identification: a new approach and an exploratory study. Softw. Qual. J. **18**(1), 145–174 (2010)

5. Gueheneuc, Y.G., Sahraoui, H., Zaidi, F.: Fingerprinting design patterns. In: Working Conference on Reverse Engineering, pp. 172–181. IEEE (2004)
6. Hill, E.F.: Jess in Action: Java Rule-Based Systems. Manning Greenwich, Greenwich (2003)
7. Rasool, G., Mäder, P.: Flexible design pattern detection based on feature types. In: International Conference on Automated Software Engineering, pp. 243–252 (2011)
8. Agrawal, A.: Reusable idioms and patterns in graph transformation languages. In: International Workshop on Graph-Based Tools, ENTCS, vol. 127, pp. 181–192. Elsevier (2005)
9. Czarnecki, K., Helsen, S.: Feature-based survey of model transformation approaches. IBM Syst. J. Spec. Issue Model-Driven Softw. Dev. **45**(3), 621–645 (2006)
10. Ergin, H., Syriani, E., Gray, J.: Design pattern oriented development of model transformations. Comput. Lang. Syst. Struct. **46**, 106–139 (2016). doi:10.1016/j.cl.2016.07.004
11. Ergin, H., Syriani, E.: Identification and application of a model transformation design pattern. In: ACM Southeast Conference, ACMSE 2013. ACM (2013)
12. Ergin, H., Syriani, E.: Towards a Language for Graph-Based Model Transformation Design Patterns. In: Ruscio, D., Varró, D. (eds.) ICMT 2014. LNCS, vol. 8568, pp. 91–105. Springer, Heidelberg (2014). doi:10.1007/978-3-319-08789-4_7
13. Gamma, E., Helm, R., Johnson, R., Vlissides, J.: Design Patterns: Elements of Reusable Object-Oriented Software. Addison Wesley Professional, Boston (1994)
14. Hutchinson, J., Whittle, J., Rouncefield, M., Kristoffersen, S.: Empirical assessment of MDE in industry. In: International Conference on Software engineering, pp. 471–480. ACM (2011)
15. Iacob, M.E., Steen, M.W.A., Heerink, L.: Reusable model transformation patterns. In: Enterprise Distributed Object Computing Conference Workshops, pp. 1–10. IEEE Computer Society (2008)
16. Lúcio, L., Amrani, M., Dingel, J., Lambers, L., Salay, R., Selim, G.M., Syriani, E., Wimmer, M.: Model transformation intents and their properties. Softw. Syst. Model. **15**(3), 647–684 (2014)
17. Lano, K., Rahimi, S.K.: Model-transformation design patterns. IEEE Trans. Softw. Eng. **40**(12), 1224–1259 (2014)
18. Lano, K., Rahimi, S.K., Poernomo, I.: Comparative evaluation of model transformation specification approaches. Int. J. Softw. Inf. **6**(2), 233–269 (2012)
19. Levendovszky, T., Lengyel, L., Mészáros, T.: Supporting domain-specific model patterns with metamodeling. Softw. Syst. Model. **8**(4), 501–520 (2009)
20. Prechelt, L., Krämer, C.: Functionality versus practicality: employing existing tools for recovering structural design patterns. J. Univ. Comput. Sci. **4**(11), 866–882 (1998)
21. Syriani, E., Vangheluwe, H.: A modular timed graph transformation language for simulation-based design. Softw. Syst. Model. **12**(2), 387–414 (2013)
22. Tsantalis, N., Chatzigeorgiou, A., Stephanides, G., Halkidis, S.: Design pattern detection using similarity scoring. Trans. Softw. Eng. **32**(11), 896–909 (2006)

Modular Solutions to Common Design Problems Using Activities and the Interface-Modular Method

Urooj Fatima[(✉)] and Rolv Bræk[(✉)]

Department of Telematics,
NTNU - Norwegian University of Science and Technology, Trondheim, Norway
{urooj,rolv.braek}@item.ntnu.no

Abstract. In order to enable automatic design synthesis it is necessary that functionality can be completely specified and that the so-called realizability problems can be detected and resolved. In this paper we focus on the second issue to resolve realizability problems. We assume a specification approach called the interface-modular method in which interfaces and core functionalities are specified and analyzed separately as modules that can be composed into complete specifications using UML collaborations and activities as the main notations. From this the designs can be derived by a process of direct synthesis whereby activities are localized to components in a manner that maintains the modularity. Such direct synthesis may contain so-called realizability problems that may need to be resolved. In this paper we propose and discuss modular solutions to the known realizability problems in terms of activities.

Keywords: Design synthesis · Interface definitions · Realizability issues

1   The Interface Modular Method

1.1   Collaborations for Structuring Interfaces and Services

In UML 2.x, collaborations are both structural and behavioural classifiers. A collaboration defines a structure of connected parts called roles. A collaboration may be used in the form of a *collaboration-use* within the context of an enclosing collaboration (or a composite class) where its roles are assigned to roles/parts in the enclosing entity. Hence collaborations support composition by role assignment. This is illustrated in Fig. 1, where a *TaxiSystem*[1] is defined as a collaboration among roles (*Taxi, User, TaxiDispatcher (TD)*) with collaboration-uses representing partial interface behaviours (*TaxiReq, UserWait, ...*). Here the roles of collaboration-use *UserWait*, for instance, is bound to the *User* and *TD* roles. Behaviour can be associated with the collaborations in order to precisely define

---

[1] In a *TaxiSystem*, *Users* can book *Taxis* by placing taxi-booking requests to a *Taxi-Dispatcher*.

© Springer International Publishing AG 2016
J. Grabowski and S. Herbold (Eds.): SAM 2016, LNCS 9959, pp. 226–241, 2016.
DOI: 10.1007/978-3-319-46613-2_15

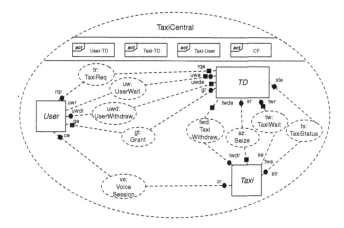

Fig. 1. UML collaboration diagram showing roles and collaboration-uses in interfaces of a *TaxiSystem*.

interface behaviour. This is illustrated by the references to activity diagrams given in a separate compartment of the collaboration in Fig. 1.

The only non-standard feature of collaborations used in the Interface-Modular (IM for short) method [2] is the indication of which roles are initiating (a black dot) and which roles that are terminating (a black square). This information, that can be provided by suitable profiling, is useful when it comes to design synthesis and detection of realizability issues as will be explained in Sect. 2. It was first proposed in [3].

In contrast to classes, roles define partial properties. Roles, role assignment and role composition goes well with the understanding of services and interfaces as partial behaviours (defined by roles) to be assigned to and composed within components. However, in UML the composition of roles and compliance between roles and classes is not clearly defined. The IM method provides a solution to this problem that will be explained below.

1.2 Using Activities for (Cross-Cutting as Well as Local) Behaviour Definition and Composition

UML 2.x activities provide a rather powerful notation for behaviour definition based on a token flow semantics. Activities can be used to define modules with cross-cutting global behaviours as well as local behaviours. Tools exist that can analyse activities for dynamic problems and generate state machines for implementation [9,10]. Using such tools, activities are useful not only to specify behaviour, but also to express design detail and generate implementations.

For local behaviours (i.e. behaviour performed by a single component, i.e. an entity performing one or more roles within a single computing node) we use standard UML activities. Modules are call behaviour actions defined as activities with pins (parameters) for connection with their environment. Figure 2 illustrates

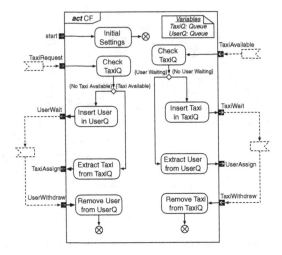

Fig. 2. The core functionality module of *TD*.

how the core functionality (abbreviated CF in the following) of the *TD* role can be defined as a local activity. Note how this diagram defines the essential behaviour of a taxi dispatcher as an interface independent module. It defines data processing in terms of queues and operations that are highly relevant for stakeholders such as users and taxi drivers and therefore important to cover in a specification of functionality, even though it will become internal to the *TD*. In order to specify dependencies and constraints on the actual external flows that can be connected to a module, one may attach so-called *external flows* to the pins as illustrated. This is a method extension that helps to specify and understand modules separately and to ensure compliance when modules are connected. It will not be elaborated further here.

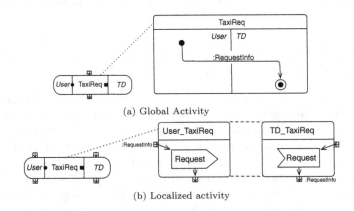

Fig. 3. Overview of global activity vs. localized activity.

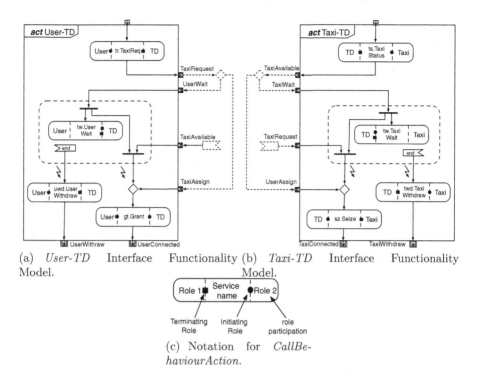

(a) *User-TD* Interface Functionality (b) *Taxi-TD* Interface Functionality
Model.   Model.

(c) Notation for *CallBe-
haviourAction.*

Fig. 4. Interface functionality modules of *TaxiCentral.*

When using activities for cross-cutting behaviour specification (i.c. behaviour involving more than one component) it is common to indicate the components that participate as so-called *partitions*. The particular notation for indicating partitions is not standardized in UML 2.x, but varieties of the so-called *swim-lane* notation are common, especially in business process modelling. Figure 3(a) illustrates how the behaviour associated with the collaboration *TaxiReq* can be expressed in this way. Note that flows crossing partition boundaries imply communication. Such flows may specify the data type that is passed, but will normally not name any particular messages or method calls to carry the data. This is in contrast to interactions (sequence diagrams) where the messages are explicitly named. In the IM method, we use this form of activity diagram to define the behaviour of elementary collaborations, i.e. collaborations not further decomposed into collaboration-uses. Most model elements of UML 2.x activities are allowed including streaming pins.

The behaviour of a composite collaboration (non-elementary) can now be defined by an activity diagram that orders the execution of elementary collaborations using activity flows. Most model elements of UML activities are allowed here as well. On this level the elementary collaboration activities are represented as *callBehaviourActions* referring to the activities defining their behaviour, in much the same way as Interaction Overview Diagrams refer to detailed interactions [3]. In the symbols for *callBehaviourActions*, roles are represented as partitions using the notation illustrated in Fig. 3 and explained in Fig. 4(c), which is in accordance by the notational variation allowed in UML 2.x. As an extension of UML, the initiating and terminating roles may be indicated by the black dots and squares as illustrated. This aids the understanding and analysis on this level of behaviour definition. This notation was first introduced in [3] to define distributed behaviours and to help identify so-called realizability problems at an early stage.

Figure 4 defines two interfaces of the *TaxiSystem* as modules. Note that the full interface functionality (abbreviated IF in the following) with its two roles and remote interactions are encapsulated in the modules. Since IF modules do not live in isolation, but will interact with CF modules at either end, the interface modules have pins to connect with the CF modules and carry this interaction. Such pins for internal composition with the CF is not so much of an over-specification as one may think at first because they represent the dependencies that exists both ways between IF and CF. Understanding these dependencies is necessary to fully understand both the core and the interface as well as to compose the two.

1.3   Interfaces as Modules

Encapsulation and well-defined interfaces is widely recognized as a key to system modularity. Thus, when specifying and designing the functionality of a system or component one may benefit from a clear separation between the encapsulated CF and the exposed IF. Interfaces as modules is a distinguishing feature of the IM method [2].

This is made possible by using UML 2.x activities to define both the IF and the CF as well as their pins for external connections. Hence, the interface is a module with cross-cutting behaviour involving two parts (formally roles in UML collaborations) and pins for connection with the CF. In the IM method composition and compliance is therefore well-defined in terms of the pins used to connect IF and CF modules and the ordering of collaboration-uses defined by activities within each interface. Altogether collaborations and activities provide languages to define interfaces as modules independently of a particular CF and to mix-and-match IF and CF modules. Activities put few constraints on the granularity of modules, and this helps to factor out IF and CF modules without the need for any additional "glue".

One might object here that the pins for connection between IF and CF within a component reveals internal detail of a component and therefore should be avoided. On the other hand this helps to achieve the benefits of separation and modularisation. The pins are internal, but they simply represent the dependencies that exist between the interfaces and the core that one need to take into account anyway both to understand and to compose. Moreover a precise definition of both IF and CF and their mutual dependencies is needed in a complete specification of functionality, and having explicit pins makes composition well defined.

2   Direct Design Synthesis

An important motivation for the IM method was to simplify the task of making specifications complete in the sense that they define the full behaviour expected by the environment. Given such a complete specification defined in terms of activities, direct design synthesis is a matter of defining local component activities that together will provide the specified behaviour. When using the IM method, direct design synthesis may be performed for each IF module and CF module separately. The CF modules are internal to components and therefore, by nature, local activities. Therefore, the problems related to distribution are confined to the IF modules only.

In specifications one normally uses global flows to order the IF collaboration activities as shown in Fig. 4. Such global flows are useful for early overview and validation. They focus on the intended overall behaviour and suppress details related to the local flows needed to enforce the global ordering. The same is the case when using Interaction Overview Diagrams (IODs) or high-level MSC diagrams. In a distributed system, however there are no global flows, only local flows and interactions. Direct design synthesis therefore involves two main steps: (1) split the elementary collaboration activities into two local role activities linked by message passing instead of flows; (2) replace the global flows by local flows. The first step is rather straight forward as illustrated in Figs. 3 and 5 and will not be elaborated further here.

The second step can be performed by copying the global flow to each component, c.f. Fig. 5. This results in two parallel local flows, one for each interface role activity. This includes also interrupting flows and control nodes like choices, forks, events etc. Once the global flows are copied to both the participating components/roles of an interface, we need to determine which of these flows are *initiating* flows and *responding* flows. Flows connected to the initiating role of the next collaboration, i.e. the role that performs the first sending action of a collaboration, are defined as initiating flows. Flows connected to the responding role, i.e. the role that participates, but is not initiating, are called responding flows. The initiating flows enable the initiating role of a collaboration to start the collaboration and send messages whereas the responding flows enable the responding role to participate in the collaboration and receive the messages sent by the initiating role. The responding flows determine when the responding role must be ready to respond in collaborations initiated by the initiating role, hence the name: *responding* flows. Responding flows and initiating flows are both ordinary flows in the UML sense, but the responding flows may give rise to design problems, also called realizability problems, that have to be resolved. Since the distinction is useful for analytical purpose, the responding flows and their control nodes are here marked as dashed.

Table 1 summarises how the global control nodes are mapped to the initiating side and the responding side. The responding flows and nodes are first dashed as an indication here and then mapped to normal flows and nodes as shown in Table 1. One can see that join nodes, merge nodes and forks can be treated the

Table 1. Synthesis rules for control nodes and interruptible region. ICR block is shaded to emphasize its re-usability as a module

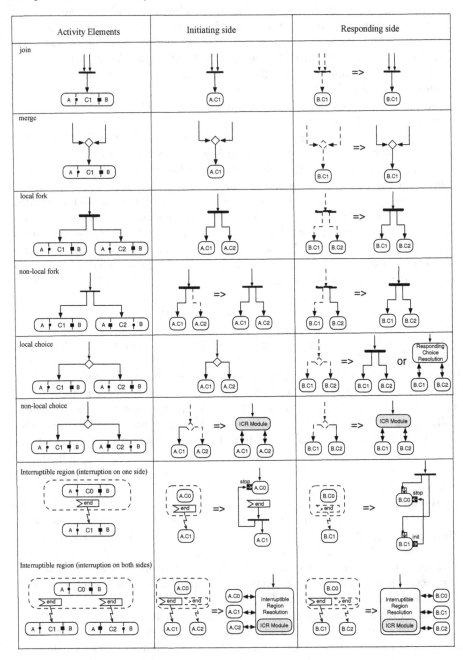

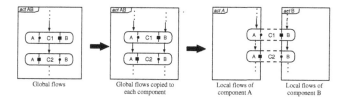

Fig. 5. An illustration of the process of direct design synthesis.

same way on the initiating and responding side and poses no problems. Choices and interruptions on the other hand, need special attention.

Choices must be treated differently on the responding side. A local choice, i.e. a choice that is performed locally on the initiating side, must on the responding side be mapped either to a fork or a special responding choice resolution module as indicated in Table 1. This is because the outcome of the decision depends on which collaboration is activated on the initiating side. Therefore, both alternatives must be activated on the responding side in order to detect the first message of the chosen collaboration. As shown in Table 1, this means that both B.C1 and B.C2 must be activated to detect the first message either from A.C1 or A.C2. Figure 6 defines the responding choice resolution module and how it can be applied in the *TaxiSystem* example. For instance, when the *User* sends a taxi request to the *TD*, either the *UserWait* collaboration or *Grant* collaboration will be activated depending upon the decision made by the initiating role, *TD*. To detect the first message, the *User* roles both in *UserWait* and *Grant* needs to be enabled.

In order to model this, the responding choice resolution module has a 'fork' with outgoing flows enabling both the responding roles *User.UserWait* and *User.Grant* via *enable* pins. If *User.UserWait* receives the event, it needs to stop *User.Grant* and vice versa because both are enabled. This is modelled in the resolution module. The resolution module gets notified about the detection of the first message by either of the responding roles via *init* input pins and stops the corresponding role via *stop* output pins.

Corresponding *init* and *stop* pins need to be added to the responding roles to communicate with the responding choice resolution module. Figure 6 illustrates how the internal details of a responding role (*User.Grant*) are modified in order to add the functionality required by the *init* and *stop* pins. An 'activity final' node is added (to stop the activity) and connected to the *stop* pin. A 'fork' is added to communicate the reception of the first event via *init* pin. Note that the additions made in the *User.Grant* role in order to communicate with the responding choice resolution block are straight forward and simple. Also note that the addition of these pins does not modify the *specified* role behaviour and can be added to all role activities to compose them with resolution modules when needed. The behaviour now described by the *User.Grant* responding role can be re-used for similar situations without further modifications. Hence it can serve as a reusable module.

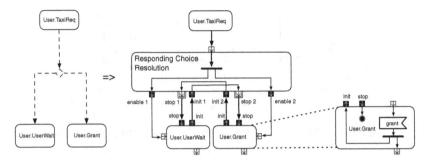

Fig. 6. Responding choice resolution and its application in the *TaxiSystem* with explanation of the required modification of role activities, here exemplified by *User.Grant*

If the output flow segments from a choice is a mix of responding and initiating flows, then we have a so-called *non-local choice*. In this case resolution is not straight forward since the decision making process is not localized to any of the components as will be explained in the following. Interruptible regions require special attention both on the initiating and responding sides, as indicated in Table 1. In the next Section we shall explain how the problems associated with non-local choices and interruptions can be resolved in a modular way.

3   Realizability Problems

If a distributed design resulting from a direct synthesis implies unspecified behaviours, sometimes referred to as implied scenarios, one has a so-called *realizability problem*. Realizability problems are not particular to the IM method, but follow from the nature of a distributed design, and have often been studied in the context of sequence diagrams and state machines, see e.g. [3].

The realizability problems that we address in this paper are related to:

– non-local choices
– Interruptible regions and interrupting flows

A third category of problems is the possibility of message reordering due to weak sequencing. Weak sequencing may be found by analysing the responding flows as explained in [5]. UML activities supports reordering before consumption, which resolves this problem. It will therefore not be elaborated further here. In order to resolve the remaining realizability problems, additional coordination among role activities are needed. The necessary coordination can be provided by, and encapsulated in general and reusable resolution modules as indicated in Table 1. The table illustrates the resolutions on both the initiating and the responding sides.

3.1   Non-local Choices

Unlike, local choices where the decision to choose the next collaboration action is localized to one component, non-local choices imply realizability problem because the decision to choose the next collaboration action cannot be localized to one component. For non-local choices, there are two cases to consider:

a. non-local data choice: the choice between alternatives depends on data not locally available.
b. non-local initiative choice: the choice between alternatives depends on events (initiatives) occurring independently in different components.

Case 'a' represents a design flaw that must be rectified by appropriate design modification, i.e. by making the data available locally in one of the components. Case 'b' is not due to design errors. Initiative choice problems follow from the nature of the system behaviour, and can normally not be prevented. One therefore has to detect and to resolve the situation when it actually occurs during execution. This may happen whenever there is a choice between collaborations initiated by different components due to local triggering events.

Initiative choice problems can be categorized as follows [3]:

– The alternatives have different goals and priority. For instance, the *UserWithdraw* initiated by the *User* and *TaxiAvailable* initiated by the Taxi. In such cases, only one of them should win.
– The alternatives have the same goal and priority. For instance, *CallDisconnect* in a *PhoneCallSystem*. Semantically there is no conflict whether the caller or the callee initiates the disconnection. The goal is *CallDisconnect*. In such cases any of them can win and the resolution may be simply to ignore the second initiative that occurs.

The first category is resolved with an initiative choice resolution module (ICR module) as depicted in Table 1 and defined in Fig. 7 with the "1" pins to be connected to the initiating side and "2" pins to the responding side.

We construct the ICR module to resolve the conflict between collaborations C1 and C2 by following two major steps:

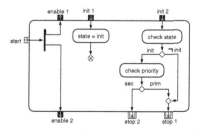

Fig. 7. Details of the initiative choice resolution module (ICR) depicted in Table 1.

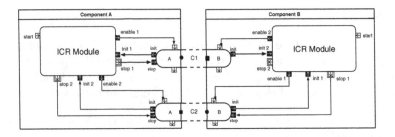

Fig. 8. Usage of the ICR module

a. **Assigning priorities**: We have assigned primary and secondary priorities to the conflicting initiatives and allow the primary side initiative to be accepted in cases of conflict, a concept we have adopted from [4].

b. **Adding *init* and *stop* pins**: The ICR module needs pins to receive indication about two events: (1) the initiating role has started the collaboration on the initiating side; (2) the first message following the initiative has been received on the responding side. These events are signalled by tokens on the *init1* and *init2* pins. By receiving information about both the initiatives via the *init* pins, the ICR module can detect the collision and stop the collaboration with the lower priority via *stop* pins.

Corresponding *init* and *stop* pins need to be added on the participating roles[2]. Note that 'enabling' of roles does not mean that the roles have taken initiative as soon as they are enabled. It only means they are ready to take an initiative or to respond to an initiative. Note that the ICR modules are local to each component and do not involve any additional communication among the components. The ICR modules can be used as shown in Fig. 8 to resolve initiative choices between collaboration C1 and C2. Note that we use the notation for collaboration ordering here as a shorthand for two local role activities linked by message passing. We assume C1 has been assigned primary priority. Let us follow an initiative on A.C1. The A.C1 activity will send its first message and indicate the initiation to the ICR module via *init1*. When the message is received by the B.C1 activity this is indicated by the *init2* to the right hand ICR module which does the following:

– If no initiative has been taken by B.C2 then B.C2 is stopped and B.C1 is allowed to continue so that the C1 collaboration will run.

– If an initiative has been taken by B.C2, which is indicated by *init1* to the right hand ICR module, then priority determines what to do: either stop B.C1 or stop B.C2. As C1 has the primary priority, B.C2 is stopped. Hence the ICR module has a state dependent behaviour. The initiative choice module has to be stopped once the choice has been made.

---

[2] The *stop* pins are added to all the participating roles except the responding role of the primary collaboration (B.C1), because the primary collaboration should not be stopped once initiated.

This solution is similar to the normal state machine solution: either side is allowed to initiate as long as they have not received an initiative from the other. If an initiative message is received after self taking an initiative, resolution applies. This solution has the advantage that resolution can be generic and independent of particular messages, as long as every activity block can signal reception of an initiative message to the ICR module and be stopped by the ICR module when decided.

3.2   Interruptible Regions and Interrupting Flows

An interruptible activity region, as defined in UML, is part of an activity diagram indicated by a dashed rectangle that surrounds a group of activity elements. The region is interrupted when a token traverses an interrupting edge and transfers the control to a target activity node outside the region (see Fig. 4). When this happens the interrupted activities are stopped and all tokens within the region are removed.

Interruptible regions are useful and convenient to model many cases of frequently occurring behaviour, but they are not so easy to implement. They involve a choice combined with stopping the interrupted activity which for collaborative activities involves stopping two distributed roles.

For Interrupts on One Side. There are several ways by which one can stop the interrupting and non-interrupting sides as discussed below:

- **Interrupting side:** The interrupting side can be stopped by:
    Ia. placing the interrupted role in a block that terminates as soon as the event triggering the interrupt happens.
    Ib. replacing the interrupting flow by a normal initiating flow followed by a fork with one branch initiating the role in the next collaboration and other branch stopping the interrupted role as shown in Table 1.
- **Non-interrupting side:** The non-interrupting (responding) side can be stopped by:
    Na. sending an additional stop message in the interrupted collaboration.
    Nb. timeout in the interrupted role
    Nc. detecting that the next collaboration following the interrupted collaboration has started and then stopping the role participating in the interrupted collaboration as shown in Table 1.

We have adopted solution 'Ib' on the interrupting side and 'Nc' on the non-interrupting side. Solution 'Nc' on the non-interrupting side is similar to the solution proposed for responding choice resolution. If component A is the interrupting side and component B the non-interrupting side, then Table 1 illustrates how to implement solution 'Nc' at B: (1) enable the responding roles of the interruptible collaboration B.C0 and the interrupting collaboration B.C1; (2) add an *init* output pin on B.C1 to indicate the start of C1 to B.C0; (3) add a *stop* input pin on B.C0 to enable its stopping once B.C1 signals the start of C1.

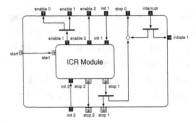

Fig. 9. Details of interruptible region resolution module depicted in Table 1. The ICR module in Fig. 7 is re-used.

For Interrupts on Both Sides. When the interruption can be triggered at both the components, it is an initiative choice situation with two conflicting activities. Therefore, in this case resolution of the interruptible region combines the treatment of interruption with initiative choice resolution as shown in Table 1[3] with C1 and C2 as potentially conflicting activities and C0 as the interrupted one. Since, both component A and B are triggering interrupts, the solution for the "interrupting-side" from single interrupts can be re-used and replicated in both A and B. This solution when combined with the ICR module results in the interruptible region resolution module shown in Fig. 9. All pins of the ICR module are extended to the enclosing interruptible region resolution module. The "0" pins are added to connect the interruptible region resolution module with the interrupted collaboration. The interruptible region resolution module has the following pins in addition to the ICR module:

- *interrupt:* The interrupting edge converted to normal initiating flow is connected to this pin.
- *initiate1:* The initiatives of the interrupting collaborations are expressed outside the collaborations to represent the interrupt events. Therefore, *initiate1* pin is added to communicate the interrupting initiative to its initiating role on the interrupting side.
- *enable0:* It enables the roles participating in the interrupted collaboration C0.
- *stop0:* It stops the roles of the interrupted collaboration C0 either when the resolution module detects the interrupt (on the interrupting-side) or when the module receives a message from one of the interrupting collaborations (on the non-interrupting side).

The ICR module is re-used in the interruptible region resolution without being modified and this illustrates its modular nature. Similarly, the interruptible region resolution module can be re-used. Figure 10 shows how the interruptible region resolution can be applied.

---

[3] For interruptible regions, the events representing the initiatives of the conflicting collaborations are shown explicitly outside the collaborations, whereas in the case of initiative choice they were encapsulated inside the conflicting collaborations.

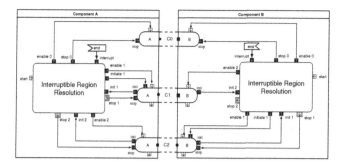

Fig. 10. General usage of interruptible region resolution module with C0 as interrupted collaboration.

Application of the direct synthesis rules and realizability resolutions described in the Sects. 2 and 3 respectively, results in separate component activities with local flows and actions only, as illustrated in Fig. 10.

In order to validate correctness, the resolution modules together with the *TaxiSystem* modules have been entered into the Reactive Blocks tool [9] and analysed using the built in model checker of the tool. An implementation has been generated that runs as expected.

4 Related Work and Conclusions

It is a very common and much recommended practice to define interfaces and to separate interface definitions from definitions of the internal behaviour of components. In most cases, however, the interfaces are defined statically as a set of operations or messages with the internal behaviour defined as an "implementation". Typical examples are APIs, web-service interfaces and Java interfaces. Although such interfaces may be reused for different implementations the definition of internal behaviour (the implementation) is tied to the interfaces and normally not separated from them. There is normally no behaviour definition for the interfaces themselves. But even if behaviour is specified using e.g. UML protocol state machines [1], the interfaces and the internal behaviour is not defined as separate modules that can be composed by directly using the composition mechanisms of the specification language as we do when using the IM method. We are not aware of other approaches where interface behaviour (IF) and internal behaviour (CF) is factored out and encapsulated in modules that can be understood and analysed separately and then easily be composed into complete specification and design models. The interface behaviours we specify, define the behaviour that is visible on each particular interface as modules that are turned into corresponding design modules during design synthesis. Earlier work has used projections of the complete behaviour of a component or a system to define interface behaviours [7]. One of the original methods of projections is proposed in [8] to reduce the complexity of analysing non-trivial communication protocols. Our method is inspired by similar reduction of complexity by constructing smaller interface behaviours. Projections are however difficult to compose within components. The IM method overcomes this problem by defining interfaces as ordinary modules, not as projections, with pins for composition.

There are several approaches to synthesize component behaviours from global scenario specifications, for instance using sequence diagrams (UML SD or MSC) or Use Case Maps for global scenario based specification and state machines (UML SM or SDL) for component design. See e.g. [11] for a survey. Several of these aims to synthesize component behaviour, but due to the incompleteness of scenario based specification the resulting design is normally not complete. In contrast, the IM method promotes complete specifications that also include the data and operations provided by the CF. The problem of scenario composition facing many of the other approaches is solved directly in the specification modules when using the IM method.

The work presented in this paper builds on our own work on the IM method [2] and on previous work, notably [3] that have resulted in the notation for ordering collaboration behaviour and criteria for identification of the known realisability problems. However [3] assumes interactions for elementary collaborations and state machines for component design. It also builds on previous work by [6] on design synthesis using activities. That work, however did not deal with responding choice resolution, and interruption. For initiative choice it re-used a solution from [13] that introduces additional interactions and therefore is more intrusive than the solution presented here. The main contributions presented here are the general, modular and distributed solutions to the design synthesis problems using activities, in particular the resolution modules for choices and interruptions entirely defined using local modules. For choices there are alternative solutions proposed for state machines, notably [4]. For activities [12,13] have proposed solutions, but these solutions require that interactions are added. We are not aware of any related solutions for interruptions.

The approach presented here provides simplifications and modularity on several levels. First, during specification, the problem is decomposed into modules for interfaces and core functionality that can be specified separately and then composed. Design synthesis may then be performed for IF and CF modules separately, and is simplified by the local nature of CF modules and the two-party nature of IF modules. Modularity on the component level is supported by well-defined interfaces provided by the IF modules. Within components more fine grained modularity is provided by the local IF and CF modules and the resolution modules that are general and re-usable.

References

1. Object Management Group.Unified Modeling Language: Superstructure, version 2.4.1 (2011). http://www.omg.org/spec/UML/2.4.1/Superstructure
2. Fatima, U., Bræk, R.: The interface-modular method for global system behaviour specification. In: Desfray, P., Filipe, J., Hammoudi, S., Pires, L.F. (eds.) MODEL-SWARD 2015. CCIS, vol. 580, pp. 339–355. Springer, Heidelberg (2015). doi:10. 1007/978-3-319-27869-8_20

3. Castejón, H.N., Bochmann, G.V., Bræk, R.: On the realizability of collaborative services. Softw. Syst. Model. **12**(3), 597–617 (2013)
4. Gouda, M.G., Yu, Y.T.: Synthesis of communicating finite-state machines with guaranteed progress. IEEE Trans. Commun. **32**(7), 779–788 (1984)
5. Kathayat, S.B., Bræk, R.: Analyzing realizability of choreographies using initiating and responding flows. In: Proceedings of the 8th International Workshop on Model-Driven Engineering, Verification and Validation, pp. 6:1–6:8. ACM (2011). URL http://doi.acm.org/10.1145/2095654.2095662
6. Kathayat, S.B., Bræk, R.: From flow-global choreography to component types. In: Kraemer, F.A., Herrmann, P. (eds.) SAM 2010. LNCS, vol. 6598, pp. 36–55. Springer, Heidelberg (2011). doi:10.1007/978-3-642-21652-7_3
7. Floch, J., Bræk, R.: Towards plug-and-play services: design and validation using roles. Ph.D. thesis, Department of Telematics, Norwegian University of Science and Technology (2003)
8. Lam, S.S., Shankar, A.U.: Protocol verification via projections. IEEE Trans. Softw. Eng. **10**(4), 325–342 (1984)
9. Reactive blocks - the tool for professional java developers. Accessed 01 Nov 2015
10. Kraemer, F.A., Slåtten, V., Herrmann, P.: Tool support for the rapid composition, analysis and implementation of reactive services. J. Syst. Softw. **82**(12), 2068–2080 (2009). Elsevier
11. Liang, H., Dingel, J., Diskin, Z.: A comparative survey of scenario-based to state-based model synthesis approaches. In: 5th International Workshop on Scenarios and State Machines: Models, Algorithms and Tools, pp. 5–12. ACM (2006)
12. Han, F., Herrmann, P.: Remedy of mixed initiative conflicts in model-based system engineering. Electron. Commun. EASST **47**, 1–14 (2012). doi:10.14279/tuj.eceasst. 47.717.723
13. Kraemer, F.A., Slåtten, V., Herrmann, P.: Engineering support for UML activities by automated model-checking - an example. In: Proceedings of the 4th International Workshop on Rapid Integration of Software Engineering Techniques (RISE 2007), pp. 51–66. ERCIM Working Group (2007)

Author Index

Printed in the United States
By Bookmasters